Willis,
Here it is! Finally done!
Thank you for all your help
in getting it this way.

Michael

The Essentials of Biblical Theology

Michael D. Wedman

2020

Scriptures taken from the Holy Bible, New International Version®, NIV®. Copyright © 1973, 1978, 1984, 2011 by Biblica, Inc.™ Used by permission of Zondervan. All rights reserved worldwide. www.zondervan.com The "NIV" and "New International Version" are trademarks registered in the United States Patent and Trademark Office by Biblica, Inc.™

For ordering information contact

Michael D. Wedman Michaelwedmanbooks@gmail.com

PRINT ISBN 978-1-09833-624-0

First Edition

There have been many people who have given a word of encouragement, offered a prayer, and provided a place to write during the journey of writing this book. To all of you, thank you! I needed every bit of every gift that you offered along the way.

And then there are some others that I would like to mention for a special thank you.

To Willis Leach, thank you. Your feedback and encouragement were so very valuable. I probably still don't have it right!

To Michael Moore, thank you. Your ability to discern between commas, quotes, and colons is remarkable. I am fortunate to have benefitted from your expertise. And from your enthusiasm!

To Nena Duran, thank you. Your skills of artistry and imagination have blessed me. If left to me, the cover of this book would be blue; yes, just blue. How very sad if not for you!

To Roland and Janet Wedman, to whom this book is dedicated, thank you. This may be as much of your work as mine. Enjoy!

To Roland and Janet

For your ceaseless work

And

Your constant belief

TABLE OF CONTENTS

PREFACE

This book comes as a result of a sermon series called, "The Essentials of the Bible" which was preached out of a desire to help more people understand the essential doctrines of scripture. More important, it is to help people understand the "essentials" of those essential doctrines. It is not, however, the intention of this book to cover every doctrine of scripture, to be an exhaustive manual of the doctrines found in the Bible, nor is it the intention to give an exhaustive account of the "essential" doctrines of scripture that I have included here. It is, rather, intended to put the "essential" doctrines of scripture into an understandable and useable form that can be easily referred to over and over.

I define the "essential" doctrines of scripture as those doctrines which are the "major" or "central" doctrines of scripture that help and guide us to know who God is, who we are before God, and how we are to be found in a right relationship with Him. This book will cover topics such as the essentials of God the Father, God the Son, God the Holy Spirit, the Trinity, Scripture, Sin, Salvation, Sanctification, the rapture, and a number of other doctrines that I have deemed as "essential".

This book is really an "essentials of systematic theology" book. What I hope to accomplish is to make systematic theology more understandable and more accessible to all people who have a desire to know God and His word in a greater and more complete way. What I don't want this book to be is a mere academic exercise in systematic theology.

Systematic theology takes a topic like God the Father and seeks to systematize everything that the whole of Scripture says about God the Father, from Genesis to Revelation. This is not that kind of book. It is not my intention to give a comprehensive and exhaustive teaching about these doctrines. This is why it is titled, "The Essentials of the Bible" and not "The Exhaustives of the Bible." No, the purpose is to lay out the "essentials". Hopefully, it is enough to get you interested so that you will do a bit more reading and studying on your own.

There is a second purpose to this book. What I hope that we gain through this is a deeper and more meaningful relationship with God, not just a greater knowledge *about* God. I see that as a danger. Anytime we engage in Bible study we tend to say, "Well, let's study our Bible to see what it says about God." So, we study the Bible, underline and highlight passages, write in notes, and even memorize scripture, with the end result often being that we have come to know lots *about* God. But I want more than that, more than just knowing more about God, I want to *know God Himself* in a deeper and more relational way; I want to *know Him personally*.

You see, there is a difference between knowing God and knowing about God. Perhaps an analogy will be useful. Let's say that I was the leading expert regarding Elvis Presley. I have read all the books about Elvis Presley. I have read all the biographies, and I can list all of his songs, and can even tell you the words to every song he has ever written. I can know his favorite color, his favorite food, his favorite people, his favorite place, his favorite car, and his favorite sports team; I can know it all. I can know his birth date and his death date. I can know everything there is to know about Elvis Presley. I could be the world's leading expert about Elvis Presley because I have studied everything there is to know about him, yet, I would not have a *relationship* with Elvis Presley. I would not actually *know* him because I do not have a personal relationship with him. Unless I actually met Elvis Presley in person and developed a personal relationship with him, I would not actually know him. The best I can say is that I know *about* him.

This is the danger we often get into when we study the Bible. We can study God and know as much about Him as there is to know, but we can still be lacking a personal relationship with Him. We can miss meeting Him in person because we are merely studying theology. The term theology means the study of God; "theo" means God and "logy" means the knowledge of. The danger is that I can know everything about God, yet not know God personally. It is my desire that we all know God in greater ways through a personal relationship with Him.

My prayer is that as you read through this book and absorb its material, you are not reading and studying for the mere purpose of knowing more about God and the words of God, but that your desire will be to know God Himself more and more deeply. And as you learn more about God, you will desire more of God Himself in your life. May our desire not be in becoming better "Bible pursuit" players, but in becoming better "God pursuit" players. Spend time not only with these essential doctrines, but with the God of these essential doctrines. My hope and prayer is that the end result of these pages would be that when you wake up in the morning, you will know God better because you want to be with Him as you learn more about Him.

Chapter 1

THE ESSENTIALS

OF

GOD THE FATHER

If someone came up to you and asked, "Who is God?" or "What is the biblical definition of God?" – how would you answer that? Have you ever thought about that? Have you ever tried to formulate a biblical definition of God? Let me suggest to you an answer. Here is a biblical definition of God:

> God is a personal, living spirit who is self-existent, distinguished from all other spirits by his attributes.

You may be wondering, "What does that really mean?" Let's look at this definition, starting with God as a self-existent spirit.

THE PERSON OF GOD	
God is spirit	John 4:24
God is self-existent	Acts 17:24-28a
	Exodus 3:13-14
	Revelation 1:8; 4:8b

God is Spirit

John 4:24 says, "God is spirit, and his worshipers must worship in spirit and in truth." We learn from this verse that God is spirit. That means that God does not have a body like we have. God the Father does not take any particular physical form; He is spirit. He is not packaged or bound or defined by any type of physical limitations. God is simply, spirit.

God is Self-Existent

Not only is God spirit, He is also self-existent. In Acts 17:24-28a| we read,

> The God who made the world and everything in it is the Lord of heaven and earth and does not live in temples built by hands. [25]And he is not served by human hands, as if he needed anything, because he himself gives all men life and breath and everything else. [26]From one man he made every nation of men, that they should inhabit the whole earth; and he determined the times set for them and the exact places where they should live. [27]God did this so that men would seek him and perhaps reach out for him and find him, though he is not far from each one of us. [28a]'For in him we live and move and have our being.'

God does not need anything or require anything to live because He is self-existent. In fact, He is the one who created all that exists. Existence has its being because God first existed and then created. Further, God does not need anybody to complete Him. He is not dependent on anybody else for His existence. There is absolutely nothing that God needs in order for Him to exist. He will never cease to exist because He has a need that cannot be fulfilled by someone or something else. Indeed, the very name that God gave to Moses to define who He is indicates that God is the "existent one". In Exodus 3:13-14 we read,

> Moses said to God, "Suppose I go to the Israelites and say to them, 'The God of your fathers has sent me to you,' and they ask me, 'What is his name?' Then what shall I tell them?"

> [14]God said to Moses, "I AM WHO I AM. This is what you are to say to the Israelites: 'I AM has sent me to you.'"

God gives His name to Moses as, "I am." Notice that God uses the present tense to describe Himself. This is because God is always present; He is always in existence. God is currently existing, always has been existing, and will continue to always exist. Think about that! God has always existed! Nobody created God, nobody birthed God, and nobody named God. God has always been. He is self-existent. God depends upon no one else. There is no other being anywhere in this universe that God needs in order to exist, nor is there any other being in this universe that created God into existence. God is the first cause of every other existence. He is the great 'I am'. He always is, always has been, always will be because He is self-existent. There is not a beginning to God, nor is there an end to God. Revelation 1:8 says, "I am the Alpha and the Omega," says the Lord God, "who is, and who was, and who is to come, the Almighty."

In other words, He has always been, He has always existed. I cannot stress it enough – God is self-existent, dependent on nobody else! He is the first cause of all creation and everything we know. God is the cause of all things and there was no one nor any other force that caused God into being, He always has been.

Think about that a little bit and let it blow your mind. We always think of things with a beginning and an end. Is there anything on the earth or in the universe that you can think of that does not have a beginning and an end? No! Not a thing! The earth, people, plants, animals, the sun, the moon, the stars, even the universe itself has a beginning and an end. There are limits to all things created, but God is without the limits of creation.

In Revelation 4:8b we read, "Holy, holy, holy is the Lord God Almighty, who was, and is, and is to come." He is self-existent. So, God is a living spirit who is self-existent. Let's look now at God as a person.

God as a Person

God is a person, or another way to put it is, God has personality or personhood. There are three elements of personality – will, intellect, and emotion. For anyone to be considered as having personhood, all three components of personhood need to exist. These three components define personality – will, intellect, and emotion.

THREE ELEMENTS OF PERSONALITY	
Will	Ephesians 1:1a
Intellect	1 John 3:20b
Emotion	Genesis 6:6

The Will of God

First, we see that God has a will. Ephesians 1:1a states, "Paul, an apostle of Christ Jesus by the will of God." Paul was called to be an apostle by the *will* of God. That is to say, God chose Paul by an act of His will. Paul repeats this phrase in many other of his epistles (See 1 Corinthians, 2 Corinthians, Colossians, etc.) – that he is an apostle of Christ Jesus by the will of God. God meets the first component of personality in that God has a will.

The Intellect of God

Second, God has an intellect. 1 John 3:20b says, "For God is greater than our hearts, and he knows everything." God knows everything. He has knowledge. This means that God knows things, that He has intellect. God meets the second component of personality in that He has an intellect.

The Emotion of God

Finally, God has emotions. Genesis 6:6 says, "The Lord was grieved that he had made man on the earth, and his heart was filled with pain." His heart was deeply troubled; it was pained. God felt something; God felt grief. Grieving is an emotion. God was grieved that he made humankind. God clearly has emotion; thus, He meets the third component of personhood. So, God has a will, God has an intellect, and God has emotion. We can conclude, therefore, that God is a person.

The Importance of the Personality of God

God has personality and that is important to us. It is important to know that God is a person and not just an inanimate object or some impersonal spirit floating out there. God is not the force of 'Star Wars'. The 'Star Wars' mantra is, "may the force be with you," as if the force is an inanimate, impersonal thing or thought that you can just tap into. The God of the Bible is far different than the force of 'Star Wars' because God is personal. God connects with us on a personal level through His intellect, His will and His emotions. We can talk to God person to person, and God does personal things for us. We can connect with him personally. God is so personal that He knows your name and even knows how many hairs are on your head (Matthew 10:30)! God interacts with us personally. He is not just some force out there that is to be tapped into.

God is not a 'Star Wars' god. The God of the Bible is a personal God – personal for each one of us. This means that God is always trying to connect with us, is always attempting to gain our attention, and is always wanting to be in our world. He is not just out there somewhere. He is here, with us, personally.

There is some erroneous theological teaching that says God created the world and then left the world to go on by itself, without Him, and that one day He will come back to it. This is not true! It is true that God created the world, but it is not true that God left the world on its own; God has stayed here with us. He even came down to earth to walk among us! One of the names of Jesus is Emmanuel (Matthew 1:23), which means "God with us." We can know that God is personally with us, with you, today. He is with you when you wake up, and He is with you every step that you take this day and every other day. He is even with you when you are asleep. I know that sometimes it does not feel that way, but you can take it as truth that He is with you because He said he will be. Psalm 121 tells us that God watches over us at all times and that He never sleeps nor does He slumber. He is always with us. He has not left us on our own. We can know by faith and by fact that even if we don't feel like God is with us today, we can take Him at His word and know that He is indeed with us.

God is a personal God who interacts with us personally. God might not answer your prayer today, but you can be sure that He has heard it and is working on it. He might not answer it tomorrow, but you can be sure that He has heard it and is working on it. He does hear our prayers, and he does take a personal interest in answering us because He is God with us; He is a personal God.

God Desires a Personal Relationship with Us

God even *desires* a personal relationship with us. Yes, He *desires* to get to know us! God is continually and concertedly trying to connect with us in the course of our day. He does this in many ways. Let me suggest four ways, essentially, not exhaustively, that God works at getting to know us.

GOD WANTS TO KNOW US	
Through Scripture	Psalm 32:8; 1 Samuel 3:21
Through His Holy Spirit	Romans 8:15-16; John 14:26
Through providence	Matthew 6:25-34; 1 Peter 5:7
Through creation	Romans 1:18-20

God Connects with Us Through Scripture

The first way God wants to connect with us personally is through His words to us, through Scripture. Because God is a personal God, he communicates to us through the letter that He has written to us – the Bible. The whole Bible, all 66 books of it, is His letter to the world.

Psalm 32:8 says, "I will instruct you and teach you in the way you should go; I will counsel you and watch over you." There is guidance and instruction that God wants to give us through words. He wants to be involved in our daily lives! Are you unsure of what decision to make? Do you need wisdom when you are not sure of some direction to take? Talk to God; He is here waiting to talk to you! He will be the one to guide you, and He *will* instruct you when you ask. God says, "Come and talk to me because I am a personal God."

Life is not just left up to the roll of the dice, or some type of impersonal fate that we cannot do anything about. We can do something about life and discerning the decisions and directions to go in! We can communicate with God about our lives and He will help because He is a personal God who takes a personal interest in what happens to us in this life. In 1 Samuel 3:21 we read, "The Lord continued to appear at Shiloh, and there he revealed himself to Samuel through his word." God reveals Himself to us through His word. God *wants* to be made known and He purposely makes Himself known. You see, God is not out there as an impersonal force that you can never know. On the contrary, God is personal and here with us. He reveals Himself to us and He wants to make Himself known to us. God desires for us to know Him personally.

God Connects with Us Through His Holy Spirit

God reveals Himself to us through the words that He has written to us in the Bible, and secondly, God maintains a relationship with us through His Holy Spirit. Romans 8:15-16 says,

> For you did not receive a spirit that makes you a slave
> again to fear, but you received the Spirit of sonship.
> And by him we cry, "*Abba*, Father." [16]The Spirit himself
> testifies with our spirit that we are God's children.

God's Spirit speaks to us because God wants to connect with us. God wants us to hear Him! We are His children because of His Spirit in us that we received when we invited Jesus into our lives. The Holy Spirit helps us to hear God and to know what God is saying to us. Jesus says about the Holy Spirit in John 14:26,

But the Counselor, the Holy Spirit, whom the Father will
send in my name, will teach you all things and will remind
you of everything I have said to you.

God, through His Holy Spirit in us, teaches us, reminds us, speaks
to us, counsels us, guides us, and instructs us because God wants to
connect with us personally. He connects with us in relationship, through
his Spirit. We can know God personally, through His Scripture, and
through His Holy Spirit.

God Connects with Us Through Providence

There is a third way in which we can know God personally – it
is through providence. Providence is simply another way of saying the
divine intervention of God in our lives through the circumstances of life
here on earth. Matthew 6:25-34 says,

Therefore I tell you, do not worry about your life, what
you will eat or drink; or about your body, what you will
wear. Is not life more important than food, and the body
more important than clothes? [26]Look at the birds of the air;
they do not sow or reap or store away in barns, and yet
your heavenly Father feeds them. Are you not much more
valuable than they? [27]Who of you by worrying can add a
single hour to his life?

[28]And why do you worry about clothes? See how the
lilies of the field grow. They do not labor or spin. [29]Yet I tell
you that not even Solomon in all his splendor was dressed
like one of these. [30]If that is how God clothes the grass of

the field, which is here today and tomorrow is thrown into the fire, will he not much more clothe you, O you of little faith? [31]So do not worry, saying, 'What shall we eat?' or 'What shall we drink?' or 'What shall we wear?' [32]For the pagans run after all these things, and your heavenly Father knows that you need them. [33]But seek first his kingdom and his righteousness, and all these things will be given to you as well. [34]Therefore do not worry about tomorrow, for tomorrow will worry about itself. Each day has enough trouble of its own.

God takes care of us. God knows what we need. He is a personal God who knows what each one of us needs personally. He tailors His divine intervention specifically for each one of our needs as individuals. He knows what I need personally and what you need personally. Furthermore, He knows what you and I need every minute of the day. He is fully aware of what we need, and He provides that for us.

There are so many things that God does for us that we may not even recognize. When we are driving along on the road, we may be unaware of how God is with us, protecting us by keeping us away from accidents that happen in front and behind us. Or perhaps our cars break down *because* God is protecting us from what would happen if we could drive that day or hour. There are so many things that God does for us that we are completely unaware of.

Sometimes God answers "no" to us *because* he is protecting us from greater harm. A "yes" answer may actually be more harmful! God has promised that He will be with us and take care of us, and He often does that through providence – His divine intervention in our lives through events and circumstances that we don't even know about. In 1 Peter 5:7, Peter encourages us to "Cast all your anxiety on him because he cares for you." God cares for us, and we can cast our cares on God because He is a personal God who cares. The force of 'Star Wars' doesn't care; the God of the Bible does because He is personal. God cares about us! And so it is that we can talk to God about our cares. We can discuss them with Him, and we can ask Him to intervene upon them.

This is the importance of knowing that the God of the Bible is a personal God. God connects with us in a personal relationship through the Bible, through the Holy Spirit, through providence and in one more major way.

God Connects with Us Through Creation

God connects with us through creation. Romans 1:18-20 says,

The wrath of God is being revealed from heaven against all the godlessness and wickedness of men who suppress the truth by their wickedness, [19]since what may be known about God is plain to them, because God has made it plain to them. [20]For since the creation of the world God's invisible qualities – his eternal power and divine nature – have been clearly seen, being understood from what has been made, so that men are without excuse.

God draws us into a relationship with Himself through creation. You can look out at the trees, you can hear the birds, you can see deer come through the forest, you can see the flowers bloom, you can feel the wind and rain on your face, and you can see the snow softly falling. Through all of our senses we can come to know God through the beauty of His creation. God connects with us through His creation, saying, "I did this for you. Enjoy what I've done for you and learn who I am."

God is a personal God who is at work personally in our lives through the words of the Bible, through His Holy Spirit, through providence, and through creation.

The Attributes of God

There is still more to this definition of God. God is a personal spirit who is self-existent, distinguishable from all other spirits, by his attributes. Let's get into the attributes of God.

THE ATTRIBUTES OF GOD		
Omniscient	all knowing	1 John 3:20b
Omnipresent	all present	Psalm 139:7-12
Omnipotent	all powerful	Matthew 19:26
Love1		John 4:8
		1 Corinthians 13:4-8a
Light		1 John 1:5-7
Consuming Fire		Hebrews 12:29
		Revelation 20:11-15

Omniscience

God is omniscient. Omniscient or omniscience is made up from the two words, "Omni" and "science". "Omni" means "all" and "scient" or "science" comes from the Latin "Scientia" which means "knowledge". Thus, omniscient or omniscience means that God is all knowing. I John 3:20b states, "For God is greater than our hearts, and he knows everything." God knows all things because He is all knowing! There is not a thing that God does not know. There is not a piece of information nor an event that takes place anywhere in creation that God is not aware of. He knows of it all. God does not have to learn anything or work at acquiring information – He knows it all already because He is omniscient.

Omnipresence

He is also omnipresent. That is, He is all present. Psalm 139:7-12 says,

> Where can I go from your Spirit? Where can I flee from your presence? [8]If I go up to the heavens, you are there; if I make my bed in the depths, you are there. [9]If I rise on the wings of the dawn, if I settle on the far side of the sea, [10]even there your hand will guide me, your right hand will hold me fast. [11]If I say, "Surely the darkness will hide me and the light become night around me," [12]even the darkness will not be dark to you; the night will shine like the day, for darkness is as light to you.

God is all present. There is no place that any of his creation can go that God is not there. God is already there because He is omnipresent. He is here with us now, in this room and He is there with those in India right now at the same time He is with us. He is here, and He is there all at the same time! Time and space mean nothing to God because God is spirit, and He is always present and equally present in all places of creation at the same time. So, when we are praying here today and half way across the world in India they are praying today, God hears us all at the same time. He is equally present with them as He is with us. There is no time difference to God just as there is no spatial difference to God. He sees everybody on the earth at the same time. God is not bound by time and space – He has no boundaries that limit Him. God is omnipresent.

Omnipotence

God is also omnipotent, that is, all powerful. We see this in Matthew 19:26, "Jesus looked at them and said, 'With man this is impossible, but with God all things are possible.'"

With God all things are possible because God is omnipotent. He is all powerful. We get the words, "potent" and "potentate" from the same root word "potens" which means powerful in Latin and often refers to supreme power. The omnipotence of God means that there is nothing that God cannot do. He is not limited by any lack of power or ability to perform that which He says He will do. And there is no 'kryptonite' which can take away His power as there is with the fictional character, Superman. So, what God promises He can and will do because He has the power to make it happen. You and I can make promises to others, but often we cannot come through with those promises because we do not have the power to control events and time and people to make our promises happen. God, however, does have the power to control the events and timing of events to fulfill every promise that He makes. The omnipotence of God means that He is capable of doing exactly what He said He will do. And He does it with ultimate cosmic power – He is omnipotent.

Love

Another attribute of God is love. 1 John 4:8 says, "Whoever does not love does not know God, because God is love." Yes, God is love. He is the definition of love. He is everything that 1 Corinthians 13:4-8a tells us about love.

> Love is patient, love is kind. It does not envy, it does not boast, it is not proud. [5]It is not rude, it is not self-seeking, it is not easily angered, it keeps no record of wrongs. [6]Love does not delight in evil but rejoices with the truth. [7]It always protects, always trusts, always hopes, always perseveres.
>
> [8a]Love never fails.

This is love, this is God.

Light

God is also light. 1 John 1:5-7 states,

> This is the message we have heard from him and declare to you: God is light; in him there is no darkness at all. [6]If we claim to have fellowship with him yet walk in the darkness, we lie and do not live by the truth. [7]But if we walk in the light, as he is in the light, we have fellowship with one another, and the blood of Jesus, his Son, purifies us from all sin.

God is light. Notice that there is no darkness in God at all. There are no shadows with God, no lesser lit areas in the character of God. There is never a time when the character and actions of God dim; all the actions that God takes are completely light and equally so. He is completely and equally light in all that He is and all that He does.

Consuming Fire

The last attribute in this list is that God is consuming fire. Hebrews 12:29 simply says that, "for our "God is a consuming fire."" The imagery of a consuming fire speaks of God's judgments upon sin. He is the one who will judge all sin, and He Himself will cast out all sin from creation when Jesus returns to judge the nations. Revelation 20:11-15 states,

> Then I saw a great white throne and him who was seated on it. Earth and sky fled from his presence, and there was no place for them. [12]And I saw the dead, great and small, standing before the throne, and books were opened. Another book was opened, which is the book of life. The dead were judged according to what they had done as recorded in the books. [13]The sea gave up the dead that were in it, and death and Hades gave up the dead that were in them, and each person was judged according to what he had done. [14]Then death and Hades were thrown in the lake of fire. The lake of fire is the second death. [15]If anyone's name was not found written in the book of life, He was thrown into the lake of fire.

These are just some of the attributes of God. There are so many more attributes of God – it would be a rewarding Bible study to identify and study all of the attributes of God that are found from Genesis to Revelation.

The Foundational Attribute of God

For this book though, there is only one more attribute of God that I want to point out as essential. I left this out of my previous list because I wanted to make a big deal about it, because it is the foundational attribute of God. If I were to ask you the question, "What underlies all of the characters of God?" What would it be? How would you answer? Most people would say that it is love that is the foundational character or attribute of God. Others might say light, or omnipotence, or a consuming fire. I suggest to you though, that none of these are the foundational attribute of God. They are true and essential attributes, but not the foundational attribute of God. What is the foundational attribute of God? The foundational attribute of God is holiness. God is above all else, or under all else, holy. Underlying all other attributes of God is his holiness. God is Holy.

The Holiness of God

THE FOUNDATIONAL ATTRIBUTE OF GOD

The Holiness of God

God is Holy   Isaiah 6:3

Psalm 19:7

1 Peter 1:16

Revelation 4:8b

Isaiah 6:3 states, "And they were calling to one another: "Holy, holy, holy is the Lord Almighty; the whole earth is full of his glory."" These statements are made by the cherubim who were attending God when Isaiah saw the vision of God in the temple. Notice they called out to one another, "holy, holy, holy" and not, "love, love, love" or "omnipotent, omnipotent, omnipotent." They were using the one attribute that describes God at the core of His character.

In Psalm 19:7 we read, "The law of the Lord is perfect, reviving the soul. The statutes of the Lord are trustworthy, making wise the simple."

The word 'perfect' and the word 'holy' are synonyms – they mean the same thing. God and His word are holy, or perfect.

I Peter 1:16 states, "for it is written: "Be holy, because I am holy."" Again, it is holiness that God uses to define Himself. And then in Revelation 4:8b, each of the four living creatures repeated day and night, saying, "Holy, holy, holy is the Lord God Almighty, who was, and is, and is to come." Once again, we see that God is spoken of by the heavenly beings, as by the cherubim, as one who is holy. Underlying all else in the character of God is holiness.

Definition of Holiness

To more fully understand the ramifications of this, we need to define what holiness is.

THE FOUNDATIONAL ATTRIBUTE OF GOD

Definition of Holiness
    Holiness is perfection or "wholly otherness"
    Without fault, blemish, stain, or any defection at all
    Without degree

The definition of holiness is – perfection or "wholly otherness." That is to say, God is completely other than any created being. He is not created; He is the Creator. He is not imperfect; He is perfect. He is completely other than anything or anyone else we know.

Holiness also means without fault, without blemish, without stain, and without defect at all. God has no blemish; God has no stain; God has no defection – God is perfect. He is perfect. We cannot imagine perfect because we have nothing on earth that is perfection. Everything and everyone on earth and in the universe has flaws, blemishes, and imperfections. But not God: He is holy; He is perfect; He is without stain or blemish or flaw. That means He is completely other than we are. That is holiness.

We may call some things here on earth perfect, but they are not perfection; they are all flawed. God does not have a flaw. Furthermore, God is without degree. There is no good, better, or best with God. Perfect is perfect. There are no degrees with God. He cannot be more God or less God. He simply *is* God. God is God and nothing compares to Him. He is completely other than we are and all that we know. Again, underlying all else in the character of God is holiness. He is completely other than we are. He is God, and we are not.

The holiness of God is foundational to His character because of what it means to the rest of His attributes. If God is not perfect, if God is not completely other, if there is a blemish or a flaw in God, then how can we trust any of His attributes? Take for example God's omniscience. He is all knowing. But, if He is not perfectly all knowing, then there might be something that God does not know or that He misses. And if there is something that God does not know, or misses, how can He be trusted when He says He knows everything. If there is a blemish in God, if He is not perfectly omniscient, then how do I know that He hears all of my prayers? And if He misses a few of my prayers – which ones? What will be answered and what will be missed? How can I trust God with my cares if He might be unaware of some of them because He is not perfectly all knowing?

And what does a not perfectly omnipresent God mean? That He is not always here for me every minute? That He just might leave us and forsake us? How can I then trust God? And maybe even worse, if God is not perfectly omnipotent, that means He may not have the power to keep His promises, that there might be things that He cannot do. How could I then trust Him? If God is flawed and not perfect, then how do we trust God's words? How do we really know that God is going to do what He says He will do? How do we know He can do what He says He will do if He is flawed and not perfect? There is a problem: we cannot completely trust a flawed and imperfect God. Hence, holiness has to underlie all the other attributes of God!

> ## THE FOUNDATIONAL ATTRIBUTE OF GOD
>
> Holiness underlies all else because if God had any blemish or non-perfection at all, then all of the rest of His characteristics could be questioned or brought into doubt.

If God has a blemish, if God is not perfect, if holiness does not underlie that attribute of omnipresence, then we can doubt that God is there for us. If God has a blemish, if God is not perfect, if holiness does not underlie that attribute of omnipotence, then we can doubt that God is powerful enough to help us. If God has a blemish, if God is not perfect, if holiness does not underlie that attribute of love, then we can doubt that God actually does love us and that what is happening to us is happening from the love of God. Without the holiness of God underlying all else in the character of God, then we can begin to wonder if maybe God slipped up and got this one wrong. If He is not perfect, then maybe He didn't hear me. If God is flawed, then maybe God doesn't love me perfectly; maybe I can doubt His love.

If God is not holy, not completely other than we are, if God is not without blemish, defect or flaw, then we can begin to doubt anything and everything that God says and does. He says He is love, but we can say, "Well to what degree are You love? If You are not perfect, then You cannot love me perfectly, so Your love doesn't really make a difference in my life. If You're not perfectly omniscient and I pray, maybe You are not hearing my prayers so it's not going to make a difference in my life. So why should I pray?" If God is not perfect then His word is not perfect, and if His word is not perfect then it might lead us in the wrong direction so why even read it?

Furthermore, if there is a flaw in God so that His words are flawed, that means that we are the ones who have to decide which words are flawed and which ones are true. That means that we are the ones who decide what God says and what God does not say. We then, get to control the words of God and subsequently, control God Himself. By choosing God's words for Him, we, as humans, end up making God in any image that we like, and we ourselves have become god.

If God is not perfect, wholly other, holy, then He really is not God at all. He ceases to become God and has now become like one of us, the creation. Do you see now why the holiness of God is so important?

God is perfect. God is holy. Holiness underlies all the other attributes of God. He is completely other. He is without degree, without blemish, without spot. He has no stains nor any imperfections at all. Therefore, everything He says about Himself can be trusted perfectly. Thus, the love He has for us is a perfect love. The omniscience He has is perfectly omniscient. He is always here; He is always present; He is always all knowing, always all powerful, and always caring. He is always a consuming fire. He is always light, and there is never a time when He is not. God does not and will not change because He is holy, perfect, completely other than us. We can trust our lives on it. We can stand on the Word and words of God. We can trust God who is perfectly trustworthy. We will never be let down by God because He is perfect, completely other; He is Holy. Holiness underlies all else.

The Consequences of God's Holiness

HOLINESS HAS CONSEQUENCES

1 Peter 1:14-16

Ephesians 5:8-20

Romans 12:1-2

The holiness of God has some consequences for us. It not only means that God is perfect, and his word is perfect, but it means something to us personally. In developing a personal relationship with God, we have to understand what holiness means to us. In 1 Peter 1:14-16 we read,

> As obedient children, do not conform to the evil desires you had when you lived in ignorance. [15]But just as he who called you is holy, so be holy in all you do; [16]for it is written: "Be holy, because I am Holy."

God calls us to look like Him. God calls us to reflect His holiness or otherness. God calls us to look more like Him than to look like anybody else. Because God is Holy means we are to be holy. We will never be perfect until Christ comes and gives us our new bodies, but He calls us to follow Him completely and to follow closely after Him. He calls us to look different than the world is, because God is different; He is completely other. But what does this really mean? What is He saying?

God is telling us that He does not want us, the way we live our lives, to look like the way the people of the world live their lives. God wants us to live our lives the way He would live. He wants us to look like Jesus in our actions and words. As disciples of Christ, we are called to reflect the character of God. We cannot be salt and light if we look and live like the world. We cannot be light if we are darkness. We read in Ephesians 5:8-20,

> For you were once darkness, but now you are light in the Lord. Live as children of light [9](for the fruit of the light consists in all goodness, righteousness and truth) [10]and find out what pleases the Lord. [11]Have nothing to do with the fruitless deeds of darkness, but rather expose them. [12]For it is shameful even to mention what the disobedient do in secret. [13]But everything exposed by the light becomes visible, [14]for it is light that makes everything visible. This is why it is said: "Wake up, O sleeper, rise from the dead, and Christ will shine on you."
>
> [15]Be very careful, then, how you live – not as unwise but as wise, [16]making the most of every opportunity, because the days are evil. [17]Therefore do not be foolish, but understand what the Lord's will is. [18]Do not get drunk on wine, which leads to debauchery. Instead, be filled with the Spirit. [19]Speak to one another with psalms, hymns and spiritual songs. Sing and make music in your heart

to the Lord, [20]always giving thanks to God the Father for everything, in the name of our Lord Jesus Christ.

Clearly, we are called to be different people. We are called to be people who look more like God than the world. We are called to speak differently, and we are called to act differently. When the world says it is okay to lie, the disciple of Christ says, "No, I will be different than the world for I will look more like God than the world, so I will not lie." When the world says it is okay to tear people down, the disciple of Christ says, "No, I will not – I will not tear people down. I will build them up." When the world says it is okay to gossip and complain, the disciple of Christ says, "I will not gossip and complain. I will praise and give thanks, because I want to look more like God than I want to look like the world."

When the world says sexual morality is not a big deal, that it is okay to have sex with someone else outside of marriage, the disciple of Christ says, "No it is not! God says it is not. I need to look more like God than the world." When the world says it is okay to be greedy and hoard money, the disciple of Christ says, "No it is not!" The disciple of Christ says, "I am going to be generous, and I am going to give because I want to look more like God than I want to look like the world."

The disciple wants to look more like Jesus than to look like the world. When the world says it is okay to be angry and mean and be a person who is not nice to be around, the disciple of Christ says, "I am going be a person of gentleness and kindness and goodness and light because I want to look more like God than I want to look like the world" – because walking with Jesus is transforming. We are to be holy people. Romans 12:1-2 says,

Therefore, I urge you, brothers, in view of God's mercy, to offer your bodies as living sacrifices, holy and pleasing to God – this is your spiritual act of worship. [2]Do not conform any longer to the pattern of this world, but be transformed by the renewing of your mind. Then you will be able to test and approve what God's will is – his good, pleasing and perfect will.

God calls us to be transformed people because of who He is, because of His holiness, His complete otherness. He calls us to look more like Him than we look like the world. Transformation – that is what God is after: for us to be transformed into His likeness. This means that we have to follow Him and follow hard after Him. We do this because God is a living Spirit, who is self-existent and distinguished from all other spirits by His attributes – especially His holiness to which He calls us.

Closing Prayer

God in heaven, I ask that You would help us. You know O God that we are sinful people and that we cannot obtain perfection. But help us to determine to get as close to You as we can. Help us, O God, to be holy people. God, we cannot do it on our own. Help us to look like You, act like You, and talk like You, so that we can be salt and light of the earth. Thank You for who you are God. You are God, and we are not.

Amen.

Chapter 2

THE ESSENTIALS

OF

GOD THE SON

In this chapter we are going to look at the essentials of God the Son. Now this material is incredibly critical because what we believe about Jesus is central to our faith. Therefore, we need to know who Jesus is, essentially. We will begin with a look at the two fundamental natures of Jesus, followed by two important characteristics of Jesus, His eternality, and His sinlessness, and then we will discuss why His two natures and two characteristics are essential for salvation.

So, let us discover what Scripture says about Jesus. We start with the two fundamental natures of Jesus.

TWO FUNDAMENTAL NATURES OF JESUS

Jesus is fully God   Matthew 1:18-20

Jesus is fully human   Matthew 1:18-20

Two Fundamental Natures of Jesus (Hypostatic Union)

There are two fundamental natures of Jesus that we must get straight. Jesus is both fully God and fully human. He is both, at the same time, existing together in the one person of Jesus Christ. The theological term for this is the hypostatic union of Christ; He is fully God and fully man. Matthew 1:18-20 states,

> This is how the birth of Jesus Christ came about: His mother Mary was pledged to be married to Joseph, but before they came together, she was found to be with child through the Holy Spirit. [19]Because Joseph her husband was a righteous man and did not want to expose her to public disgrace, he had in mind to divorce her quietly.
>
> [20]But after he had considered this, an angel of the Lord appeared to him in a dream and said, "Joseph son of David, do not be afraid to take Mary home as your wife, because what is conceived in her is from the Holy Spirit."

Essentially, the person of Jesus Christ came about by the supernatural act of the Holy Spirit who fertilized the egg in Mary's womb so that Jesus has both a God nature and a human nature; divine from the Holy Spirit and human from Mary. Thus, Jesus is fully God, and He is fully human. He is not three-quarters God and one quarter human, or two parts human and one part God. He has a 100% fully human nature and a 100% fully divine nature. He is both fully God and fully man.

So many mistakes are made of this hypostatic union of Christ. Some believe that Jesus is a great prophet or that Jesus is a great moral teacher but that He is not fully God. This is not the Jesus of the Bible. Others believe that Jesus is God but that he was never fully human – or even human at all, but rather some sort of super-human. Both beliefs deny the true nature of Jesus by denying either his God nature or his human nature. It is essential that we know that Jesus is fully God and fully human.

Any belief that accepts anything less than both natures of God falls short of the truth of God's word. This is what makes a cult considered to be a cult – what they believe about Jesus. Every cult does not accept that Jesus is both fully God and fully human. They have some different explanation for who Jesus is. Orthodoxy, proper and true doctrine, however, does not view Jesus as some sort of combination and strange mixture of God and human. Jesus is fully or 100% God and fully or 100% human. This is an essential point that we need to get straight, because, as we will see later on, our very salvation hinges on Jesus being fully God and fully human.

Let us move into a bit of Bible study now to show how Scripture supports the claim that Jesus is both fully God and fully man.

Jesus Is Fully God

JESUS IS FULLY GOD	
The word was God	John 1:1
In very nature, God	Philippians 2:6a
Exact representation of God	Colossians 1:15-17

John 1:1

Let's look at John 1:1. It states, "In the beginning was the Word, and the Word was with God, and the Word was God." The key phrase is that "The Word was God." The Word refers to Jesus. Jesus is the divine Word, thus, Jesus is God. Modern day cults generally want to put an indefinite article "a" in between "was and God" to cause it to say, *"the Word was a god"* rather than *"the Word was God."* Further, a small "g" for God is written in. This is terribly wrong. The original language in which it was written, Greek, does not put an indefinite article in front of God, nor does it use a small case "g" for God. In fact there is absolutely no way this can be done while still being true to the original Greek because the original Greek is written in such a way as to be very clear and undeniable – The Word was God. Jesus was *God* – the one and only God, equal to God the Father, and not any less. "The construction the evangelist chose to express this idea was the most *concise* way he could have stated that the Word was God and yet was distinct from the Father."[1] What is very clear is that Jesus is God, the one and the same as the Father.

Philippians 2:6a

Philippians 2:6a also confirms this position that Jesus is fully God when Paul writes about Jesus saying, "Who, being in very nature God." The phrase, "who being in very nature God" is used to show that the nature of Jesus is the same nature as God the Father. Jesus has the same divine nature as God the Father because Jesus is God. Not "a" god, but "The God".

Colossians 1:15-17

So, we see that the Word was God, that Jesus is in very nature God and now, through Colossians 1:15-17, we discover that Jesus is the exact representation of God. Colossians 1:15-17 says about Jesus,

> He is the image of the invisible God, the firstborn over all creation. [16]For by him all things were created: things in heaven and on earth, visible and invisible, whether thrones or powers or rulers or authorities; all things were created

---

1   Wallace, Daniel B., *Greek Grammar Beyond the Basics*, (Grand Rapids: Zondervan, 1996), 269.

by him and for him. [17]He is before all things, and in him all things hold together.

These verses show us that Jesus is God by showing us that Jesus created all things in the entire universe, even things in heaven! All creation owes its existence to Jesus. Now we know that God created the heavens and the earth. Thus, Paul, in writing these verses is clearly telling us that Jesus is God; that He is fully God. The creative act is attributed to God the Son as equally as it is to God the Father.

Furthermore, we read that Jesus is before all things, He is eternal, and in Him all things hold together. Notice that Jesus holds all things together. The very molecules that hold this book together are held together by Jesus. If Jesus did not exist and if Jesus was not fully God, this book could not exist in this form because the very pages would fall apart. Jesus holds the very molecules together. Only the creator God can hold the universe together, and the apostle Paul tells us that Jesus is that creator God. He is fully 100% God. These three Scriptures are only a sample of the Scriptures that confirm that Jesus is divine in nature, that He is God.

Jesus Was Aware of His Divinity

There are other Scriptures that show us that Jesus is God by showing us that Jesus was aware of His divinity. Let us take a look at how Jesus was aware of His own divinity and knew that he was fully God in being, nature, and purpose.

Jesus knew very clearly who He was. He did not stumble into it or wake up one day and cry out in new-found discovery, "I have just found out who I am." No, Jesus knew who He was from the beginning; there was never any doubt.

JESUS WAS AWARE OF HIS DIVINITY

Accepted worship as God
> John 20:24-29; Matthew 16:13-20; Luke 19:37-40
> Revelation 19:10a; Acts 14

Came to fulfill the law
> Matthew 5:17

Knew his purpose
> Matthew 26:39b; John 3:14-16; John 10:7-18

Claimed to be God
> John 10:30; 8:54-59; 4:25-26; Exodus 3:14

Jesus Accepted Worship as God

We know that Jesus was aware of His divinity because He accepted worship as God. John 20:24-29 is the story of Thomas, dubbed, 'doubting Thomas' because Thomas did not believe that Jesus was alive and had been raised from the dead. John 20:24-29 reads,

> Now Thomas (called Didymus), one of the Twelve, was not with the disciples when Jesus came. [25]So the other disciples told him, "We have seen the Lord!"

> But he said to them, "Unless I see the nail marks in his hands and put my finger where the nails were, and put my hand into his side, I will not believe it."

[26]A week later his disciples were in the house again, and Thomas was with them. Though the doors were locked, Jesus came and stood among them and said, "Peace be with you!" [27]Then he said to Thomas, "Put your finger here; see my hands. Reach out your hand and put it into my side. Stop doubting and believe."

[28]Thomas said to him, "My Lord and my God!"

[29]Then Jesus told him, "Because you have seen me, you have believed; blessed are those who have not seen and yet have believed."

Thomas is unwilling to believe that Jesus has been raised from the dead until he actually sees Jesus with his own eyes and touches Jesus with his own hands. One week later, Thomas received his chance as Jesus showed up in the room where they were meeting. Jesus instructs Thomas to put his finger in the nail prints of His hand and for Thomas to put his hand in the side of Jesus where He had been pierced. After Thomas touches Jesus with his own hands, he realizes that this really is the same Jesus that he saw crucified and that Jesus really is now alive right in front of him. And the response that Thomas gives is one of worship, "My Lord and my God!" Thomas clearly worships Jesus as more than just his master, he worships Jesus as God Himself. Thomas recognizes that Jesus really is God and offers up worship to Him. Now, what is telling is how Jesus responds. Jesus does not deny that He is God, Jesus does not rebuke Thomas for calling Him God; rather, Jesus clearly accepts worship as God.

In another of the gospels, we have the account of Matthew in 16:13-20.

When Jesus came to the region of Caesarea Philippi, he asked his disciples, "Who do people say the Son of Man is?"

[14]They replied, "Some say John the Baptist; others say Elijah; and still others, Jeremiah or one of the prophets."

[15]"But what about you?" he asked. "Who do you say I am?"

[16]Simon Peter answered, "You are the Christ, the Son of the living God."

[17]Jesus replied, "Blessed are you, Simon son of Jonah, for this was not revealed to you by man, but by my Father in heaven. [18]And I tell you that you are Peter, and on this rock I will build my church, and the gates of Hades will not overcome it. [19]I will give you the keys of the kingdom of heaven; whatever you bind on earth will be bound in heaven, and whatever you loose on earth will be loosed in heaven." [20]Then he warned his disciples not to tell anyone that he was the Christ.

Jesus is talking to the disciples and asks them who people are saying that He is. They answer that some say He is John the Baptist, or Elijah, or Jeremiah, or a prophet, or some other good prophet type guy. Peter however gives the correct answer when he says, "You are the Messiah, the Son of the living God." Peter is giving worship to Jesus as being the Messiah which is an Old Testament reference for 'God with skin on'. Jesus accepts this worship as the Messiah, showing that He is God. Even more telling is what Jesus does next! Jesus blesses Peter for getting the answer right, not because Peter knew it himself, but because Peter had it revealed to him by God the Father. Yes, God Himself confirms that Jesus is God!

In still another gospel, the gospel of Luke, we see another story of Jesus accepting worship as God. We read in Luke 19:37-40,

> When he came near the place where the road goes down the Mount of Olives, the whole crowd of disciples began joyfully to praise God in loud voices for all the miracles they had seen:
>
> [38]"Blessed is the king who comes in the name of the Lord!" "Peace in heaven and glory in the highest!"
>
> [39]Some of the Pharisees in the crowd said to Jesus, "Teacher, rebuke your disciples!"
>
> [40]"I tell you," he replied, "if they keep quiet, the stones will cry out."

This is often referred to as the triumphal entry. This is the time when Jesus enters Jerusalem during Passover and is worshiped as the Messiah. When Jesus came near where the road goes down to the Mount of Olives the whole crowd of disciples began joyfully to praise God in loud voices for all the miracles they had seen. They proclaimed, "Blessed is the king who comes in the name of the Lord!" "Peace in heaven and Glory in the Highest." Some of the pharisees in the crowd said to Jesus, "Teacher rebuke your disciples," to which Jesus responds, "I tell you if they keep quiet the very stones will cry out." Why did the pharisees want Jesus to rebuke the people? Because they were proclaiming Jesus as the Messiah, as 'God with skin on'. Jesus did not rebuke the people however, but actually accepted worship as God, precisely because He knew that He was God! Jesus was very much aware of His divinity.

To put Jesus' acceptance of worship in perspective, we read the apostle John's writing in the book of Revelation 19:10a,

> At this I fell at his feet to worship him. But he said to me,
> "Do not do it! I am a fellow servant with you and with
> your brothers who hold to the testimony of Jesus. Worship
> God!

The apostle John heard from an angel and fell at the feet of the angel to worship him. But the angel clearly tells John that God alone is to be worshiped and not anyone else, not even an angel.

There is another exhortation to worship God alone in the life of the apostle Paul. In Acts 14, after Paul had healed a crippled man in the city of Lystra, the crowd came out to worship Paul as the god Zeus, but Paul stopped them from worshiping him. He knew that only God was worthy of worship. So, the fact that Jesus accepted worship as God meant that Jesus knew He was God and could be worshiped as God.

Jesus Came to Fulfill the Law as God

Jesus not only knew that He was God by accepting worship as God, but He also showed that He was God by telling us that He came to fulfill the law. Matthew 5:17 states, "Do not think I have come to abolish the Law or the Prophets; I have not come to abolish them but to fulfill them."

Who could possibly fulfill the whole Old Testament law and all that the prophets said? Who could fulfill the role of the Messiah? Only God! By making this statement, Jesus showed that He knew why he had come. He knew He had come to fulfill all of the law and the prophets because He is God.

Jesus Knew His Purpose as God

Jesus accepted worship as God, He knew He came to fulfill the law as God and, thirdly, He knew his purpose. While Jesus was in the garden of Gethsemane praying just before His arrest, trial, and crucifixion, Jesus shows us that He knew what His purpose in coming was – to die on the cross. As he agonizes in prayer with the Father, He prays, "My Father, if it is possible, may this cup be taken from me" (Matthew 26:39b). Jesus knew that the cup that he was about to drink was crucifixion on the cross. Jesus clearly knew His purpose was to pay the penalty of sin for humankind by becoming sin for us on the cross (2 Corinthians 5:21).

Another instance of Jesus knowing His purpose as God is found in John 3:14-16.

> Just as Moses lifted up the snake in the desert, so the Son of Man must be lifted up, [15]that everyone who believes in him may have eternal life.
>
> [16]For God so loved the world that he gave his one and only Son, that whoever believes in him shall not perish but have eternal life.

Clearly Jesus knew He had come to bring forgiveness of sins and everlasting life, something only God could do. Jesus knew He was God who was coming to give everlasting life. It was not a mystery to Him. He knew who He was. Again, John states in his gospel in 10:7-18.

> Therefore Jesus said again, "I tell you the truth, I am the gate for the sheep. [8]All who ever came before me were thieves and robbers, but the sheep did not listen to them. [9]I am the gate; whoever enters through me will be saved. He will come in and go out, and find pasture. [10]The thief comes only to steal and kill and destroy; I have come that they may have life, and have it to the full.
>
> [11]I am the good shepherd. The good shepherd lays down his life for the sheep. [12]The hired hand is not the shepherd who owns the sheep. So when he sees the wolf coming, he abandons the sheep and runs away. Then the wolf attacks the flock and scatters it. [13]The man runs away because he is a hired hand and cares nothing for the sheep.
>
> [14]"I am the good shepherd; I know my sheep and my sheep know me – [15]just as the Father knows me and I know the Father – and I lay down my life for the sheep. [16]I have other sheep that are not of this sheep pen. I must bring them also. They too will listen to my voice, and there shall be one flock and one shepherd. [17]The reason my Father loves me is that I lay down my life – only to take it up again. [18]No one takes it from me, but I lay it down of my own accord. I have authority to lay it down and authority to take it up again. This command I received from my Father."

Who has the authority to lay his life down and authority to take it up again? Only God! He knew who He was. Jesus was aware of His divinity because he accepted worship from people and He knew His purpose to fulfill the law and bring salvation to the world. Yet, there is still another way that we know Jesus is fully God. Jesus Himself claimed to be God.

Jesus Claimed to Be God

Jesus just simply and outright claimed to be God. In John 10:30 we read, "I and the Father are one." Jesus was claiming to be the same as God the Father. He claims that again in John 8:54-59. The background of what is happening here is that Jesus is being attacked by the pharisees who are trying to discredit Him. The pharisees are really impressed by their own rightness before God and are claiming that Jesus is from satan. In John 8:54-59 Jesus replied,

> If I glorify myself, my glory means nothing. My Father, whom you claim as your God, is the one who glorifies me. [55]Though you do not know him, I know him. If I said I did not, I would be a liar like you, but I do know him and keep his word. [56]Your father Abraham rejoiced at the thought of seeing my day; he saw it and was glad.
>
> [57]"You are not yet fifty years old," the Jews said to him, "and you have seen Abraham!"
>
> [58]"I tell you the truth," Jesus answered, "before Abraham was born, I am!" [59]At this, they picked up stones to stone him, but Jesus hid himself, slipping away from the temple grounds.

They actually picked up the stones and were ready to kill him. Now that is a pretty serious action to take! What would cause them to do that? It was because Jesus claimed to be God! Jesus used the name of God for Himself that God spoke to Moses at the burning bush.

God spoke to Moses and used the name, "I Am" as found in Exodus 3:14. God said to Moses, "I AM WHO I AM. This is what you are to say to the Israelites: 'I AM has sent me to you.'" Jesus did not say, before Abraham I *was* – He says before Abraham I *Am*. The pharisees picked up stones to stone Jesus because they clearly knew that Jesus was saying that *He is God*. Thus, according to the law of the Old Testament, that was blasphemy, and the punishment was stoning to death. If anyone claimed to be God, that person could be stoned to death according to the law, but Jesus is God so there was no blasphemy. Jesus was speaking the truth.

One more Scripture on this point: John 4:25-26. In this passage, Jesus is travelling in Samaria with his disciples. While there He sits down at a well, and He meets a woman at the well. He engages her in conversation about spiritual life. She comments that the Samaritans, like the Israelites, are children of Abraham too. "The woman said, "I know that Messiah" (called Christ) "is coming. When he comes, he will explain everything to us." [26]Then Jesus declared, "I who speak to you am he.""

Jesus Declares that He is the Messiah. He is God.

In summary then, Jesus was aware of His divinity because He accepted worship as God, He came to fulfill the Scriptures as God the Messiah, He knew his purpose as God, and he declared himself as God.

Our Response to the Claims of Jesus

As a result of all of this, we are faced with making a decision about who Jesus is. We have three options to the claims of Jesus. Jesus is either a liar, a lunatic, or He is who He actually says He is – the Lord, which means He is God.

THREE OPTIONS TO THE CLAIMS OF JESUS	
Jesus is a liar	not to be believed in anything
Jesus is a lunatic	not to be trusted in anything
Jesus is Lord	He is God, who He says
	He is Believable and
	trustworthy – Acts 2:36

Jesus as Liar

First, if Jesus is lying about who He is, then we can conclude that He is not to be believed or trusted in anything that He says about any other subject. Would you believe the words of someone who you know continually and regularly lies to you? Of course not! If Jesus is lying about who He is, then we cannot believe any other statement that Jesus makes. If Jesus is not who He claims to be then He has lied to us. If Jesus is claiming to be God, but He is really not God, then we can throw out every other claim that He makes because we cannot believe the words of a liar. Furthermore, if Jesus is lying, then He ceases to be a good prophet or a good moral teacher but is instead a lying prophet and a teacher with bad morals. Now, would you be inclined to call someone good who lies to you? No! Nor would you believe anything they said to you.

Jesus as Lunatic

The second response to Jesus is to say that He is a lunatic. That is to say, the claims of Jesus that He is God are claims made by someone who is mentally unstable, perhaps schizophrenic, or just out of touch with reality. This option says that Jesus really has no clue who He is but is claiming to be God, even though He is not. And, after all, who calls himself God except someone who is crazy, or… perhaps actually God. If Jesus is a lunatic, then He can't be trusted in anything else that He says. Would you trust a lunatic? Would you trust a guy who says crazy things? Would you lay your life down for that guy? Of course not! Yet clearly the disciples did lay their life down for Jesus, so maybe Jesus is actually God!

Jesus as Lord

So, if Jesus is lying, that means he can't be believed in. If Jesus is a lunatic that means he can't be trusted. But, if He really is who He claims to be – God, then He *is* believable, and He *is* trustworthy. In Acts 2:36 Peter is preaching to the crowd and says to those there, "Therefore let all Israel be assured of this: God has made this Jesus, whom you crucified, both Lord and Christ." Peter recognizes Jesus as God and Saviour.

We can rightly come to the conclusion then that Jesus is indeed fully God. The weight of evidence from the Scriptures cannot be denied. The claims of others about Jesus and the claims and actions of Jesus lead to the conclusion that He truly is God.

The Humanity of Jesus

We have thus far established that Jesus is fully God. We will now turn our attention to establish that Jesus is also fully human. The humanity of Jesus can be seen throughout the life of Jesus. Both the birth of Jesus and the experiences of Jesus show us that He is fully human. Let us begin with the birth of Jesus.

The Birth of Jesus

Here is how I know Jesus is fully man. He was born as a human being. The narrative found in Matthew 2 is the narrative about the birth of Christ. He was born as a baby. Jesus was born the same way that humans are born. Mary definitely knew that she had given birth to a baby boy; that could not be denied. You would never convince Mary, nor Joseph either, that she had not just gone through the process of giving birth to a baby. Jesus was born as a human being. Furthermore, the shepherds confirmed His birth when they saw Jesus in the stable where he was born. They went to see Jesus and could confirm that Jesus was a real baby, that He was a human being.

Physical Experiences of Jesus

Not only was Jesus born as a human baby is born, but He experienced physical experiences just as other humans do.

PHYSICAL EXPERIENCES AS HUMANS	
Hunger	Matthew 4:2
Thirst	John 19:28b
Weariness	John 4:6
Temptation	Matthew 4:1
	Hebrews 4:15
Suffering	Hebrews 2:18

Matthew 4:2 states that he experienced hunger. Jesus went out into the desert and, "After fasting forty days and forty nights, he was

hungry." Human beings experience hunger, Jesus had the experiences of hunger because He was a human being. Jesus was also thirsty. In John 19:28b we read about Jesus as He is hanging on the cross and He says, knowing everything now had been finished so that Scripture would be fulfilled, "I am thirsty." Human beings experience thirst, so too Jesus experienced thirst.

Jesus was thirsty, Jesus was hungry, and Jesus was weary, another human experience. In John 4 we have the story of Jesus travelling through Samaria, and He decides to rest at the well. We read in John 4:6 that, "Jacob's well was there, and Jesus, *tired* as he was from the journey, sat down by the well. It was about the sixth hour." Let me ask you a question, "Is God ever tired?" No. God is never tired, but human beings are tired. Jesus was fully God and He was tired. What does that mean? It means that Jesus had a human nature. Jesus was tired; He experienced humanity, as we experience humanity.

The Temptation of Jesus

Jesus was also tempted just like all humanity is tempted. That may be a little bit of a surprise since we do not usually think of Jesus as one who was tempted, or even capable of being tempted. But clearly, He was tempted because He was fully human. Matthew 4:1 says, "Then Jesus was led by the Spirit into the desert to be *tempted* by the devil." This is very clear that Jesus was tempted. Even more instructive to us is Hebrew 4:15 which states,

For we do not have a high priest who is unable to sympathize with our weaknesses, but we have one who has been tempted in every way, just as we are – yet was without sin.

Jesus was tempted as we are tempted. Only humanity can be tempted. Jesus had a human nature. And in his human nature He was tempted in every way, just as we are. His temptations were every bit as real and tempting as those we go through today. Jesus experienced exactly what we experience in being tempted. He was tempted to lie, He was tempted to serve idols, He was tempted to cheat, and He was tempted towards sexual immorality; He was tempted in all the ways that we are tempted because He was fully human.

The Suffering of Jesus

Jesus also suffered as humanity suffers. Hebrew 2:18 says, "Because he himself suffered when he was tempted, he is able to help those who are being tempted." Jesus suffered. God does not suffer. Humanity suffers. Thus, Jesus has a human nature; He is fully human.

In His humanity, Jesus suffered, Jesus was tempted, Jesus was tired, Jesus was thirsty, and Jesus was hungry. Jesus was born as a human being, and Jesus also died as a human being.

The Death of Jesus

In the Matthew 27 account, Jesus hung on a cross and died. He was proclaimed and proven to be dead. The Roman soldiers whose job it was to crucify people knew when people were dead. They did not guess at it; they knew. They made certain that those who were supposed to die were dead. It was their job, and they took it seriously. They took the spear and stuck it in the side of Jesus and knew that He was dead. They were going to break the legs of Jesus because they normally break the legs of people who had been crucified, so that they cannot raise up on their feet and get oxygen in their lungs anymore. Once the legs of those being crucified are broken, they suffocate. The soldiers were going to break the legs of Jesus with a big mallet, but they did not because they knew that Jesus was already dead. Jesus, in his humanity, experienced death.

Scriptural Statement of the Humanity of Jesus

The life and experiences of Jesus prove that He was fully human. But there is one more proof – Scripture outright tells us so. In Hebrews 2:14a we read, "Since the children have flesh and blood, he too *shared in their humanity*." We are clearly told that Jesus shared in our humanity; Jesus was fully human.

Through all of these proofs, we know that Jesus is both fully human and fully God. These are the two essential natures of Jesus.

Characteristics of Jesus

We have established the two essential natures of Jesus. Now let us look at just a few other characteristics of Jesus.

Jesus is Eternal

JESUS IS ETERNAL
Revelation 1:8; 4:8; 22:13

In Revelation 1:8 we read, ""I am the Alpha and the Omega," says the Lord God, "who is, and who was, and who is to come, the Almighty."" Alpha and Omega are Greek letters of the alphabet. The first letter of the Greek alphabet is Alpha and Omega the last letter.

Jesus is saying that He is the first and the last. There is nothing before the first and nothing after the last. Everything else is in between. Revelation 4:8 states,

> Each of the four living creatures had six wings and was covered with eyes all around, even under his wings. Day and night they never stop saying: "Holy, holy, holy is the Lord God Almighty, who was, and is, and is to come."

They were worshiping Jesus, who was, and is and is to come. They were worshiping and celebrating His eternality. They were clearly worshiping Jesus as "The Lord God Almighty." Jesus Himself proclaims in Revelation 22:13, "I am the Alpha and the Omega, the First and the Last, the Beginning and the End." These statements show that Jesus is the eternal God.

Jesus is Sinless – Without Sin

JESUS IS SINLESS – WITHOUT SIN
Hebrews 4:15
2 Corinthians 5:21

Not only is Jesus eternal, He is sinless. Jesus is without sin. We find this in Hebrews 4:15 which states,

> For we do not have a high priest who is unable to sympathize with our weaknesses, but we have one who has been tempted in every way, just as we are – yet was without sin.

Jesus was without sin. He never committed one sin in His whole life. He was perfect in all that He did and said. Paul, in 2

Corinthians 5:21 confirms this when he says, "God made him who had no sin to be sin for us, so that in him we might become the righteousness of God."

Again, Scripture tells us that Jesus is sinless. He is perfect, spotless, and without blemish. Remember that holiness means to be without spot, blemish, wrinkle, stain, or sin. Holiness is to be completely other than creation. Jesus, being perfect, or holy, is completely other. He is God, fully God.

The Importance of Jesus as Fully God and Fully Man

We have taken the time to prove and establish the two essential natures of Jesus, fully human and fully God, and to highlight two other characteristics about Him, His sinlessness and His eternality. Now let us take some time to discover what that means to us. Why is it important that Jesus is fully God and fully man?

The Payment of Sin Required Perfection

There are two main reasons. First, let me suggest to you that Jesus had to be fully God and fully man to pay the penalty of sin. Humankind sinned against God and, as a result, was separated from God, and the only way to get back together with God was through a perfect sacrifice. That is, a sacrifice that does not have sin. But since every human was and is sinful, no human being could make the sacrifice to appease God and to pay the penalty of sin.

Someone might be a really good and even morally upright person, but that person could not pay the penalty of sin because that person is still a sinner; there is sin in their lives. Buddha may have been a really good person and prophet, but Buddha could not pay the penalty of sin, because Buddha was a sinner. Hari Krishna might be a good person and very religious, but he could not pay the penalty of sin because he was a sinner. All humankind has sinned. There is no person in the whole world who has ever lived or now lives who is perfect and without sin. There is no human being who could pay the penalty that sin required. Only God can pay that penalty, because only God is perfect. And Jesus is perfect. Jesus, because of His fully divine nature, was qualified to pay that penalty of sin. It took the perfection of Jesus to pay the penalty of sin.

The Payment of Sin Required Humanity

Second, only humankind could pay the penalty of sin because it was humankind who sinned. Humanity are the ones that owe the debt, we are the ones who had to pay the wages of sin. The perfect sacrifice for sin had to come from humanity. Of course the trouble with humanity is that all of humanity is imperfect! There is not one perfect human who could pay the penalty. It was an impossible requirement. Humanity had nothing to offer God to pay the penalty of sin. Nothing!

But Jesus was fully human. And Jesus was perfect! Thus, Jesus was the perfect human to pay the penalty of sin. He had to be fully God to be perfect, and he had to be fully man to make the payment for us. Jesus took upon humanity to represent us and stand in our place before God. When Jesus hung on the cross to pay the penalty of sin, he was the perfect, sinless, spotless, lamb without blemish who could pay the penalty of sin. And only Jesus could do that, because only Jesus is fully God and fully man.

That is why it is important that Jesus is fully God and fully man. That is why Jesus can say, "I am the way and the truth and the life. No one comes to the Father except through me" (John 14:6). No one else in all of creation could pay the penalty; no one at all could do what Jesus did.

Conclusion

The two natures of Jesus are essential to the salvation of the world. Salvation could not come about except by the hypostatic union of Jesus Christ. This is why it is important to know that Jesus is fully man and fully God. Jesus is the one who saves us from sin. He is the perfect one, the eternal one, and the only one who gives us salvation from sin.

Closing Prayer

God, I thank You that You know us and that You took humanity upon Yourself. Thank You that You walked in this world in a human body of flesh and blood and that You subjected Yourself to all that we are subjected to. Thank You that You experienced all that we experience. And thank You that You are fully God and that You have the power to save us from our sins. Thank You for being fully God and fully man for us. In Your name we pray.

Amen.

Chapter 3

THE ESSENTIALS

OF

GOD THE SPIRIT

So far, we have covered the essentials about God the Father and God the Son. Now, in this chapter, we are going to look at the essentials of God the Spirit. The purpose of this chapter is fourfold; to show that the Holy Spirit has personhood, to show that the Holy Spirit is fully God, to show the many works that the Holy Spirit is actively undertaking in the world today, and to make an application of what that means for our own life.

The Holy Spirit as a Person

The first place to start is to show that the Holy Spirit is a person. Just as God the Father is a person and God the Son is a person, so too, is the Holy Spirit. The Holy Spirit has personhood. He is a person. Notice that I refer to the Holy Spirit as "He" and not an "it". Since we do not refer to God as an "it", nor do we refer to Jesus as an "it", we therefore do not refer to the Holy Spirit as an "it". The Holy Spirit has personhood, and therefore we use a personal pronoun rather than an impersonal pronoun.

The Personal Pronoun

Jesus refers to the Holy Spirit as a person by using a personal pronoun. He does this in the gospel of John.

John 16:7-13

John 14:16-17

John 16:7-13,

But I tell you the truth: It is for your good that I am going away. Unless I go away, the Counselor will not come to you; but if I go, I will send him to you. [8]When he comes, he will convict the world of guilt in regard to sin and righteousness and judgment: [9]in regard to sin, because men do not believe in me; [10]in regard to righteousness, because I am going to the Father, where you can see me no longer; [11]and in regard to judgment, because the prince of this world now stands condemned.

[12]I have much more to say to you, more than you can now bear. [13]But when he, the Spirit of truth, comes, he will guide you into all truth. He will not speak on his own; he will speak only what he hears, and he will tell you what is yet to come.

Jesus uses a personal pronoun for the Holy Spirit ten times in this passage! It is very clear that Jesus views the Holy Spirit as a person and not as some sort of impersonal force.

In John 14:16-17 Jesus says,

And I will ask the Father, and he will give you another Counselor to be with you forever – [17]the Spirit of truth. The world cannot accept him, because it neither sees him

nor knows him. But you know him, for he lives with you
and will be in you.

In this passage, Jesus uses the personal pronoun for the Holy Spirit five
times, again showing us that He views the Holy Spirit as a person and
not an impersonal force or "it". So, the Holy Spirit is a person and should
be referred to as "him" or "he" rather than an "it," as we would with an
impersonal force.

Three Indicators of the Personality of the Holy Spirit

As was indicated in chapter one, the tests or indicators of
personality are will, intellect, and emotion. Just as we saw in chapter one
that God the Father had these three indicators of personality, so too we
will show that God the Spirit has the three indicators of personality: will,
intellect, and emotion.

THREE INDICATORS OF PERSONALITY		
Will	He determines	1 Corinthians 12:11
Emotion	He can be grieved	Ephesians 4:29-30
	He can be insulted	Hebrews 10:29
Intellect	He teaches	John 14:26
	He can be lied to	Acts 5:2-4, 8-9
	He knows the thoughts of God	
		1 Corinthians 2:11

The teaching in 1 Corinthians 12:11 shows us that the Holy Spirit
has a will. In this passage, the apostle Paul is teaching about spiritual

gifts. Concerning the gifts of the Spirit he writes, "All these are the work of one and the same Spirit, and he gives them to each one, just as he determines." The word, "determines" can also be translated as "wills". Every disciple of Christ has a spiritual gift by the will or determination of the Holy Spirit. It is clear that the Holy Spirit has a will, one of the indicators of personality.

Secondly, the Holy Spirit has emotion. In Ephesians 4:29-30 we read,

> Do not let any unwholesome talk come out of your mouths, but only what is helpful for building others up according to their needs, that it may benefit those who listen. [30]And do not grieve the Holy Spirit of God, with whom you were sealed for the day of redemption.

To grieve someone means to give them grief, to make them feel sorry, to make them feel sad, or to make them feel, in some way, out of sorts. Grief is an emotion. Paul tells us that we can grieve the Holy Spirit through our actions and words, what we do and say. The Holy Spirit can be saddened by our actions and words. If He can be saddened by our words and actions, then He has emotion.

Hebrews 10:29 shows us another emotion of the Holy Spirit. He can be insulted. Hebrews 10:29 says,

> How much more severely do you think a man deserves to be punished who has trampled the Son of God under foot, who has treated as an unholy thing the blood of the covenant that sanctified him, and who has insulted the Spirit of grace?

Our words and actions can insult the Holy Spirit. To be insulted means that there is emotion involved. This shows that the Holy Spirit has emotion.

We can both grieve the Holy Spirit and insult the Holy Spirit by our words and our actions. So it is that the Holy Spirit meets the second proof of personality.

The Holy Spirit not only has will and emotion, but He has intellect as well, the third indicator of personality. In John 14:26 we read, "But the Counselor, the Holy Spirit, whom the Father will send in my name, will teach you all things and will remind you of everything I have said to you." The Holy Spirit teaches and reminds. Both these actions require an intellect. Since the Holy Spirit performs these actions, He has intellect.

Another way in which we see the intellect of the Holy Spirit is through the fact that He can be lied to. In the book of the Acts of the Apostles, in Chapter 5, there is a story about Ananias and Sapphira. Ananias and Sapphira have some property that they sell and then go to Peter and say to him, "Peter, here is the money we got for the property." They make the claim that they have given all the proceeds from the sale of the land to the church. However, as Acts 5:2a says, "With his wife's full knowledge he kept back part of the money for himself." They did not give all of it to the church but wanted the church to believe that they did. As a side note, they certainly did not have to give all of it. The sin was not that they did not give it all but rather that they lied about the amount they gave. They told Peter that it was the full price when it was not. Peter responds to them in Acts 5:3-4,

> Ananias, how is it that Satan has so filled your heart that you have

lied to the Holy Spirit and have kept for yourself some of the money

you received for the land? [4]Didn't it belong to you before it was sold?

And after it was sold, wasn't the money at your disposal? What made

you think of doing such a thing? *You have not lied to men but to God.*

That is pretty pointed. Peter looks him right in the eye and says, "You have lied. But you have not lied to me only, you have lied to the Holy Spirit." Notice also that Peter says first that they lied to the Holy Spirit, and then he says that they have lied to God. Peter is clearly indicating that the Holy Spirit is God.

So, the Holy Spirit has intellect. He knows when we are lying. To finish the story, Ananias, upon hearing that he has lied to the Holy Spirit, falls down and dies. Then, three hours later, his wife, Sapphira comes to Peter who asked her, "Tell me, is this the price you and Ananias got for the land (Acts 5:8a)?" She lies too, "Yes," she said, "that is the price (Acts 5:8b)." Peter answers, "How could you agree to test the Spirit of the Lord (Acts 5:9a)?" She then falls down and dies too! That is a pretty significant lesson for the early church. They discovered that the Holy Spirit is God and knows when they were lying. Since He has knowledge, He has intellect.

Another verse, 1 Corinthians 2:11 even uses the word "to know". It says, "For who among men *knows* the thoughts of a man except the man's spirit within him? In the same way no one *knows* the thoughts of

God except the Spirit of God." The Holy Spirit is the Spirit of God and knows the thoughts of God. He has intellect.

The Holy Spirit is a person because He fulfills the three proofs or indicators of personality: will, emotion, and intellect. And just like God the Father and God the Son, The Holy Spirit is not some impersonal force of nature. The gods of other religions are just an impersonal force but not the God of the Bible. He is a personal God, and we have His personal Spirit with us and in us. The Holy Spirit is a person who connects with us personally.

One last thought about the personhood of the Holy Spirit. And for this, let's look at John 14:17b. I want to make a little bit of a deal about the words, "you know Him, for he lives with you and will be in you" because this shows us that the Holy Spirit is with us personally. He is with us because He is in us. Jesus says the Holy Spirit is not only living with you, but he is going to be in you. One of the names for Jesus is Emmanuel, which means, "God with us." The Holy Spirit is God with us and in us. Every single person who has received Jesus as Lord and Saviour has the Holy Spirit in him/her. In fact, you cannot be a Christian without the Holy Spirit. Titus 3:5-6 tells us that it is the Holy Spirit that does the work of regeneration. It is impossible to be a Christian without the Holy Spirit because it is the Holy Spirit that washes us and gives us rebirth. Thus it is that we have the Holy Spirit in us. We have God's personal presence with us at all times through the Holy Spirit in us because the Spirit is a person just as God the Father is a person and as God the Son is a person.

The Holy Spirit – Fully God

Now that we have established the personhood of God, let us turn our attention to showing that the Holy Spirit is fully God. In the next chapter, we will cover the essentials of the Trinity, how all three persons of God are all God and work together as God, but for now, we will focus our attention on the divinity of the Holy Spirit.

It is essential to know that the Holy Spirit is fully God, co-equal and co-eternal with the Father and Son.

> THE HOLY SPIRIT IS GOD
>
> Matthew 28:18-19
> 2 Corinthians 13:14
>
> Genesis 1:2

The Holy Spirit as God is seen in Matthew 28:18-19. Matthew 28:18-19 is the Great Commission passage in which Jesus tells his disciples to go and make disciples. He says,

> All authority in heaven and on earth has been given to me. [19]Therefore go and make disciples of all nations, baptizing them in the name of the Father and of the Son and of the Holy Spirit.

Jesus uses Father, Son, and Holy Spirit co-equally. He does not distinguish between the three as if they are all separate entities. The Holy Spirit is no less God than the Son and the Father.

The next passage, 2 Corinthians 13:14, simply says, "May the grace of the Lord Jesus Christ, and the love of God, and the fellowship of the Holy Spirit be with you all." Again, Jesus uses all three persons co-equally, no distinguishing between the three as if they are all separate entities.

Next, Genesis 1:2 states, "Now the earth was formless and empty, darkness was over the surface of the deep, and the Spirit of God was hovering over the waters." The Holy Spirit is God acting upon creation, hovering over the waters. These three passages of Scripture show that the Holy Spirit is a person who is equal to the Father and the Son; the Holy Spirit is fully God.

The Work of the Holy Spirit

We have seen that the Holy Spirit is fully God and has personality, like the Father and the Son. Now, let us turn our attention to the work of the Holy Spirit in the world around us. There are many works of the Holy Spirit. We will just look at a few of them, not an exhaustive list, just some essential ones.

The first four works of the Holy Spirit are linked together in that all of these actions are meant to draw us into a deeper relationship with God. The Holy Spirit teaches, counsels, convicts, guides and reveals God to us.

THE WORK OF THE HOLY SPIRIT	
Teaches	John 14:26
Guides	Psalm 32:8a
Convicts	John 16:8
Reveals God to us	John 16:14-15

The Holy Spirit is always guiding us closer to Christ and helping us to understand and know God more and more. He is at work helping us live out our relationship with Christ.

According to John 14:26 the Holy Spirit teaches and counsels us, "But the Counselor, the Holy Spirit, whom the Father will send in my name, will teach you all things and will remind you of everything I have said to you." Because we have the Holy Spirit in us, we can say, "God, I do not know what decision to make; I do not know what to do; I do not understand; please give me wisdom." God is our counselor and will help us and teach us. We can come to the right decision because of the Holy Spirit in us. God also tells us in Psalm 32:8a, "I will instruct you and teach you in the way you should go." We can count on God to lead and guide us in the decisions of life through His Holy Spirit who lives in us.

The Holy Spirit also has the job of convicting people of sin. John 16:8 says, "When he comes, he will convict the world of guilt in regard to sin and righteousness and judgment." It is interesting that the Holy Spirit convicts people of sin. Mankind has something called a conscience, something in our psyche, our very personhood that indicates to us what is right and what is wrong. Where does this conscience or this knowledge of right and wrong come from? It comes from God, the creator of the universe. God created the universe and endowed it with truth, His truth. There is an objective truth that comes from God. It is not truth because you or I call it truth or accept it as truth; it is truth simply because it comes from God. There is a truth that is, well, truth! It cannot be anything other than truth because God said it is true.

An example of God's truth that exists in the universe is the law of gravity. Gravity is true. Gravity exists because God set up gravity. The truth is, every time something drops it is because gravity is true. The law of inertia is another example of objective truth that God put into the universe. All the laws of science exist because God created those laws; they remain truth and always will. They are objectively true and can be tested and proven to be true every time. The very fact that we have something called science exists because we have objectivity. Objectivity exists because God created it.

There is truth that comes from God. Thus, there is also non-truth, or un-truth. All that is not from God is un-truth, or non-truth, or falsehood. There is right and there is wrong, and it is this right and wrong that the Holy Spirit convicts us of. Whenever we do something that is against God's truth, the Holy Spirit convicts us of our wrongdoing. He lets us know that we are doing wrong, that we are sinning. We may try to justify it away or ignore it, but the Holy Spirit comes along and convicts us of that wrongdoing.

So, the Holy Spirit teaches, guides, convicts, and The Holy Spirit further reveals God to us. The actions of convicting of sin and revealing God go together. A person cannot recognize his/her need for God until he/she recognizes his/her own sin. The Holy Spirit loves to draw us into a deeper relationship with God by showing us both our sin and the solution to our sin. Jesus says in John 16:14-15,

> He will bring glory to me by taking from what is mine and making it known to you. 15All that belongs to the Father is mine. That is why I said the Spirit will take from what is mine and make it known to you.

The Holy Spirit's job is to reveal God to the world. It is important to note that the Holy Spirit will not speak on His own, He will speak only what comes from the Father. The Holy Spirit will not say anything that is contradictory to what God has already said through His word. The Father and the Spirit will say the same things. In other words, the guidance, counselling, teaching, and convicting of the Holy Spirit is always in line with God's will and way. The Holy Spirit will never contradict what God has already said. The Spirit will convey to us what the Father is saying by taking God's words and making them known to us. In this way, by promoting God in our lives, the Holy Spirit brings glory to God the Father.

Further Workings of the Holy Spirit

We have seen that the Holy Spirit teaches, guides, convicts, and reveals. Let us look at some more workings that the Holy Spirit undertakes. He empowers, intercedes, and gives gifts.

THE WORKINGS OF THE HOLY SPIRIT	
Empowers	Acts 1:8
Intercedes	Romans 8:26
Gives spiritual gifts	1 Corinthians 12:11

The Holy Spirit empowers. In Acts 1:8 Jesus says,

But you will receive power when the Holy Spirit comes on you; and you will be my witnesses in Jerusalem, and in all Judea and Samaria, and to the ends of the earth.

The Holy Spirit gives us power for living, for following God. We cannot, by our own power, make ourselves better people or more right people before God; it is the Holy Spirit who does that for us. The Holy Spirit empowers us to live as God asks us to live. Then, as we are empowered to live for God, we will begin to be witnesses for God. Our lives will give witness to who Jesus is, both in how we live and what we say.

Perhaps one of our greatest fears, as Christians, is to tell people about Jesus. We often do not feel comfortable witnessing about Jesus. Remember this, though: every Christian has the Holy Spirit in them giving them power to witness for Jesus. Trust that the Holy Spirit in you will give you the power to live right before God and to be a witness for God.

Another work that the Holy Spirit does for us is the work of intercession. The Holy Spirit intercedes for us. Romans 8:26 says, "In the same way, the Spirit helps us in our weakness. We do not know what we ought to pray for, but the Spirit himself intercedes for us with groans that words cannot express."

Have you ever been in a position in life where the circumstances of life leave you wondering about how you would even pray? What do you ask for? How do you proceed? What should you say before God? Sometimes we do not even know where to start in our circumstance. Thankfully, the Holy Spirit does.

The disciple of Christ has the Holy Spirit in him who is in constant communication with the Father. The Holy Spirit intercedes for us. Another way to put it is that the Holy Spirit communicates with God for us. He connects us with God when we do not know how. He leads the way to God for us. He moves us in the direction of the Father. He moves us closer to God and connects us with Him.

It is interesting that the Holy Spirit intercedes for us with groans and expressions that cannot be put into words. Do you feel that sometimes? That emotion or sense of communicating with God? You may not know what to say to God, yet there is a definite, but undefined connection with God. You do not know what to say, how to say it, but you do know that you are somehow communing with God… and that is sometimes enough. During those times, it is very likely that the Holy Spirit in you is helping you to commune with God the Father on a level that does not need words. This is a wonderful ministry that the Holy Spirit does for us.

Yet another work that the Holy Spirit undertakes for us is to give us spiritual gifts that help to promote and build the kingdom of God. The apostle Paul writes in 1 Corinthians 12:11, "All these are the work of one and the same Spirit, and he gives them to each one, just as he determines." The apostle Paul is talking about spiritual gifts – supernatural empowering from God's Spirit that we could not and do not have on our own. It is the Holy Spirit who gives them to us. Every single Christian has a spiritual gift – at least one! When you receive Jesus as Lord and Saviour, the Holy Spirit gives you a gift that you will use to help build and promote God's kingdom.

If you think about the kingdom of God in terms of a 'Lego' building, God is building His kingdom through us, His people, by fitting each one of us 'Legos' into the right place so that the building rises and fits together well. We are all 'Lego' pieces being fitted into the building just as the Holy Spirit determines. It is up to Him as to which 'Lego' piece each one of us will be and how we will fit into the building. Our fitted-ness and our purpose are determined by the spiritual gift that He gives to us. In fact, the very opportunities of ministry we have in building the kingdom of God comes from the Holy Spirit who gives us gifts to do it.

We have seen so far that the Holy Spirit teaches, counsels, convicts, guides, reveals God to us, empowers us, intercedes for us and gives us supernatural gifts to help build the kingdom of God. There are many more activities of the Holy Spirit, but for the sake of our "essentials" we will take a look at one more.

THE WORK OF THE HOLY SPIRIT

Regenerates   Titus 3:4-7
                   John 3:3
                   Galatians 5:16-25

As previously stated in this chapter, the Holy Spirit regenerates us. Let us take a look at Titus 3:4-7.

> But when the kindness and love of God our Savior appeared, [5]he saved us, not because of righteous things we had done, but because of his mercy. He saved us through the washing of rebirth and renewal by the Holy Spirit, [6]whom he poured out on us generously through Jesus Christ our Savior, [7]so that, having been justified by his grace, we might become heirs having the hope of eternal life.

Scripture tells us that it is the Holy Spirit who regenerates us when He comes into our life. When anyone prays to ask Jesus to "come into my life", they are inviting the Holy Spirit to come into their life so that He can regenerate them and renew them. This is what Jesus calls being "born again" in John 3:3 when He talks to Nicodemus about salvation. It is the work of the Holy Spirit to regenerate us, to give us a new nature, a nature that is right before God. One cannot become a Christ follower without the regenerating work of the Holy Spirit to begin with.

The activity and ministries of the Holy Spirit are essential to the Christian. It can be plainly seen, by the list of activities or workings of the Holy Spirit, that we, as Christ followers, are completely dependent upon Him. We cannot live our lives without Him. He lives in us, constantly teaching and guiding, helping and counselling, convicting and revealing

God to us. The Holy Spirit is constantly connecting us with God and helping us to remain in a right relationship with God. Wherever we go, God is with us, and whatever we do God is constantly working for us.

Application of Knowing the Holy Spirit

So, what does it all mean? What does it mean that the Holy Spirit is a person? What does is mean that the Holy Spirit is God? What does it mean that the Holy Spirit regenerates and guides and teaches and convicts? What does all of this mean to us personally? The answer is found in Galatians 5:16-25.

In verse 16 Paul says, "So I say, live by the Spirit, and you will not gratify the desires of the sinful nature." How do I not sin? How do I not gratify the sinful nature? I live by the spirit who lives in me. I rely upon His power in me to guide me away from temptation and deliver me from evil. Paul continues in verse 17, "For the sinful nature desires what is contrary to the Spirit, and the Spirit what is contrary to the sinful nature. They are in conflict with each other, so that you do not do what you want."

Do you have that conflict sometimes? Of course you do! It is called temptation. We are tempted to do something, and we know we should not but we want to anyway. The conflict you feel is due to the Holy Spirit living in you and guiding and counselling you to not sin. The Holy Spirit is saying, "Walk with me. Do not walk away; stay with me. Do not walk over there where the world wants you to go. Stay with me."

Paul goes on in verses 18-21,

But if you are led by the Spirit, you are not under law.

> [19]The acts of the sinful nature are obvious: sexual immorality, impurity and debauchery; [20]idolatry and witchcraft; hatred, discord, jealousy, fits of rage, selfish ambition, dissentions, factions [21]and envy; drunkenness, orgies, and the like. I warn you, as I did before, that those who live like this will not inherit the kingdom of God.

Now that is quite a list! Have you ever done anything from that list? Of course you have! We all have! And we can be sure that any one of those actions that are listed here are not actions that originate from the Holy Spirit in us. There most certainly is a way to live that promotes God's kingdom, and there is a way that does not promote God's kingdom. The activities of the sinful nature that Paul lists do not promote God and His kingdom. These are activities that would indicate that we are not living according to the Holy Spirit in us.

But, there is another way! Paul goes on to write that there is a better way. There is a way to walk with the Holy Spirit which he calls the "fruit of the Spirit" or the result of the Spirit living in us. In verses 22- 23 we read, "But the fruit of the Spirit is love, joy, peace, patience, kindness, goodness, faithfulness, [23]gentleness and self-control. Against such things there is no law."

If we are going to look like a disciple of Jesus, this list from Paul tells us what we are going to look like. We will be people of love and joy and peace, etc… These character qualities will be produced in our life. What you are is identifiable by your character. You know what an apple tree is because it produces apples. You know what a pear tree is because it produces pears. You know the kind of fruit tree it is by the fruit it produces. Jesus says that His followers will be known by the fruit they produce.

Christ followers will look and act and talk like Jesus because of His Holy Spirit in us. Furthermore, verse 24 says, "Those who belong to Christ Jesus have crucified the sinful nature with its passions and desires." Jesus uses the word crucified. What does crucified mean? It means hung on a cross until it is dead. Now, Paul is not telling us to go out and be crucified. He is using the word to indicate to us that we are to be taking drastic measures with our sinful nature. We must crucify our sinful nature; we must put it to death. We must be completely against sin and completely for God. We are to learn to walk in the new nature and to consider the old sinful nature as dead. We are dead to the sinful nature but alive to the new spiritual nature. This is what Paul means when he goes on in verse 25 to say, "Since we live by the Spirit, let us keep in step with the Spirit."

When we are not in step with the Spirit, we cause Him grief, we insult Him, and we may find ourselves lying to Him. When we say, "No, Jesus, I am going to do my own thing. I am not going to listen to you; I am not going to take your advice, your counsel, your wisdom, or your guidance, nor am I going to listen to your conviction," we are not keeping in step with the Spirit. That puts us in opposition to God, and that is not where we want to be!

Disciples of Christ are to look different than those who are not disciples of Christ. Disciples of Christ look different, behave differently, think differently, view the world differently, approach the world differently and relate to the world differently because the Holy Spirit is in them.

We cannot do it on our own. The Holy Spirit does it for us. I encourage you to get to know God, who is in you, by walking with the Spirit. Keep in step with the Spirit.

Closing Prayer

Jesus, thank You that You have sent us Your Holy Spirit. Thank You that Your Holy Spirit is with us and in us. I simply ask Jesus that You would help us to keep in step with Your Spirit. Help us this week to look like You and act like You and think like You and be like You to those around us. I ask and pray in Your name Jesus,

Amen.

Chapter 4

THE ESSENTIALS

OF

THE HOLY TRINITY

In this chapter we will look at the essentials of the Holy Trinity. The topic of the Trinity is kind of a mysterious topic, but an essential topic that we must get straight because so many have gone astray. Every false religion, in part, is false because of how they deal with the Holy Trinity. Many Christians avoid the topic of the Trinity because it is difficult to understand and hard to define and explain. But that is no excuse to avoid the topic and no excuse to misunderstand it. We can neither ignore the doctrine of the Trinity, nor can we throw out the doctrine of the Trinity just because it is difficult and carries an air of unknown or mystery about it. If we fail to understand the Trinity, if we ignore it, or if we get it wrong, then we will find that our understanding of God – the true and living God – will be wrong as well. It is imperative that we come to understand the essentials of the Holy Trinity so that our concept and knowledge of God, not to mention our relationship with God, will be founded on truth and correctness.

We ought to keep in mind, however, that we may not be able to fully wrap our minds around the concept of the Trinity because God is God after all. He is Holy, completely other than we are. He is God and we are His creatures, His creation. He is so much more beyond us than we can even think or imagine. There will always be a sense of mystery; there will always be the fact that we, as created beings, cannot wrap our minds around a totally "other" being than us. He is God and we are not.

There is a measure of faith that is required when we approach God: not a blind faith or an un-informed faith, but a faith based on the facts of Scripture. This faith is not unlike a faith that you exercise here on earth. For example, when you write an e-mail and send it to the recipient that you have addressed it to, you have a certain measure of faith that the e-mail will actually be received by that person to whom it was addressed. That person could be halfway around the world, but you take it by the faith that you have in technology that the e-mail you wrote will indeed be delivered to that e-mail address in the next few seconds. It is likely that you cannot fully explain or maybe even understand exactly *how* that e-mail gets there, but you trust that it does. In fact, you just *know* that it does because of the faith you have in the truth of technology, even though you cannot fully explain the process of sending and delivering e-mails. The same thing is true about fax machines and sending faxes to one another. We know that it works and that it is true that the paper I put in somehow is translated to the paper that comes out of the fax machine to which it was sent. We cannot fully explain the technology of the process, but we have a certain measure of faith that what was sent over there is exactly what is received over here. So, if we can put our faith in man-made technology, is it so difficult to put our faith in God and what He says about Himself?

Let us now get into the Essentials of the Trinity and do so with faith and trust in God and His word. In this chapter, we will look at a definition of the Trinity, work through five essential Scripture passages that help us understand the Trinity, and show how God is one God who exists in three persons. We will then explore the co-equality and co-eternity of the Trinity and take a look at some of the attributes and works that all three persons of the Trinity share together as one.

Definition

If someone were to ask you what the definition of the Holy Trinity is, how would you answer? What definition would you give? Here is how I would put it – God is one God who exists co-equally and co-eternally in the persons of the Father, the Son and the Holy Spirit.

> THE HOLY TRINITY
>
> Definition: The Holy Trinity is the doctrine/ theology that says, "God is one God who exists co-equally and co-eternally in three persons; the Father, the Son and the Holy Spirit."

God is one being, existing in three persons. God is one God, not three separate gods. He is one God and exists in three persons. To help us understand this more, perhaps a more technical definition would help. God is one substance, existing in three subsistences. The word "subsistence" just means someone who is a real being or someone who meets the condition of remaining in existence. Thus, God is one substance existing in three subsistences. That is just another way of saying God is one God existing in three persons.

Essential Scripture About the Holy Trinity

In order to understand this definition, we need to look at some essential Scriptures about the Holy Trinity. There are five essential Scriptures that we are going to look at for this.

ESSENTIAL SCRIPTURES

Deuteronomy 6:4
John 10:30
Acts 5:3-4
Genesis 1:26-27
2 Corinthians 13:14

These five Scriptures are the basics or the basis of the concept of the Holy Trinity.

Deuteronomy 6:4 tells us God is one God. We read, "Hear, O Israel: The Lord our God, the Lord is one." We learn that God is God and He is one God. Now remember, Israel came out of a time in ancient Near East culture in which there were many gods. Each one of those nations had their own set of gods, plural. But Israel – Israel is different. Israel has only one God! This was unheard of that you would only have one God! The nations surrounding Israel believed that multiple gods were required for different needs. There was a god for the sun, a god for the rain, a god for war, a god for peace, a god for prosperity, a god for the trees, a god for the rivers, and on it went. According to the ancient Near East mindset, many gods were needed to cover all aspects of life.

Yet, the God of Israel claims that He is only one God. God came along and set up His nation Israel to be a completely different nation than all those around them. This was a nation that had a God who could do it all! He was a God that was powerful enough for every and all aspects of life – this was the God of gods! He made it clear that there was only one God and it was He. This was revolutionary and life changing!

In John 10:30 Jesus, in speaking to the pharisees, says, "I and the Father are one." Jesus and the Father are one. He does not say, "I and the

Father are two," or "I and the Father make a good pair." He says, "I and the Father are one." Jesus was saying that the Father and the Son are the same. They are the same substance; they are both God, and the same God. Jesus is just God with skin on – yes, God with skin on. There is one God who exists as the person of God the Father and the person of God the Son. Jesus is God, the same God as God the Father.

Then in Acts 5:3-4 we find out that the Holy Spirit is God.

> Then Peter said, "Ananias, how is it that Satan has so filled your heart that you have lied to the Holy Spirit and have kept for yourself some of the money you received for the land? ⁴Didn't it belong to you before it was sold? And after it was sold, wasn't the money at your disposal? What made you think of doing such a thing? You have not lied to men but to God.

Here we see that the Holy Spirit is made equal to God. The first phrase was that Ananias had lied to the Holy Spirit, and then Peter uses the phrase that Ananias had lied to *God*. The Holy Spirit is God! He is one and the same God as God the Father. Peter did not say Ananias had lied to *a* god, he said Ananias had lied to God –the same God – the Father, Son, and Holy Spirit.

Genesis 1:26-27 is another essential verse for the Trinity. It says,

> Then God said, "Let us make man in our image, in our likeness, and let them rule over the fish of the sea and the birds of the air, over the livestock, over all the earth, and over all the creatures that move along the ground."
>
> ²⁷So God created man in his own image, in the image of God he created him; male and female he created them.

Did you notice that God says "Let *us* make man in our image," and then the very next verse says that God created man in *His* own image. What is the "us" part? Well, it is a reference to the Holy Trinity – Father, Son, Holy Spirit – "let us make man in our image." Scripture does not say that three gods created man, but that one God created man – one God who exists in three persons.

The last essential Scripture is 2 Corinthians 13:14. This Scripture is simply supplied to show that God the Father, Son and Holy Spirit are being used co-equally and co-eternally. The apostle Paul writes in 2 Corinthians 13:14, "May the grace of the Lord Jesus Christ, and the love of God, and the fellowship of the Holy Spirit be with you all." Here we see the grace of Jesus, the love of God, and the fellowship of the Holy Spirit. They are used co-equally. Note that there is no hierarchy in the Trinity. There is not a division of 60% Father, 30% Son and 10% Holy Spirit. They are all the same – the same substance, existing in three subsistences - one God, three persons being co-equal.

God Is One God

God is one God who exists in three persons. Now, the question is: Why do we say there is one God? That statement tends to confuse people. Most other religions have more than one god so why does Christianity say there is only one God? Let's take a look at some essential Scriptures to answer this question.

ONE GOD	
God is one God	Deuteronomy 6:4
One God the Father	1 Corinthians 8:4-6
There is one God	1 Timothy 2:5-6
Demons believe in one God	James 2:19

Again, we go to Deuteronomy 6:4, "Hear, O Israel: The Lord our God, the Lord is one." At the very beginning of God's introduction to who He is, He lets His newly founded nation know that He is one God and not a combination of many gods.

For further proof of God's one-ness we turn to 1 Corinthians 8:4-6 which says,

> So then, about eating food sacrificed to idols: We know that an idol is nothing at all in the world and that there is no God but one. ⁵For even if there are so-called gods, whether in heaven or on earth (as indeed there are many "gods" and many "lords"), ⁶yet for us there is but one God, the Father, from whom all things came and for whom we live; and there is but one Lord, Jesus Christ, through whom all things came and through whom we live.

Notice that the phrase, "from whom all things came and for whom we live," appears twice in these verses. The first time it is used is in reference to God the Father, and the second use of the phrase is in relation to Jesus, the one Lord. The apostle Paul, by attributing the phrase to both the Father and the Son indicates to us that the Father and the Son are indeed the same. Yes, they are one and the same God. In this passage, Paul is saying that there are a lot of people who say there are a lot of gods out there and that there are many small letter 'lords' out there, but we know biblically, scripturally, and truthfully that there is only one capital letter "G", God. There is only one capital letter "L", Lord and, furthermore, they are the same. There is one God existing in three persons – one substance existing in three subsistences.

Then we read in 1Timothy 2:5-6, "For there is one God and one mediator between God and men, the man Christ Jesus, ⁶who gave himself as a ransom for all men – the testimony given in its proper time." There is one God, not many gods, not multiple gods, just the one God. So it is that we confess there is one God.

Finally, James 2:19 is an interesting verse because it says even demons believe that there is one God. James writes, "You believe that there is one God. Good! Even the demons believe that – and shudder." Even in the spiritual realm, where demons exist, the demons know and recognize that there is one God and only one God. The demons, who do not worship God, know. The demons who have walked away from God, who have cursed God, who shudder before God, know there is just one God and that He is one. It is truth from Scripture that there is one God.

One God, Three Persons

There is one God, but that one God exists in three persons. Why is it that we say that God exists in three persons? Let us have a look at how Scripture answers that question.

THE HOLY TRINITY - THREE PERSONS

One God, the Father	1 Corinthians 8:4-6
The Son is God	Hebrews 1:8
The Holy Spirit is God	Acts 5:3, 4b
	John 14:9-10a

A passage that we go back to is 1 Corinthians 8:4-6,

So then, about eating food sacrificed to idols: We know that an idol is nothing at all in the world and that there is no God but one. [5]For even if there are so-called gods, whether in heaven or on earth (as indeed there are many "gods" and many "lords"), [6]yet for us there is but one God, the Father, from whom all things came and for whom we live; and there is but one Lord, Jesus Christ, through whom all things came and through whom we live.

The point here is that the Father is called God.

Turning to Hebrews 1:8, we read, "But about the Son he says, "Your throne, O God, will last for ever and ever, and righteousness will be the scepter of your kingdom."" We know from 1 Corinthians 8 that the Father is God, and now we know from Hebrews that the Son is God. In speaking about Jesus, the writer says, "Your throne, O God will last forever." Jesus is very clearly called God. There is no mistaking that Jesus is God, just as the Father is God.

And then, to show us that the Holy Spirit is God, we turn to Acts 5:3, 4b. Peter is responding to Ananias who has just lied to Peter about the price of some land that he has sold saying,

> "Ananias, how is it that Satan has so filled your heart that you have lied to the Holy Spirit and have kept for yourself some of the money you received for the land? 4bWhat made you think of doing such a thing? You have not lied to men but to God."

Peter very clearly equates the Holy Spirit to God when he tells Ananias that he has lied to the Holy Spirit and then follows it up by re-iterating that Ananias has lied not to men, but to God. This shows us that the Holy Spirit is God, just as the Father is God and the Son is God.

In summary then, there is ample evidence from Scripture that there is one God who exists in three persons – the Father, Son, and Holy Spirit. This is the Holy Trinity. Whenever we talk about God, we are talking about a Trinity. We are talking about the Father, we are talking about the Son, and we are talking about the Holy Spirit. That is why Jesus tells His disciples that if they have seen Him, they have seen God the Father because they are one and the same. After Philip asks Jesus to show them the Father, Jesus answers by saying in John 14:9-10a,

> Don't you know me, Philip, even after I have been among you such a long time? Anyone who has seen me has seen the Father. How can you say, 'Show us the Father'? [10a]Don't you believe that I am in the Father, and that the Father is in me?

Jesus makes it clear to Philip and the disciples that by seeing Jesus, they were seeing the Father. Jesus is telling them that He and the Father are one – that Jesus is God, the same as God the Father. Imagine that! The disciples who were walking with Jesus were walking with God! They were walking with 'Immanuel' who is "God with us" (Matthew 1:23).

The Trinity – Co-Equal

We have seen that there is one God existing in three persons, the Father, the Son and the Holy Spirit. They are all one and the same God. Now, let us take a look at how the three persons of the Holy Trinity are co-equal, thus proving that they are all one and the same God.

CO-EQUAL

Matthew 28:19
2 Corinthians 13:14
1 Peter 1:1-2

The three persons of the Trinity are co-equal. In Matthew 28:19 Jesus says, "Therefore go and make disciples of all nations, baptizing them in the name of the Father and of the Son and of the Holy Spirit." All three are used co-equally by Jesus. They are to be baptized in the name of all three persons of the Trinity. One is not any more important or weightier than another. All three are God, the one and the same God. Thus, all three persons of the Trinity are used co-equally in the act of baptism.

Then we have 2 Corinthians 13:14 in which we read, "May the grace of the Lord Jesus Christ, and the love of God, and the fellowship of the Holy Spirit be with you all." In this benediction that Paul pronounces upon the Corinthian Church, he uses the Father, Son and Holy Spirit co-equally. There is no division, separation, or hierarchy; they are co-equal because they are one and the same God existing in three persons.

Jesus and Paul see the persons of the Trinity as co-equal, as does the apostle Peter in 1 Peter 1:1-2.

Peter, an apostle of Jesus Christ,

To God's elect, strangers in the world, scattered throughout Pontus, Galatia, Cappadocia, Asia and Bithynia, ²who have been chosen according to the foreknowledge of God the Father, through the sanctifying work of the Spirit, for obedience to Jesus Christ and sprinkling by his blood:

Grace and peace be yours in abundance.

Peter shows that the work of salvation in a person's life is enacted by the triune God. All three persons are at work in salvation. We are called by God; we are sanctified through the Spirit and made right by the blood of Jesus. All three persons of the Trinity are involved in our salvation. Each person has his part; each person is God. God the Father, God the Son, and God the Holy Spirit are co-equal.

The Trinity - Co-eternal

The Holy Trinity is also co-eternal. That means that each person of the Trinity shares in the eternal nature of God. All three persons of the Trinity are co-eternal; they all exist together from eternity to eternity. Neither the Father, the Son, nor the Holy Spirit are created beings – they are all the one and the same eternal God.

CO-ETERNAL	
Father	Isaiah 57:15; Psalm 90:2
Son	John 8:58; Isaiah 9:6
Holy Spirit	Genesis 1:1-2

That the Father is eternal is generally accepted. Isaiah 57:15 reads,

> For this is what the high and lofty One says – he who lives forever, whose name is holy: "I live in a high and holy place, but also with him who is contrite and lowly in spirit, to revive the spirit of the lowly and to revive the heart of the contrite."

Also, Psalm 90:2 says, "Before the mountains were born or you brought forth the earth and the world, from everlasting to everlasting you are God." Clearly the Father is eternal.

The Son is also eternal. A very telling verse is found in John 8:58 where Jesus, in speaking to the pharisees about who He is says, "I tell you the truth," Jesus answered, "before Abraham was born, I am!" The significance here is that Jesus uses the name of God, "I am" that is found in Exodus 3:14. He calls Himself God, by using the same name that God the Father used when speaking to Moses. Jesus says that He too is the always existing One, that He is eternal. Jesus says that He existed before

Abraham existed! Jesus is claiming eternality. By using the name that God gave to Moses for Himself, Jesus was clearly indicating to the pharisees that He was putting Himself as equal to the everlasting God. That is why the pharisees wanted to stone Him! They knew He was claiming to be the everlasting God.

Isaiah, in prophesying about Jesus, referred to Him as "the Everlasting Father" (Isaiah 9:6). There is no doubt about it; Jesus is co-eternal with the Father because He is the one and the same God.

The Holy Spirit is also spoken of as eternal. I go back to Genesis 1:1-2. "In the beginning God created the heavens and the earth. ²Now the earth was formless and empty, darkness was over the surface of the deep, and the Spirit of God was hovering over the waters." The Holy Spirit was there at creation taking part in the creative act of the universe. He is not a created being; He is God. He was there creating, just as the Father and Son were creating. Thus, we can conclude that the Holy Spirit is co-eternal with the Father and the Son.

The Shared Attributes of the Trinity

Another way in which we can know that the three persons of the Trinity are all the one and the same God is through their attributes – the characteristics of God which are attributed to all three persons. These Scriptures give us proof of the co-equality of the three persons of the Trinity as being one and the same God. We will look at four attributes of God to show that all three persons share in these attributes, thus showing that they are all one and the same God. We will look at omniscience, omnipotence, omnipresence, and the attribute of truth. We begin with the omniscience of God.

Omniscience

```
THE ATTRIBUTE OF OMNISCIENCE

Father              1 John 3:20b
Son                 John 6:64b
Holy Spirit         1 Corinthians 2:10b-11
```

The Father, Son and Holy Spirit are all omniscient. That is, all three persons are all knowing. 'Omni' means all, and 'science' means the knowing of, or knowledge.

The Father is all knowing. In 1 John 3:20b we read, "For God is greater than our hearts, and he knows everything." God knows everything, He is all knowing. The Son is also all knowing." John 6:64b says, "For Jesus had known from the beginning which of them did not believe and who would betray him."

Jesus already had knowledge of those who would believe in Him and who would betray Him. The point is that Jesus knew – He knew from the beginning. Jesus the Son is omniscient.

Then we see the omniscience of the Holy Spirit in 1 Corinthians 2:10b-11.

> The Spirit searches all things, even the deep things of God.
> [11]For who among men knows the thoughts of a man except the man's spirit within him? In the same way no one knows the thoughts of God except the Spirit of God.

The Spirit of God, the Holy Spirit, knows the thoughts of God. To know the thoughts of God means to be all knowing, to be omniscient. The Holy Spirit knows the thoughts of God because He is God! Thus, the Holy

Spirit is all knowing, just the same as the Son and the Father. All three are omniscient.

Omnipotence

ATTRIBUTE OF OMNIPOTENCE	
Father	Matthew 19:26
	Jeremiah 32:17
Son	Matthew 28:18b
Holy Spirit	Luke 1:35a

All three persons of the Trinity are also co-equal by omnipotence. Omnipotence means all powerful, to have all power. Matthew 19:26 says, "Jesus looked at them and said, "With man this is impossible, but with God all things are possible."" All things are possible with God. That means nothing is impossible for God, and that is because God is all powerful. There is no lacking in His power to accomplish whatever He decides to accomplish. He is all powerful. Jeremiah 32:17 tells us, "Ah, Sovereign Lord, you have made the heavens and the earth by your great power and outstretched arm. Nothing is too hard for you."

Jesus is also all powerful. About Jesus, Matthew writes in his gospel, Matthew 28:18b, "All authority in heaven and on earth has been given to me." Jesus has all authority. There is no authority that does not belong to Jesus. He has all authority, or power. Jesus the Son is all powerful just as God the Father is.

The Holy Spirit is also omnipotent. In Luke 1:35a we read about the angel speaking to Mary regarding the birth of Jesus, "The Holy Spirit will come upon you, and the power of the Most High will overshadow you." The Holy Spirit is called the power of the Most High. The name Most High is a very clear reference to God Himself and the Holy Spirit is equated with the Most High. Thus, the Father, Son, and Holy Spirit are all omnipotent; they are co-equally the all powerful God.

Omnipresence

ATTRIBUTE OF OMNIPRESENCE	
Father	Ephesians 4:6
Son	Matthew 18:20
Holy Spirit	Psalm 139:7-12

Another attribute of God is His omnipresence. God is omnipresent which means that He is always present. He is present everywhere at the same time on earth.

God the Father is always present. In Ephesians 4:6 we read, "one God and Father of all, who is over all and through all and in all." To be over all and through all and in all, is to be always present. There is never a time when God the Father is not present. There is not a place on earth or under the earth or above the earth or in the universe where God is not present. He is currently present in all places, at all times, at the same time.

We also learn that God the Son is omnipresent. In Matthew 18:20 Jesus tells His disciples that, "For where two or three come together in my name, there am I with them." Jesus was telling His disciples that wherever they would go in this world that He would be present there with them. Further, it indicates that whenever even the smallest groups of Christians gather together at various places in the world, Jesus would be with all of them equally as much. His presence would be with the small group in one country in equal measure as with a small group in another country at the same time. Wherever they are meeting and praying, wherever they are together, Jesus is with them. How can Jesus be with everybody, in all places, at the same time? It is because He is omnipresent, just as God, the Father is.

The Holy Spirit is omnipresent as well. Psalm 139:7-12 reads,

> Where can I go from your Spirit? Where can I flee from your presence? [8]If I go up to the heavens, you are there; if I make my bed in the depths, you are there. [9]If I rise on the wings of the dawn, if I settle on the far side of the sea, [10]even there your hand will guide me, your right hand will hold me fast. [11]If I say, "Surely the darkness will hide me and the light become night around me," [12]even the darkness will not be dark to you; the night will shine like
>
> the day, for darkness is as light to you.

It is clear that the Holy Spirit is being spoken of here as the One who is in all places at all times. There is no place to go to hide or get away from the presence of the Holy Spirit because He is omnipresent. He is present in all places, at all times, for all people.

Truth

Let's take a look at one last attribute, the attribute of truth. The Father, Son and Holy Spirit all share the attribute of truth – they are co-equal in truth.

ATTRIBUTE OF TRUTH	
Father	John 3:33
	Hebrews 6:18b
Son	John 14:6
Holy Spirit	John 14:16-17a
	John16:13a

Of the Father it says in John 3:33, "The man who has accepted it has certified that God is truthful." Also, Hebrews 6:18b says, "it is impossible for God to lie." We know then that God is truth and everything that God says is truth.

We can know that Jesus is the truth also by His very own words in John 14:6 where He says, "I am the way and the truth and the life. No one comes to the Father except through me." Jesus claims to be truth, putting Himself as equal to God the Father. Jesus is, therefore, claiming to be God by claiming to be the truth. Note that He is not claiming to be another version of the truth, or another facet of the truth, but is claiming to *be* truth, just as God the Father is truth.

The Father is truth, the Son is truth, and the Holy Spirit is truth as well. In John 14:16-17a, Jesus says, "And I will ask the Father, and he will give you another Counselor to be with you forever – [17a]the Spirit of truth." Jesus clearly calls the Holy Spirit the "Spirit of truth." Again, not a different version of the truth, but *the truth*, just as the Father and the Son are *the truth.* Jesus also says of the Spirit in John 16:13a, "But when he, the Spirit of truth, comes, he will guide you into all truth." Again, Jesus refers to the Holy Spirit as the Spirit of truth whose work it is to lead people into the truth. Thus, we see that the Father is truth, the Son is truth and the Holy Spirit is truth. All three are the same truth – all three are the same God.

We have seen that the attributes of God; omniscience, omnipotence, omnipresence, and truth are applied to all three persons of the Trinity, thus showing they are co-equally one and the same God.

The Shared Work of the Trinity

There is yet one more way to show that all three persons of the Trinity are co-equally and co-eternally God: by the work that they share. Let us look at the work of the Trinity in creation, revelation, and salvation.

Creation

The three persons of the Trinity are co-equal in their work of creation.

CREATION	
Father	Genesis 1:1, 26-27
Son	John 1:1-3
Holy Spirit	Genesis 1:2

Genesis 1:1 tells us, "In the beginning God created the heavens and the earth." God the Father was at work creating the world. Then in Genesis 1:26-27 we read,

> Then God said, "Let us make man in our image, in our likeness, and let them rule over the fish of the sea and the birds of the air, over the livestock, over all the earth, and over all the creatures that move along the ground."
>
> [27]So God created man in his own image, in the image of God he created him; male and female he created them.

This is a curious thing that God speaks of Himself in the plural. He says, "our image" and "our likeness" in verse 26 but then verse 27 goes on to speak of God creating in the singular, "in *his* own image" and "*he* created them". What is going on here? We are seeing the Trinity at work. The three persons of the Trinity being spoken of are in the plural, yet they are the one and the same God which is reflected by using the singular tense.

At the very beginning of creation God reveals Himself to us as the Trinity, one God existing in three persons.

We have also seen in Genesis the specific mention of the Holy Spirit at work in creation in Genesis 1:2. We read, "Now the earth was formless and empty, darkness was over the surface of the deep, and the Spirit of God was hovering over the waters." God the Father is creating in verse one and the Holy Spirit is also part of that creating in verse two.

Jesus, too, is part of that creative work. We know that from the New Testament. John 1:1-3 says,

> In the beginning was the Word, and the Word was with God, and the Word was God. ²He was with God in the beginning.
>
> ³Through him all things were made; without him nothing was made that has been made.

Jesus was there at creation. All things were created by Jesus. Without Jesus, the world could not be created because Jesus is God, co-equally with both the Father and the Holy Spirit.

Revelation

Another way the three persons of the Trinity are shown to be co-equal is in their work of giving us revelation. Revelation is the act of God revealing Himself to the world so that His creation might know Him.

REVELATION	
Father	2 Timothy 3:16-17
Son	Hebrews 1:1-2
Holy Spirit	2 Peter 1:20-21

God the Father was at work revealing Himself to humankind. We see this in 2 Timothy 3:16-17,

> All Scripture is God-breathed and is useful for teaching, rebuking, correcting and training in righteousness, [17]so that the man of God may be thoroughly equipped for every good work.

Every bit of Scripture that we have is given to us by God. God is the one who has breathed it out to us so that we can know who He is and how to be in a right relationship with Him. The Holy Bible is revelation; it is God's revealed words to us. It is not just the book that we call Revelation but our whole Scripture that is the revealed word of God. That is what revelation really means, the revealing of God's words to us. The fact is, we could not know anything about God if God did not reveal Himself to us. The Bible is the revealed words of God. It is the God-breathed writings used for letting us know how to be in a right relationship with God, to be used for teaching, correcting, training and rebuking in righteousness, or rightness before God.

God the Son is also involved in revelation. Hebrews 1:1-2,

> In the past God spoke to our forefathers through the prophets at many times and in various ways, [2]but in these last days he has spoken to us by His Son, whom he appointed heir of all things, and through whom he made the universe.

Here we see that the words of Jesus are God's revealed words to us. Jesus gives us revelation just as the Father does. Furthermore, John 1:1 speaks of Jesus as being the 'Word'. Jesus Himself is the word of God, He is the very revealer Himself!

So, the Father and the Son are both at work in revelation. What about the Holy Spirit? We see the Spirit's work in revelation through 2 Peter 1:20-21, which says,

> Above all, you must understand that no prophecy of Scripture came about by the prophet's own interpretation. [21]For prophecy never had its origin in the will of man, but men spoke from God as they were carried along by the Holy Spirit.

The words we have as Scripture were written by men, but not on their own or by their own ideas and design. It was the Holy Spirit who guided them to write what God wanted to reveal to us. Humankind did not come up with the idea of writing a book to later be claimed as a book that God wrote. It was not by the design of humankind that we have this most marvelous piece of literature called the Holy Bible. The Holy Bible was a result of God speaking His words for humankind to write down as they were controlled by the Holy Spirit. The words that we have in the Bible are God's words, given to us by the working together of the Father, Son and Holy Spirit. They are co-equal by their work or revelation.

Salvation

The Trinity is at work in creation, revelation, and also in the work of salvation. The Father, the Son, and the Holy Spirit are all involved in our salvation. Salvation was the plan of the Father, through the death of Jesus, and by the regeneration of the Holy Spirit.

SALVATION	
Father	Ephesians 2:8b
Son	John 14:6
Holy Spirit	Titus 3:4-6

Our salvation is the very gift of God. It was He who determined that salvation could be ours. It was His plan or will. Ephesians 2:8b tells us that salvation is "the gift of God". God the Father is the giver of salvation, and Jesus is the one through whom salvation comes. Jesus tells us in John 14:6 that He Himself is the way and the truth and the life, and that no one comes to the Father but by Him. Jesus is the way of salvation. It is His work to make the gift of salvation available to us. Then, it is the Holy Spirit's work to bring about our salvation. Titus 3:4-6 says,

> But when the kindness and love of God our Savior appeared, ⁵he saved us, not because of righteous things we had done, but because of his mercy. He saved us through the washing of rebirth and renewal by the Holy Spirit, ⁶whom he poured out on us generously through Jesus Christ our Savior.

It is the Holy Spirit's work to regenerate us and give us a new nature, to cause us to be re-born. Without the work of the Holy Spirit, we cannot be regenerated; we cannot be Christ followers. So, all three persons of the Trinity are at work in our salvation: God the Father, God the Son, and God the Holy Spirit.

Conclusion

We have shown through some essential Scriptures that the three persons of the Trinity – Father, Son and Holy Spirit, are all the one and the same God, though this can be fairly difficult to understand. We have to agree with the words of Romans 11:33, "Oh, the depth of the riches of the wisdom and knowledge of God! How unsearchable his judgments, and his paths beyond tracing out!" We cannot expect to fully understand God who is unlike us. He is God… and we are not. He cannot be fully known, but we can know, through Scripture, that God is One God, existing in three persons who are co-equal and co-eternal – Father, Son and Holy Spirit.

Perhaps a non-scriptural way of explaining this would help. I, Michael Wedman, am a father to my two daughters. To them, I am Dad, and I function as a father. But at the same time, I am a son. When I am in the presence of my father and mother, I am their son, and I function as their son. So, I am a father and a son at the same time. I am the same person existing in two subsistences. Then, to complicate matters, I am also a brother. When I am around my brothers, I function as their brother. So, I am a father, I am a son and I am a brother, all at the same time. I am, in a sense, three in one. When I am with my extended family, I function as a father to my children, a son to my parents and a brother to my siblings. This does not make me schizophrenic; I am not different people living in one body. I am one and the same Michael Wedman, but I function as three persons,– father, son, and sibling. I am one substance existing in three subsistences. It is similar with the Trinity – One God, three persons. God is One God existing in three persons: Father, Son and Holy Spirit.

God also reflects His Trinity in creation, in the substance of water. Water exists in three forms. There is the solid form or ice. It is still water, H_2O; it is found in a frozen form. Then there is the liquid state of water, the kind we drink or swim in. It is still water, H_2O; it is found in liquid form. It is the same substance as ice yet takes a different form. Thirdly, there is water existing in a gaseous form that we call steam. You put your kettle on, boil water, and steam comes out. It is still water, H_2O; it is found in gaseous form. All three forms are all the one and the same water, but they exist in three different states: solid, liquid and gas. Furthermore, there is scientifically reproducible evidence of something called a triple point, or flash point, wherein water exists as solid, liquid and gas all at the same time! Water exists as a type of trinity. There is one substance and three subsistences. It is similar with the Trinity: One God, three persons. God is One God existing in three persons: Father, Son and Holy Spirit.

Closing Prayer

God in Heaven, thank You that You show us who You are through Your words to us. Thank You that You have revealed Yourself to us and that we can know You as the Triune God who is at work in the world. We know that we will never be able to fully understand who You are because You are God and we are not but help us to know and understand as fully as we can through Your revealed words to us.

Amen.

Chapter 5

THE ESSENTIALS

OF

SIN

In this chapter we turn our attention to the essentials of sin. We will begin with a definition of sin, take a look at the universality of sin, and then investigate three aspects of sin. After that we will cover the topics of total depravity, the penalty of sin, and finally, the remedy of sin.

The topic of sin is not a topic that many people like to hear and talk about or be confronted with and even informed about. In an article that appeared in the magazine, "Table Talk", Rev. Steffen Meuller wrote, "In twenty-one of twenty-four Easter Sunday sermons (in evangelical churches), the words, 'sin', 'repentance', 'death', and 'cross' were not mentioned at all."[2] The fact is, most people, even church people, do not like to hear about the topic of sin, and pastors do not generally like to preach on the topic of sin because sin is a hard topic to preach on. We live in a day in which many people come to church for the purpose of "feeling good and uplifted", and thus, they view the topic of sin as one in direct opposition of "feeling good and uplifted".

---

2   Steffen Mueller, "Table Talk" Magazine, May 2018, p 43.

Hearing about sin in general, and especially our own sin that exposes us as sinners, is not what many church goers come to hear and be reminded of. I had an interesting experience in a church that I once pastored. I preached on sin and after I was approached by a person who let me know that he/she was really disappointed that I used the word sin. As I probed the reasons why, the person responded by telling me that the word "sin" is a bad word to use. This person felt that we should not use the word "sin" because it is bad for our egos and for our self-esteem. The person felt that speaking about sin was not helping people but actually hurting them and that I should use more uplifting words; certainly not the word "sin".

That is the unfortunate reality of the thinking that is out there, even in our churches! Many people who come to church come to hear the message that God loves you, that God will bless you, and that God will make everything in your life great. The fact that we each do have sin in our own life, which separates us from both God and others, is dropped in favor of, well, favor from God. The measure of a good sermon, a good church and a good pastor is based on people leaving the church service with warm fuzzies. Again, Meuller writes, "Yes, we need to talk about love, peace, joy, and life to the full, but we also need to talk about sin, the need to repent, and God's grace and forgiveness."[3]

Sin is a Reality

The existence and penalty of sin is a reality. Sin is not a human concept that we made up. Sin is a reality that God tells us about. All throughout Scripture God informs us of what sin is, how it affects us, and what we need to do in response to it. It is interesting that in the Old

3   Steffen Meuller, *"Table Talk" Magazine*, May 2018, p 43.

Testament, in the Hebrew language, there are eight basic words for sin. Eight basic words for categories of sin, but there are also many other words for sin that appear. In the New Testament, in the Greek language, there are more basic words – there are twelve. This is quite interesting when we think about it because when it comes to the Old Testament, we tend to think about God's laws, about God's judgment and about God's wrath. When we think of the New Testament we tend to think about love and grace and peace and mercy. Yet, the New Testament, which is less than half the size of the Old Testament, has more words for sin than the Old Testament! It is really a fallacy to think that the Old Testament is law and wrath and the New Testament is love and mercy. The Testaments are the same in their message because they are both speaking of the one and the same God: the Father, Son and Holy Spirit. Further, the same God wrote them both. Thus, the teaching about sin in both Testaments is the same; it has not changed.

Jesus, in his teaching, emphasized the reality of sin and the consequences of sin when it is left unforgiven. One might be surprised at how many times Jesus speaks or teaches about sin, its effects, and our response to sin. Jesus defines what sin is. He calls hypocrisy sin, He calls idolatry sin, He calls pride sin, He calls greed sin, and He calls immorality sin. Jesus says there are sins of the tongue, sins of the mind and sins of our actions. Jesus is clear that sin is a reality that needs to be addressed and taught about so that every person can come to a right relationship with God through Jesus. That is why this chapter teaches about the essentials of sin. We need to know what sin is and how it affects us. So, let's begin with a definition of sin.

Definition of Sin

We will start with a simple definition of sin and then begin to expand that definition as we go. Definition: sin can be defined as any defection from God's standards.

God does have standards. These standards are called truths. There is truth that God has given to humankind, truth that tells us what is right and what is wrong. Truth lets us know what sin is and what sin is not. God has given us truth; a truth that is not subjective but rather, objective. That is to say, God's truth is a truth that always remains the same, no matter what time, what culture, or where in the world you are. Truth given by God is an absolute truth, one that is absolutely and always true because God is always and absolutely true. God says this is right and that is wrong. There is no mixing of the two. Sin is any defection from God's standards of truth. If God says lying is a sin, then lying is a sin. Thus, every time we lie, we sin. We have defected from His standard. No matter how you want to justify it, or how "white" the lie might seem to us, it is always a sin. There is no getting around or changing God's standards of truth. So, sin can be defined as a defection from God's standards.

> SIN
>
> Defection from God's standards
> Deviation from the character of God
> Missing the mark; hitting the wrong mark

To broaden our definition of sin, we can define sin as anything that deviates from the character of God. Sin is not only breaking the standards of truth that God has set; it is also any action, thought, or word that goes against the character of God. Do you remember what underlies everything else in the character of God? It is holiness! Underlying everything else in the character of God is Holiness. Thus, sin is anything that we do which is in opposition to the holiness, or perfection, of God. We can sin against His standards of truth, and we can sin against His character of holiness.

Yet another way of defining sin is, "missing the mark". To sin is to miss one mark – the standards and holiness of God – and to hit another mark, that which is not the character and holiness of God. As disciples of Christ, we have a target to aim for – the standards and character of God. We want to live our lives in such a way that we reflect the character of God in our character and that we hold the same standards of truth that God holds. That is our aim. Yet, we do not always hit the target when it comes to our action, thoughts, and words. We often miss the target. Our aim is taken elsewhere, and we hit a different target, the wrong target.

When you go target shooting, you want to hit the target that is in front of you. When you do not hit the target, it is said that you missed the target. That is true; we did miss the target in front of us, but we did hit something else. We hit exactly what we were aiming for! Our aim was off the intended, or hoped for, target, but nonetheless, we hit another target; the target we aimed for. We hit exactly where we were aiming for. The problem is, our aim is not always correct. We have to continually adjust our aim to make sure that we are really aiming for the right target. If we do not, we will be off target, exactly where we aimed. You hit your target – it is just that the target you hit was not the one that you were supposed to hit – rather it was the one that you were aiming at.

Sin is like that. We can miss the mark that God has set out for us when we do not take the time to properly aim at that target. It takes concentration, adjustment and focus to hit the right target of God's standards and character. To sin is to aim at the wrong target and hit what we aim for. We always hit what we aim for. God desires that we aim for the "right" target – His holy standards of living.

Sin is all encompassing. Sin is any thought, word, or action that does not meet the standards of God, that does not express, or which is contrary to the Holy character of God, and which misses the target that God set up for us. Every action we take, every thought we think, every word we speak, if it is contrary to God's holy standards, it is sin. So then there is no way that humankind could ever proclaim to be without sin. If we claim to be without sin, we are claiming to be God – and that itself is a sin. As Romans 3:23 says, "for all have sinned and fall short of the glory of God."

The Universality of Sin

This brings us to something called the universality of sin. The universality of sin means that all humankind has sinned. Every single person has sinned, except Jesus, who never sinned. He is the only human being who never sinned. All the rest of humankind who ever lived, are now living, and will yet live are sinners.

THE UNIVERSALITY OF SIN

All humankind are sinners

Romans 3:9-24
Ecclesiastes 7:20
Luke 11:11-13

Let us look at some Scripture to know what God says about sin.
Paul writes in Romans 3:9-24,

> What shall we conclude then? Are we any better? Not
> at all! We have already made the charge that Jews and
> Gentiles alike are all under sin. [10]As it is written:
>
> There is no one righteous, not even one; [11]there is no
> one who understands, no one who seeks God. [12]All have
> turned away, they have together become worthless; there
> is no one who does good, not even one. [13]Their throats are
> open graves; their tongues practice deceit. The poison of
> vipers is on their lips. [14]Their mouths are full of cursing
> and bitterness. [15]Their feet are swift to shed blood;[16]ruin
> and misery mark their ways, [17]and the way of peace they
> do not know. [18]There is no fear of God before their eyes.
>
> [19]Now we know that whatever the law says, it says to
> those who are under the law, so that every mouth may be
> silenced and the whole world held accountable to God.
> [20]Therefore no one will be declared righteous in his sight
> by observing the law; rather, through the law we become
> conscious of sin.
>
> [21]But now a righteousness from God, apart from law,
> has been made known, to which the Law and the Prophets
> testify. [22]This righteousness from God comes through faith
> in Jesus Christ to all who believe. There is no difference,
> [23]for all have sinned and fall short of the glory of God, [24]and
> are justified freely by his grace through the redemption
> that came by Christ Jesus.

Did you notice how many times Paul says that all have sinned, and none
are righteous before God? That no one seeks God and that no one is good?
Eight times! In the gospels, Jesus was called the "good teacher". Jesus
responded by saying, "Why do you call me 'good', only God is 'good'."
Jesus was making a point that no human being is good on their own; only

God is good. No human being is right before God on their own. We have all sinned and fallen short of God's standards of holiness.

Paul further says in Romans 3:13-15 that our throats are open graves. What does that mean? It means we use our tongues to destroy people and tear people down and kill them. And it is not only by our tongues that we sin, for this Scripture says that our feet are quick to rush into sin. When temptation comes calling to us, we are prone to follow along in that temptation. We use our feet to carry us to places we should not go and to do things that we should not do. We are all sinful. All of humankind have gone their own way, away from God's way.

Ecclesiastes 7:20 is a great little verse that says, "There is not a righteous man on earth who does what is right and never sins." There is not a right person on earth who does what is always right and never sins. Again, all have sinned.

Then we have Luke 11:11-13 which says,

Which of you fathers, if your son asks for a fish, will give him a snake instead? ¹²Or if he asks for an egg, will give him a scorpion? ¹³If you then, though you are evil, know how to give good gifts to your children, how much more will your Father in heaven give the Holy Spirit to those who ask him!

Jesus clearly says that we are evil, meaning that we have sin in our life and that we are prone to follow the ways of sin rather than the ways of God.

This is the universality of sin – that all people are sinners. Not one person can claim he/she have never sinned. Sin affects us all.

Three Aspects of Sin

Sin is a condition of humanity that affects every single person. And, as if to prove to us further that all human beings have sin, we learn from Scripture that there are three aspects of sin. There is inherited sin, imputed sin, and personal sin. Let's take a look at these in order.

Inherited Sin

Inherited sin means that every human being is born into a sinful state. We are born into sin.

```
INHERITED SIN

All humanity is born into a sinful state

    Psalm 51:5
    Ephesians 2:3
```

Psalm 51:5 says, "Surely I was sinful at birth, sinful from the time my mother conceived me." The Psalmist, David, recognizes that he was sinful from the time of birth, from the time his mother conceived him. How could David be sinful at birth when he had yet to do anything wrong or bad? He was innocent as a baby, wasn't he? Aren't we all without sin when we are born? The answer to that is yes, and no. Yes, we are innocent of any personal sin that we have yet to commit, but we are born with a sinful nature. This is what is referred to as inherited sin. We get sin from our parents. Since our parents have a sinful nature, the children are born with a sinful nature. Unfortunately, like father, like son. We are all born with a sinful nature from our very birth.

Ephesians 2:3 says, "All of us also lived among them at one time, gratifying the cravings of our sinful nature and following its desires and thoughts. Like the rest, we were by nature objects of wrath." Paul tells us that we were objects of God's wrath by our very nature, our sinful nature. We were born with a sinful nature because we inherited a sinful nature.

It does not happen that we are born partly good and partly bad and we get to choose which way we are going to go. We are born with a sinful nature and so we naturally sin. This is why young children, when they are old enough to speak and understand, begin to defy what their parents ask them to do. They have a sinful nature inherited from their parents that naturally leads them to disobey or defy their parents. The "terrible twos" come from an inherited sinful nature. Perhaps you have observed that you have to teach children *not* to lie. We do not have to be taught how to lie; it comes naturally from our sinful nature. Also, children do not naturally share with others; they have to be taught to share. Selfishness comes naturally; from our sinful nature that we are born into.

We are all born with a sinful nature. That is inherited sin.

Imputed Sin

Then there is something called imputed sin. Imputed sin simply means all humankind has a sinful nature that is given to us from Adam. Imputation or imputed means: that which is ascribed to us, accredited to us, given to us, or assigned to us. If you impute an action to someone you are ascribing that action to them or accrediting it to them or assigning it to them.

Perhaps I can explain this is through an example. Say you are part of a group of high school students that decides that they are going to write graffiti on the side of their high school. So you all go out, as planned, on a certain date, at a certain time, in a certain place, and the group begins to graffiti the high school walls with spray paint cans. The group is having a great art session, but you yourself are only watching as you somehow have a twinge of conscience that maybe this is not a good idea. So, you yourself do not actually spray anything at all on the walls of the school, not even one spray; you just watch as the others do the artwork. Then suddenly the police cars show up, and you are all caught! The whole group is arrested and taken away in the police cars, including yourself, even though you have not sprayed anything on the wall. You are found guilty because you are part of the group; you are implicated in the crime. The sin of the crime of the whole group is imputed onto you, even though you did not actually physically take part in spraying the paint. It is assigned to you because you were there; you were part of the group. Thus, their fate is your fate. Their sin of graffiti is imputed to you; it is assigned to you, it is accredited to you, and it is given over to you. That is imputed sin.

All of humanity has sin that is imputed to us from the sin of Adam. Adam was the first sinner, and because Adam sinned, and because we all share in Adam's race, we are all assigned or accredited or ascribed sin. We are part of the group.

IMPUTED SIN

All humankind have a sinful nature that is imputed to us from Adam.

Imputed = ascribing, accrediting, assigning
Romans 5:12-21

The apostle Paul writes about imputed sin in Romans 5:12-21,

Therefore, just as sin entered the world through one man, and death through sin, and in this way death came to all men, because all sinned – [13]for before the law was given, sin was in the world. But sin is not taken into account when there is no law. [14]Nevertheless, death reigned from the time of Adam to the time of Moses, even over those who did not sin by breaking a command, as did Adam, who was a pattern of the one to come.

[15]But the gift is not like the trespass. For if the many died by the trespass of the one man, how much more did God's grace and the gift that came by the grace of the one man, Jesus Christ, overflow to the many! [16]Again, the gift of God is not like the result of the one man's sin: The judgment followed one sin and brought condemnation, but the gift followed many trespasses and brought justification. [17]For if, by the trespass of the one man, death reigned through that one man, how much more will those who receive God's abundant provision of grace and of the gift of righteousness reign in life through the one man, Jesus Christ.

In this passage, Paul is comparing death that is imputed to us by Adam to everlasting life that is imputed to us by Jesus. Paul goes on to say,

[18]Consequently, just as the result of one trespass was condemnation for all men, so also the result of one act of righteousness was justification that brings life for all men.

Did you get that? The result of Adam's sin was condemnation for all people – that is imputed sin.

Likewise, Paul writes that the death of Jesus on the Cross and the resurrection of Jesus gives us imputed life when we receive Him.

[19]For just as through the disobedience of the one man the many were made sinners, so also through the obedience of the one man the many will be made righteous.

[20]The law was added so that the trespass might increase. But where sin increased, grace increased all the more, [21]so that, just as sin reigned in death, so also grace might reign through righteousness to bring eternal life through Jesus Christ our Lord."

The whole human race has imputed sin from Adam. Because Adam sinned, death entered all of us. Because Adam sinned, we all have sinned.

So there is inherited sin, there is imputed sin, and thirdly there is personal sin. Personal sin is what most of us think of when we think of sin. We do not think of the sin nature, either inherited sin or imputed sin. No, we think of our own personal sin.

Personal Sin

PERSONAL SIN

All humankind have personally and individually sinned – action we have taken ourselves.

All have turned away	Romans 3:12
All have sinned	Romans 3:23
Cannot claim to be without sin	1 John 1:8
Sample list of personal sins	Galatians 5:16-23, 25
Sinful nature vs spiritual nature	Romans 7:14-25a

Personal sin is a result of having a sinful nature which we then act upon or act out. When a two-year-old says, "No! I am not going to listen to you," that is the acting out of his/her sin nature. Any time we say to God, "No, I am not going to listen to you," we are personally sinning; we are acting out of our sinful nature.

Personal sin is an action that we have taken ourselves, individually or personally. The sin nature is not necessarily something we have done ourselves, whereas personal sin is. Romans 3:12 says, "All have turned away, they have together become worthless; there is no one who does good, not even one." Romans 3:23 says, "for all have sinned and fall short of the glory of God." All of humanity has sinned; we all have personal sin. Nobody can ever raise their hand and claim that they have never sinned. We all have personal sin. In fact, 1 John 1:8 says that we cannot claim to be without sin. John writes, "If we claim to be without sin, we deceive ourselves and the truth is not in us." We can never claim to be without sin, we all have personally sinned.

Galatians 5:16-23 also clearly tells us that we have personal sin. Here we get a sample list of personal sin. Paul writes,

> So I say, live by the Spirit, and you will not gratify the desires of the sinful nature. [17]For the sinful nature desires what is contrary to the Spirit, and the Spirit what is contrary to the sinful nature. They are in conflict with each other, so that you do not do what you want. [18]But if you are led by the Spirit, you are not under law.
>
> [19]The acts of the sinful nature are obvious: sexual immorality, impurity and debauchery; [20]idolatry and witchcraft; hatred, discord, jealousy, fits of rage, selfish ambition, dissensions, factions [21]and envy; drunkenness, orgies, and the like. I warn you, as I did before, that those who live like this will not inherit the kingdom of God.
>
> [22]But the fruit of the Spirit is love, joy, peace, patience, kindness, goodness, faithfulness, [23]gentleness and self-control. Against such things there is no law.

In these verses, Paul gives us two lists. The first list is a list of sins that each person on earth has participated in. Perhaps you have not participated in every one of them, but there is no doubt that you have personally been involved with at least one of the sins on the list and likely more. There are other lists that we have in Scripture, but we do not need to go to them as it is clear from just one of these lists that we have personal sin in our lives.

The second list that Paul gives is a list of what the characteristics of a Christ follower are to look like. You have likely noticed that these two lists are vastly different. That is because the sinful nature and its actions are contrary to the spiritual nature and its actions. These two lists exist as options for all of us, every day, and it is up to us, as disciples of Christ, to choose the second list – the list of what the characteristics of walking with Jesus looks like. We want to conform to the character of God, rather than deviate from it. Even after we become disciples of Jesus, we continue to fight against our sinful nature. Paul would not have written this to the Galatian Christians unless he knew that the choice to sin continues to exist within us through our sinful nature even after we have received Jesus as our Lord and Saviour.

The apostle Paul in Romans 7 clearly teaches that everyone has a sinful nature, even after salvation. He writes of even himself when he writes about the sinful nature that wars against the spiritual nature so that he does what he does not want to do, and hates doing what he does not want to do. He writes about the battle that rages within him, between his sinful nature and his spiritual nature. He writes in Romans 7:14-25a,

> We know that the law is spiritual; but I am unspiritual, sold as a slave to sin. [15]I do not understand what I do. For what I want to do I do not do, but what I hate I do. [16]And if I do what I do not want to do, I agree that the law is good. [17]As it is, it is no longer I myself who do it, but it is sin living in me. [18]I know that nothing good lives in me, that is, in my sinful nature. For I have the desire to do what is

good, but I cannot carry it out. [19]For what I do is not the good I want to do; no, the evil I do not want to do – this I keep on doing. [20]Now if I do what I do not want to do, it is no longer I who do it, but it is sin living in me that does it.

[21]So I find this law at work: When I want to do good, evil is right there with me. [22]For in my inner being I delight in God's law; [23]but I see another law at work in the members of my body, waging war against the law of my mind and making me a prisoner of the law of sin at work within my members. [24]What a wretched man I am! Who will rescue me from this body of death? [25a]Thanks be to God – through Jesus Christ our Lord!

Even after we receive salvation through Jesus Christ, we still have a sinful nature. It is not wiped out or taken away; it is our very nature that we inherited and that was imputed to us.

Paul knows that the disciple of Christ must behave, talk, and think differently than those who are not disciples of Christ. Thus he gives us a type of check list in which to evaluate our walk with Jesus. We can ask ourselves, "Am I displaying the characteristics of the spirit-filled life (the second list), or am I displaying the characteristics of the sin-filled life (the first list)?" Paul exhorts us to look more like the second list in Galatians 5:25 when he says, "Since we live by the Spirit, let us keep in step with the Spirit."

Without a doubt, we all have personal sin that arises out of inherited sin and imputed sin. Any argument otherwise is futile in light of the Scriptures that we have seen.

Total Depravity

There is a term that we use for our total sinfulness; it is called depravity.

> TOTAL DEPRAVITY
>
> All humankind fails the test of pleasing God.
>
> Every facet of our being is corrupted by sin; our very nature is sin.
>
> All people have sin and are powerless to do good on their own.

Humanity, because of sin, is totally depraved. Depravity is really a word that means to have failed the test of pleasing God. Humanity failed the test; we are depraved. Every facet of our being is corrupted by sin. Indeed, it is our very nature to sin. Depravity, total depravity, refers to the fact that there is no goodness that exists in us without the grace of God. We cannot, by our own nature and character, do anything good. Goodness comes from God, not us. We are devoid of goodness without God. There is not a good thing in us; we are totally depraved. In fact, I would argue that without God in this world humanity would not have laws that protect and help people because these laws promote goodness, and all goodness comes from God. Humanity's sinful nature does not promote the goodness of God.

The nature of sin is destruction, not goodness. It is evil, not good. The sin nature seeks that which is only for self, not which is helpful to others. The sinful nature does not spread goodness, but spreads harm to others. The sinful nature causes our total depravity. All people have sinned and are powerless to do good on their own.

Penalty of Sin

This is a pretty bleak picture of humanity, isn't it? Yes, it is, but sorry to say, the story gets worse. Not only are we all sinful before God, but sin has a penalty. And that is a problem. If there were no penalty for sin, then sin would not matter; it would make no difference to our lives. We would all just sin as we pleased and carry on. If there is no penalty for sin, then who cares? If there were no penalty for robbing banks, we would be robbing banks all the time. If there were no penalty for cheating on our taxes, we would be cheating all the time. If there were no penalty for lying, we would be lying all the time. The truth is, though, there is a penalty for sin. And that is our real problem.

PENALTY FOR SIN	
There is a penalty for sin	Romans 6:23a
Both a physical and spiritual death	Genesis 3:1-12
Separation from God	Ephesians 2:1-2

Scripture tells us that "For the wages of sin is death" (Romans 6:23a), and that death is both a spiritual death and a physical death.

In Genesis 3:1-12 we read,

Now the serpent was more crafty than any of the wild animals the Lord God had made. He said to the woman, "Did God really say, 'You must not eat from any tree in the garden'?"

²The woman said to the serpent, "We may eat fruit from the trees in the garden, ³but God did say, 'You must not eat fruit from the tree that is in the middle of the garden, and you must not touch it, or you will die.'"

⁴"You will not surely die," the serpent said to the woman. ⁵"For God knows that when you eat of it your eyes will be opened, and you will be like God, knowing good and evil."

> ⁶When the woman saw that the fruit of the tree was good for food and pleasing to the eye, and also desirable for gaining wisdom, she took some and ate it. She also gave some to her husband, who was with her, and he ate it.

Please note that Adam was right next to Eve; he was right there with her! At what point did Adam step in and say, "No, no, no, do not do it?" He did not. He, too, was being deceived by satan.

> ⁷Then the eyes of both of them were opened, and they realized they were naked; so they sewed fig leaves together and made coverings for themselves.

> ⁸Then the man and his wife heard the sound of the Lord God as he was walking in the garden in the cool of the day, and they hid from the Lord God among the trees of the garden.

They hid from God. That was the first separation from God. That is the first death that occurred, a death in their relationship with God. Because of their sin, they now wanted to hide from Him rather than enjoy His company. They did not want to be near God because they knew they had sinned; they knew they had done something wrong. They did not want to face God with it. The oneness and transparency in their relationship with God had died. They now wanted separation and hiddenness.

> ⁹But the Lord God called to the man, "Where are you?"

> ¹⁰He answered, "I heard you in the garden, and I was afraid because I was naked; so I hid."

Adam was afraid. Fear was not in the world before sin entered the world. There is another consequence of sin – fear. And what was the particular reason for Adam's fear? Adam now knew that he was naked. He was now afraid of being completely transparent before God.

[11]And he said, "Who told you that you were naked? Have you eaten from the tree that I commanded you not to eat from?"

[12]The man said, "The woman you put here with me – she gave me some fruit from the tree, and I ate it."

God was giving him a chance. It is not as if God did not know. He knew, He was offering Adam a chance to come clean, to confess, to be transparent. A similar thing happens with our own children. When they do something wrong and we know it, we ask them about it. We give them a chance to come clean, to confess, to be transparent. "Did you take that extra cookie? No? Okay, do you want to try it again? Did you take that cookie?" God is doing the same thing; He was giving them a chance to tell the truth. And take note of what God says, "Who told you that you were naked, and did you eat of the fruit I told you not to?" Come on Adam, here is your chance! Get right with God! But does he? No! Just like our own children, Adam makes is worse! He now even blames Eve! His only other human companion, his wife! It was not me! It was her!

As a result of the very first sin, disobedience to God, humankind now has fear, a death in their relationship with God, blame, and separation from one another. This is death taking place here – death in a relationship with God and death in a relationship with the only other person alive. This is what sin does. It destroys our relationship with God and destroys our relationship with each other.

Another passage that helps us to understand the consequence of sin is Ephesians 2:1-2.

As for you, you were dead in your transgressions and sins, [2]in which you used to live when you followed the ways of this world and of the ruler of the kingdom of the air, the spirit who is now at work in those who are disobedient.

We are clearly told that there is death in transgressions and sins. There is no life in sin but always death. The wages of sin is always death, of some sort, in some way.

Eternal Consequences of Sin

> ETERNAL CONSEQUENCES OF SIN
>
> John 3:16
> 1 John 5:12
> Revelation 20:11-16

We have so far been speaking of temporal consequences of sin. But there are not just temporal consequences of sin; there are eternal consequences of sin as well. When we ignore sin and do not seek God's forgiveness through Jesus Christ, there is an eternal separation from God forever. This is called hell, a place which God does not want anyone to end up in. John 3:16 tells us that God does not want anyone to perish. "For God so loved the world that he gave his one and only Son, that whoever believes in him shall not perish but have eternal life."

Perishing and everlasting life are terms that are opposite each other. Another way of putting it is – everlasting death and everlasting life. We read in 1 John 5:12, "He who has the Son has life; he who does not have the Son of God does not have life." (That is, does not have everlasting life.) The book of Revelation confirms this teaching as well. Revelation 20:11-16 is the teaching about the great white throne judgment in which all of those whose names not written in the book of life are judged unto eternal torment, or an eternal separation from God forever. It is a place called hell. There is the real and eternal consequence of sin – death, or separation from God forever. But not all is lost! There is a remedy for sin!

Remedy for Sin

That there are eternal consequences for sin is the bad news. But there is good news! There is great news! There is a remedy for sin! I don't want to leave you with the eternal consequences of sin and have you finish this chapter with the bad news. No, I want you to know that there is a sure and certain remedy and hope. There is salvation from sin in Jesus Christ.

Though this is the topic of the next chapter, I will briefly write about the remedy for sin to close this chapter.

```
REMEDY FOR SIN

God's love and forgiveness

     John 3:16
     1 Timothy 2:3-4
     2 Peter 3:9
     Romans 5:8b
     Romans 6:23
```

The remedy for the consequences of sin is God's love and forgiveness. John 3:16 says, "For God so loved the world that he gave his one and only Son, that whoever believes in him shall not perish but have eternal life." Whoever! That means anyone and everyone. 1 Timothy 2:3-4 tells us that God wants all people to come into salvation. It says, "This is good, and pleases God our Saviour, ⁴who wants all men to be saved and to come to a knowledge of the truth." Also, 2 Peter 3:9 confirms that God wants all people to come to salvation! "The Lord is not slow in keeping his promise, as some understand slowness. He is patient with you, not wanting anyone to perish, but everyone to come to repentance."

Salvation, the forgiveness of our sins, is found in Jesus Christ. Romans 5:8b, says, "While we were still sinners, Christ died for us." Romans 6:23 states, "For the wages of sin is death, but the gift of God is eternal life in Christ Jesus our Lord." There is a gift of God, the salvation of our souls. Jesus paid the penalty of our sin through His death and Resurrection on the cross and offers salvation to us as a free gift for us to receive.

When we receive Jesus as Lord and Saviour into our lives, He forgives us our sins and gives us everlasting life. Have you received Jesus? Have you asked Him into your life for the forgiveness of your sins? He is wanting to save you from your sins. Jesus invites you to receive the gift of forgiveness of sins and everlasting life. If you have never received Him as Lord and Saviour, will you?

Maybe you have never received Him and need to today. I am going to pray. It is a prayer that simply says, "Jesus, come into my life and be my Saviour and Lord." If you have never prayed that prayer and you know that you are a sinner, that you can't do anything for salvation on your own, pray this prayer.

Closing Prayer

Jesus, I know that I am a sinner. I know that I cannot do anything on my own to get to heaven. I know that there is no good thing in me. So Jesus, I ask You to forgive my sins. I believe You died on the cross for me. I believe You were raised again on the third day so that You now offer me salvation. Jesus, I receive You. Come into my life as both my Lord and my Saviour and help me to live for You. In Jesus' name.

Amen

Chapter 6

THE ESSENTIALS

OF

SALVATION

In this chapter we will look at the Essentials of Salvation. You have likely heard sermons about salvation, read about salvation and even memorized Bible verses about salvation, but if your neighbor were to ask you what salvation is, how would you answer that question? What would you tell that person? How would you go about defining and describing salvation? In this chapter, we will answer those questions by giving a definition of salvation, show the need for salvation (a quick review of the previous chapter), and walk through some key verses to help you understand salvation and therefore help lead others unto salvation. This chapter will also cover the topics related to salvation: atonement, justification, and regeneration.

Definition

Let me suggest an essential definition of salvation. Salvation is God saving His creation, particularly humankind, from the penalty of sin, from the power of sin, and ultimately from the presence of sin. Salvation can also be defined as God rescuing humankind from eternal death unto eternal life, from condemnation before God to peace with God, and from an old life that is in opposition to God to a new life that is in conformity with God. Salvation is an action that God initiates in order to bring people from death to life, darkness to light, and from satan to Himself.

DEFINITION OF SALVATION

God saving His creation, humankind, from the penalty of sin, the power of sin and the presence of sin.

Rescuing humankind from death to life and from condemnation before God to peace with God.

Let's take a closer look at the various parts of that definition: God saving His creation, humankind, from the penalty, the power and ultimately the presence of sin.

The Need for Salvation

So many people today question even the need for salvation. They argue that they have no need for salvation, nor do they need a Saviour. Since they have never murdered someone or committed the 'big sins', they are good people and, therefore, not in need of God for salvation. In fact, some would say that the notion of salvation itself is somehow old-fashioned or outdated, arguing that even if they did need some sort of salvation, they would not need God for it since humankind has evolved enough in our thinking and in our humanity so that we can save ourselves. Humankind, they argue, is saving the environment and saving the planet, so why can't we save ourselves? Why would we need to be saved? And why would *God* need to save me? However, if you read the previous chapter, you would know that humankind *is* sinful and is in need of saving and is unable to do so on our own. Here is a quick re-cap.

All Humankind Is Sinful.

Romans 3:23 says, "for all have sinned and fall short of the glory of God." There is no person here on earth, nor has there ever been a person on earth, nor will there ever be a person on earth except, of course, Jesus, who is without sin. Every single person has sinned. You know from the last chapter that there is inherited sin, imputed sin, and personal sin. All of humanity is born with a sin nature, or inherited sin. Sin has been passed along to us from our birth. Then there is imputed sin, a sin nature that has been given to us by Adam, our forefather. And it is this sin nature that causes our own personal sin. It is the sin nature that causes us to lie; it is the sin nature that causes us to steal; it is the sin nature that causes us to act out in our anger. It is the sinful nature that causes us to yell at the driver in front of us because we think he/she is not driving the way he/she should. It is the sin nature that makes us think that we are God and that the whole world should bow to the way we think because we are clearly master and commander of the universe above and beyond anyone else!

The truth, however, is that everybody is equally a sinner. Even if you sin just once in your life, just once, you are still a sinner. James 2:10 tells us "For whoever keeps the whole law and yet stumbles at just one point is guilty of breaking all of it." If you have sinned just once, just broken one command, it is as if you have broken them all. Thus, the argument that one does not need salvation because one is a "good" person, not committing the "big sins", is not valid. According to James 2:10, if you broke one command, even the smallest, you are as guilty as if you have broken them all, even the "big ones". One sin is all it takes to be in need of a saviour.

Sin is like putting just one drop of food coloring in a jar of water. When the food coloring enters the water, it disperses throughout the whole jar, turning all the water to color. All it takes is one drop, and the whole jar of water is colored. So too it is with sin – just one sin affects our whole entire life. One sin means that we are a sinner – and this has consequences.

Sin Has a Penalty

Roman 6:23a says, "For the wages of sin is death." The penalty of sin is death. Every time we sin something dies.

The physical death of humanity is a direct consequence of sin, as is the spiritual death of humanity. The death we die physically is a result of the sin of Adam and Eve. Their disobedience to God gave sin an entrance into the whole world which led to physical death. Yet, not only is there a physical death, there is a spiritual death as well. The spiritual death we die is a spiritual separation from God: separation from God here on earth and also separation from God eternally. There is an eternal separation from God that has taken place because of sin. That is what sin does. That is the penalty of sin.

Salvation from the Penalty of Sin

But there is good news! Romans 5:8b says, "While we were still sinners, Christ died for us." While we were still sinners Jesus died for us. Jesus paid the penalty of sin and is, in fact, the only one who can pay the penalty of sin. The penalty of sin required a perfect payment; it required a perfect person to make that perfect offering. But there are no perfect people, and as a result humanity could not make a perfect offering. Something had to be done to pay the penalty of sins and offer salvation from sin. What is the solution? What would God do?

If you remember the chapter on the essentials of God the Son, Jesus is fully man and fully God. Since Jesus is fully God, He is perfect and without sin. And since Jesus is fully human, He can represent humanity. Jesus took humanity upon Himself in order to represent humanity as a perfect sacrifice for sin. He could pay the price, and He did. Jesus hung on the cross and took our sins upon Himself. In

2 Corinthians 5:21 we read, "God made him who had no sin to be sin for us, so that in him we might become the righteousness of God." Jesus, who was perfectly sinless, willingly took sin upon Himself to save us.

In John 14:6 Jesus says, "I am the way and the truth and the life. No one comes to the Father except through me." Jesus is the only way to salvation because Jesus is the only one who is fully God and fully man, the perfect sacrifice for us. Acts 4:12b says, "there is no other name under heaven given to men by which we must be saved." Only Jesus could pay the penalty of sin.

There is a theological term for paying the penalty of sin. It is called atonement.

Jesus, the Atonement for Sin

THE PENALTY OF SIN IS PAID

Atonement – to pay the penalty, to satisfy the wrong

1 John 4:9-10
John 10:17-18

Jesus is the atonement for sin. Atonement means to pay for something. You have probably heard the phrase "You are going to have to atone for this, young man or young lady!" What is that phrase saying? It is saying that you are going to have to make up for this; you are going to have to pay for this. You are going to have to satisfy a set of requirements to pay for the wrongdoing in order to make it right. This is what Jesus did for humanity; Jesus was the atoning sacrifice. He was the one who satisfied the payment requirements of God and made it right in God's books. 1 John 4:9-10 says,

> This is how God showed his love among us: He sent his one and only Son into the world that we might live through him. [10]This is love: not that we loved God, but that he loved us and sent his Son as an atoning sacrifice for our sins.

Notice it says that Jesus was the atoning sacrifice for our sins. The penalty was paid by Jesus.

Please note that Jesus did not *have* to pay the penalty of sin. He was under no pressure or obligation to do so. He was sinless and had no penalty for sin of his own that he needed to pay. Yet, even though He did not need to pay for sin, Jesus *chose* to pay for sin. John 10:17-18 says,

> The reason my Father loves me is that I lay down my life – only to take it up again. [18]No one takes it from me, but I lay it down of my own accord. I have authority to lay it down and authority to take it up again. This command I received from my Father.

\Jesus was not forced to pay the penalty. Jesus was not guilted into paying the penalty. Jesus did not *have to* come down to earth; Jesus did not *have to* hang on a cross; Jesus did not *have to* stay on the cross. Jesus *wanted* to! Jesus wanted to die for us because He loves us. He loves you. Even while we were yet sinners Christ died for us.

Salvation Is a Free Gift

The salvation that Jesus paid for and offers to all today is a free gift! Yes, it is absolutely free. Ephesians 2:8-9 says,

> For it is by grace you have been saved, through faith – and this not from yourselves, it is the *gift* of God – [9]not by works, so that no one can boast.

There is nothing that humanity can do to work for salvation. Salvation is not gained through good works or impressive offerings to God. Humankind was at a complete loss to pay the penalty that God required for sin. Remember that only Jesus could pay for that sin. Only He was qualified to make the acceptable payment, no one else. Romans 6:23 tells us that "For the wages of sin is death, but the gift of God is eternal life in Christ Jesus our Lord." Yes, eternal life! Salvation is a gift of God. So now, through the death and resurrection of Jesus, through His atoning sacrifice, humanity has been offered the gift of salvation by God through Jesus. There is nothing we can do or have to do to earn salvation. It is simply a gift to be received.

We Must Receive Him

The gift of salvation needs to be received, however, in order for it to come into effect in a person's life. At Christmas time, gifts are put under the tree with the names of those whom they were bought for. When Christmas day arrives, those gifts are passed around to the appropriate people and they are opened.

The gifts were free to those who received them. They gladly received them and opened them so that they could enjoy them. What would happen if someone rejected the gift or did not actually open that gift but instead, they looked at the gift, admired the wrapping paper, checked out its size and weight, but then put it back under the tree? Without it being received and opened, that gift does not fulfill the purpose that it was intended for – the enjoyment of the person to whom it was given. The gift of salvation is like that; it was intended to be received and opened. In order to enjoy this free gift of salvation, we have to receive it from Jesus.

> WE MUST RECEIVE HIM
>
> Romans 10:9-10
> 1 John 1:9

It is not enough just to believe in the salvation of Jesus, it is not enough just to give assent to it or say yes it sounds cool, we must receive Him. Romans 10:9-10 says,

> That if you confess with your mouth, "Jesus is Lord," and believe in your heart that God raised him from the dead, you will be saved. [10]For it is with your heart that you believe and are justified, and it is with your mouth that you confess and are saved.

An action must be taken; we must receive Him. In order to receive salvation from Jesus, we need to use our mouth and actually ask Him for it. And when we ask Jesus for salvation, He gives it to us, free of charge. He promises to do that. He promises to forgive our sins and cleanse us from all unrighteousness. The apostle John says in 1 John 1:9, "If we confess our sins, he is faithful and just and will forgive us our sins and purify us from all unrighteousness." That means He gives you salvation.

That is what Jesus does; that is what salvation is all about – forgiveness of sins and being made right before God both now and forever because we are born again by His Spirit. This is called regeneration, a theological term meaning to be made new spiritually, to be born again with a new nature.

Regeneration

REGENERATION

To be made new spiritually, given a new nature
   Titus 3:3-6
   2 Corinthians 5:17

Our nature is right before God.

According to Titus 3, we are regenerated or made new spiritually. Titus 3:3-6 states,

> At one time we too were foolish, disobedient, deceived and enslaved by all kinds of passions and pleasures. We lived in malice and envy, being hated and hating one another. [4]But when the kindness and love of God our Savior appeared, [5]he saved us, not because of righteous things we had done, but because of his mercy. He saved us through the washing of rebirth and renewal by the Holy Spirit, [6]whom he poured out on us generously through Jesus Christ our Savior.

When we receive Jesus as Lord and Saviour we are reborn through the power of the Holy Spirit. This is what Jesus talks about when He says to Nicodemus that he must be born again.

In John chapter 3, Nicodemus does not understand the statement made by Jesus that we must be born again. Nicodemus is thinking in terms of physical rebirth, but Jesus is speaking about spiritual rebirth, about spiritual regeneration, about "rebirth and renewal by the Holy Spirit," as we read in Titus.

When we receive Jesus as our Lord and Saviour, we are given a spiritual rebirth to a new spiritual nature. Our old nature is the sinful nature, but our new nature is a spiritual nature that is given over to following Jesus. This is made clear in 2 Corinthians 5:17 which says, "Therefore, if anyone is in Christ, he is a new creation; the old has gone, the new has come!" We become new creations when we receive Jesus as our Saviour. Jesus has broken the power of sin in our lives.

Jesus Offers Us Salvation

In Revelation 3:20 Jesus says, "Here I am! I stand at the door and knock. If anyone hears my voice and opens the door, I will come in and eat with him, and he with me." In other words, Jesus will come into your life, forgive your sins, and will make you pure and holy before God. That is what Jesus does. That is salvation. He takes the sin from our lives and He cleanses us. He washes our sin away, and He gives us a new nature that is now inclined and capable of following Him.

Salvation from the Power of Sin

Not only does He save us from the penalty of sin, Jesus also saves us from the power of sin. Yes, there is more! Jesus saves us from the power of sin. The power of sin and death is eternal separation from God, but Jesus saves us from that eternal separation from God. The apostle Paul writes in Ephesians 2:1-5,

As for you, you were dead in your transgressions and sins, [2]in which you used to live when you followed the ways of this world and of the ruler of the kingdom of the air, the spirit who is now at work in those who are disobedient. [3]All of us also lived among them at one time, gratifying the cravings of our sinful nature and following its desires and thoughts. Like the rest, we were by nature objects of wrath. [4]But because of his great love for us, God, who is rich in mercy, [5]made us alive with Christ even when we were dead in transgressions – it is by grace you have been saved.

Paul writes again in Colossians 2:13-15,

When you were dead in your sins and in the uncircumcision of your sinful nature, God made you alive with Christ. He forgave us all our sins, [14]having canceled the written code, with its regulations, that was against us and that stood opposed to us; he took it away, nailing it to the cross. [15]And having disarmed the powers and authorities, he made a public spectacle of them, triumphing over them by the cross.

Jesus triumphed over sin by dying on a cross! Isn't that an unexpected twist! Jesus, while hanging on the cross was actually in the process of triumphing! The world thought that the spectacle to watch was Jesus as he hung on the cross, but the real spectacle was what was happening to satan – he was being defeated! Jesus, in the process of dying was triumphing over death! Jesus was making a spectacle of satan, destroying the power of satan and sin.

The Power of Sin Is Broken

Through Jesus, the power of sin and satan is broken from our lives. Jesus clears us from all sin. This is called justification.

> JUSTIFICATION
>
> To be declared clear of all sin
>
>   Romans 5:1-2
>   Romans 8:1-2

Justification means to be made right before God. Romans 5:1-2 says,

> Therefore, since we have been justified through faith, we have peace with God through our Lord Jesus Christ, [2]through whom we have gained access by faith into this grace in which we now stand. And we rejoice in the hope of the glory of God.

When we are justified before God, we are made right before God. We are declared clear of all sin so that our position or standing before God is right.

Romans 8:1-2 reads,

> Therefore, there is now no condemnation for those who are in Christ Jesus, [2]because through Christ Jesus the law of the Spirit of life set me free from the law of sin and death.

Did you get that? By Christ's death and resurrection, because He justified us, He made us right before God. We are set free from the power of sin. We are set free! Because of the atonement and justification through Jesus's death on the cross we are freed from the power of sin.

Salvation Over the Presence of Sin

Jesus not only paid the penalty of sin and broke the power of sin, Jesus also promised to eradicate the presence of sin. Yes, Jesus will eradicate even the very presence of sin!

Sin will be done away with from the earth forever

1 Corinthians 15:51-57
Revelation 21

We read in 1 Corinthians 15:51-57,

> Listen, I tell you a mystery: We will not all sleep, but we will all be changed – [52]in a flash, in the twinkling of an eye, at the last trumpet. For the trumpet will sound, the dead will be raised imperishable, and we will be changed. [53]For the perishable must clothe itself with the imperishable, and the mortal with immortality. [54]When the perishable has been clothed with the imperishable, and the mortal with immortality, then the saying that is written will come true: "Death has been swallowed up in victory."
>
> [55]"Where, O death, is your victory? Where, O death, is your sting?"
>
> [56]The sting of death is sin, and the power of sin is the law. [57]But thanks be to God! He gives us the victory through our Lord Jesus Christ.

Jesus, when He comes back again, will eradicate sin altogether. There will be no more sin in the new heaven and the new earth.

Revelation chapter 21 tells us that there will be no tears, no pain, no mourning, no suffering, no trials, and no temptations. There will be no blackness, no darkness, nothing ugly, nothing that makes us feel bad, nothing that makes us feel guilty, and nothing that will even be unpleasant in any way. Simply put, there will be no sin or its effects whatsoever. Heaven will be a place where sin and satan no longer exist. There will be no more penalty of sin, no more power of sin and no more presence of sin. That is what Jesus does for us in salvation. That is what He wants to do for every person on this planet. It is the desire of Jesus that all people come unto salvation through His death and resurrection on the cross. This is confirmed in 2 Peter 3:9 which says, "The Lord is not slow in keeping his promise, as some understand slowness. He is patient with you, not wanting anyone to perish, but everyone to come to repentance." God wants all people to come unto salvation – yes, all people.

Conclusion

Salvation is an act of God, saving His creation, humankind, you and I, from the penalty of sin, the power of sin, and eventually, even the very presence of sin. If you have never asked Jesus to come into your life, never asked to receive His forgiveness, you can do that now. Simply pray this prayer and receive Jesus today.

Closing Prayer

Jesus, I know that I am a sinner. I ask You to forgive me of my sin. Cleanse me from all unrighteousness. I believe that You are the Saviour, and I ask You to save me. Come into my life, Jesus, and give me a new nature. Be my Saviour and my Lord. Help me to live for You.

Amen.

Chapter 7

THE ESSENTIALS

OF

SANCTIFICATION

We now turn our attention to the essentials of sanctification. In the last few chapters we have been moving in a natural progression – from the essentials of sin, to the essentials of salvation and now to the essentials of sanctification. This is a natural progression because the proper understanding of sin leads to the need for salvation which then leads to the process of sanctification. Thus, in this chapter, we are going to look at the essentials of sanctification.

The term sanctification might be a bit of a new word or even an unknown word for many readers. The reality is, biblical teaching on sanctification is not common teaching that is heard in many churches, even though teaching on sanctification is commonly found in the Bible. Sanctification needs to be taught, understood, and put into practice in our Christian lives. So then, let us start with an essential definition of sanctification.

Definition of Sanctification

SANCTIFICATION

The activity of God in setting Christians apart from the world unto Himself by making them holy.

> The process of spiritual maturity – Christ-likeness.
>
> The lifelong process of submitting to Christs's authority in our lives.

Sanctification is the activity of God in setting Christians apart from the world unto Himself by making them holy. It is the process of spiritual maturity that comes from following Christ. As we follow Christ, we develop a Christ-likeness in our actions, words, and thoughts so that we begin to think like Jesus, speak like Jesus, and act like Jesus. Sanctification is not a one or two-time event; rather, sanctification is a lifelong process of daily following Jesus – "following" being described as continually submitting to Christ's authority in our lives. It is saying yes to the will and ways of Jesus while saying no to our own will and way. Sanctification is a continual process of recognizing that God is God and we are not. It is submitting to His authority over our lives on a continual and constant basis. In summary, sanctification is the process of spiritual maturity, becoming more like Christ through submitting to His will for our lives.

The Command to be Sanctified

Of course, the question needs to be asked, "Why is sanctification important? Why bother with the essentials of sanctification? What is the point?" To explore the answer, we begin with 1 Peter 1:13-16 which says,

> Therefore, prepare your minds for action; be self-controlled; set your hope fully on the grace to be given you when Jesus Christ is revealed. [14]As obedient children, do not conform to the evil desires you had when you lived in ignorance. [15]But just as he who called you is holy, so be

holy in all you do; [16]for it is written: "Be holy, because I am holy."

Do you remember the definition of holiness? In chapter one, The Essentials of God the Father, I asked the question, "What underlies all other characteristics of God?" The answer is, God's holiness. Remember also that holiness means to be set apart. It is to be set apart from sin. Holiness is to be without any blemish, any spot, and without any wrinkle of sin. God is this; He is Holy. God is completely other than sin and therefore completely other than His creation, even humanity. It is this creator God that now tells us, His creation, to be holy, just like Him. God is calling His disciples to be holy – to be completely other than the sin that characterizes the world who are without Christ. In other words, Jesus is calling His disciples to be different. He is calling them to be people who reflect Jesus to the world around them.

The phrase "be holy because I am Holy" is not a suggestion. It is not a "well if you feel like it, if you have time for it, if it really fits your schedule, or if you think you might want to do it today." The Greek tense indicates that it is an imperative. An imperative is a type of command, not a suggestion. Disciples of Christ are therefore commanded, as obedient children, to no longer conform to the pattern of the world but rather to be transformed to the pattern of God. Disciples are to be reflecting the character of God in their lives. Disciples of Christ are called to be holy because God, Himself, is holy.

God wants His disciples to be different people from those who are not disciples of Christ. That is, they are to act differently, react differently, and interact differently with both God and others than the rest of the world does. Disciples are to be transformed in their thinking, transformed in their actions, and transformed in the way they speak. A person who is following Jesus, who is a disciple of Jesus, who understands that he/she needs to be a transformed person is a person who is changing. We cannot be a disciple of Christ and stay the same. We just cannot do it. To remain the same without a Christ-like change in our life indicates that we are not following Jesus. Following Jesus is to look more and more like Jesus. And this always involves change.

It means that we may have to change some of the places we used to go because they are no longer appropriate and healthy for the disciple of Christ. It may mean that the people who were our closest friends are no longer our closest friends anymore. Perhaps the things we used to watch are not watched anymore, and some of the things we used to read are not read anymore. Sanctification changes the way we talk so that the way we used to talk is not the way we talk anymore. This is what sanctification does; it transforms our life and our lifestyle.

The process of sanctification is the formation of Christ's characteristics being instilled in us as disciples of Christ. If you are being discipled by somebody, it means that you are becoming more and more like the person who is discipling you. Others will know that you are so-and-so's disciple because your characteristics will match the characteristics of the one discipling you. Your life will begin to reflect the life of the other. Thus, the disciple of Christ will look more and more like Jesus as time goes by. A transformation will take place, change will happen, and we will not be the same person that we used to be.

When I first received Christ and I was learning to follow Him, I said "Man this is tough." I asked the question, "How long is this going to take for me to figure this out?" The answer given to me was, "It only takes a lifetime!" Yes, it only takes a lifetime. Sanctification is a lifelong process of submitting to Christ's authority in our lives. It is not just a Sunday thing. It is not enough to go to church on Sunday, to look good, to talk right, and to make sure to say the right things to the right people. No, sanctification is a Monday thing, a Tuesday thing, a Wednesday thing – it is an all-week thing. It is looking, acting, behaving, and talking like Jesus, every day.

Sanctification is the process of the Spirit of Christ working in every Christian, over time, to set him/her apart from the sin of the world, through the transformation of character that comes from following the command of Christ to be in submission to His will and ways.

Two Aspects of Sanctification

We have addressed the definition and the demand of sanctification; now let's discuss the dual aspects of sanctification. These are positional sanctification and progressive sanctification.

TWO ASPECTS OF SANCTIFICATION

Positional Sanctification
Progressive Sanctifiction

Positional Sanctification

Positional sanctification addresses the believer's position before God as one of being set apart. To be sanctified positionally means that the believer's position before God is one of being holy, right, and perfect. Because you are sanctified by Jesus, you are perfect before God. That means you are right before God! Imagine that! Because you have believed in and received Jesus as your Lord and Saviour, you are now right before God. For the disciple of Christ, your position before God is one of being holy, right and perfect. You are without any blemish or stain of sin.

POSITIONAL SANCTIFICATION

The believer's position before God is one of being set apart.

The believer's position before God is one of being holy, right and perfect.

You may wonder how I can say that because you are thinking to yourself, "I sure do not feel holy, and I know I have sin in my life. So how can you say that I am right and perfect before God?" I can say those things with confidence because of something called justification.

Justification

Justification means to be made right before God. Paul writes about it in Romans 5:1-2 which says,

> Therefore, since we have been justified through faith, we have peace with God through our Lord Jesus Christ, [2]through whom we have gained access by faith into this grace in which we now stand. And we rejoice in the hope of the glory of God.

We have been made right through faith in Jesus Christ, and as a result, we have peace with God. Our relationship with Jesus brings us peace with God. We are justified; we are made right before God through Jesus.

Through Jesus, our position before God is no longer wrong; we have been made right before God. Paul writes further in Romans 8:1-4,

> Therefore, there is now no condemnation for those who are in Christ Jesus, [2]because through Christ Jesus the law of the Spirit of life set me free from the law of sin and death. [3]For what the law was powerless to do in that it was weakened by the sinful nature, God did by sending his own Son in the likeness of sinful man to be a sin offering. And so he condemned sin in sinful man, [4]in order that the righteous requirements of the law might be fully met in us, who do not live according to the sinful nature but according to the Spirit.

There is no condemnation before God for those who are disciples of Christ! Disciples of Christ are no longer condemned before God because of Christ in them. They are right before God because the requirements of the law have been fully met through Jesus. In our standing before God, our position before Him, every disciple of Christ is made right and holy.

Regeneration

Not only are disciples of Christ justified before God, we are also regenerated. Regeneration is another proof of positional sanctification.

REGENERATION

Titus 3:3-5
John 3:7b
2 Corinthians 5:17
1 Corinthians 1:1-2
1 Corinthians 6:11

Hebrews 10:10
Ephesians 2:4-6

One of the best passages about regeneration is found in Titus 3:3-5, which says,

> At one time we too were foolish, disobedient, deceived and enslaved by all kinds of passions and pleasures. We lived in malice and envy, being hated and hating one another. ⁴But when the kindness and love of God our Savior appeared, ⁵ he saved us, not because of righteous things we had done, but because of his mercy. He saved us through the washing of rebirth and renewal by the Holy Spirit.

Regeneration means that we have a new nature. We have been reborn. Jesus talks to Nicodemus in John 3:7b where He says, "You must be born again." Nicodemus is fairly confused and asks how he can possibly be born again. "I don't get it," he says. Jesus responds by telling him that he can be born again by the Holy Spirit. It is by the Holy Spirit, the Spirit of Jesus, that we have a new nature. In our new nature we are right before God. We are regenerated. We are made right because we are given a new nature.

Another passage about regeneration is 2 Corinthians 5:17, "Therefore, if anyone is in Christ, he is a new creation; the old has gone, the new has come!" We are new creations. We are positionally holy before God because not only has He justified us before God, but He has also regenerated us, giving us a new nature.

The apostle Paul understood this positional sanctification well and therefore calls us saints. Have you ever thought of yourself as a saint? Probably not! But that is what disciples of Christ are! We are saints! Yes, Christians are saints, not in the catholic sense of a saint, but we are saints in the biblical sense of the word "saints". In 2 Corinthians 1:1, Ephesians

1:1, and Philippians 1:1, Paul addresses the Christians in each church as saints. He says, "to the saints in Corinth, to the saints in Ephesus, and to the saints in Philippi." Was Paul writing to only certain "saintly" people? No! Paul was speaking to all people in those churches who were followers of Jesus. He wrote to the saints, to everyone who was set apart and made right before God through Jesus Christ, including you. Just think about that: you are a saint!

Take a look at 1 Corinthians 1:1-2,

Paul, called to be an apostle of Christ Jesus by the will of God, and our brother Sosthenes,

²To the church of God in Corinth, to those sanctified in Christ Jesus and called to be holy, together with all those everywhere who call on the name of our Lord Jesus Christ – their Lord and ours.

Notice the words, "To those sanctified in Christ." Paul writes it in the past tense. It is an action that has already been taken. It has already happened. Paul says that Christians have already been sanctified. It is an action that has taken place; it has been completed. Positionally, before God, the disciple of Christ has been made holy. The work has already been done.

Paul also writes in 1 Corinthians 6:11, "And that is what some of you were. But you were washed, you were sanctified, you were justified in the name of the Lord Jesus Christ and by the Spirit of our God."

Did you get that? You were washed, you were sanctified – you were justified. You are, right now, holy before Jesus. You are a saint, in your position before God. The writer of Hebrews also adds, in 10:10, "And by that will, we have been made holy through the sacrifice of the body of Jesus Christ once for all." We have been made holy. You have been made holy. You are a saint. You are holy before God. You are perfect in the sight of God because of Christ in you.

But that is not all; there is more to our position before God! In Ephesians 2:4-6 we read,

> But because of his great love for us, God, who is rich in mercy, [5]made us alive with Christ even when we were dead in transgressions – it is by grace you have been saved. [6]And God raised us up with Christ and seated us with him in the heavenly realms in Christ Jesus.

Not only are we declared to be right before God in our standing, but we are also seated in the heavenly realms with Christ Jesus. Today! Right now!

So get the picture – positional sanctification says you are right before God because Jesus is in you, because you have recognized your sin, because you have asked for forgiveness of sin, because you have received Jesus as Lord and Saviour, because you have asked Him into your life. You are right before God because Jesus has regenerated you and given you a new nature. Because He has justified you in the sight of God, positionally, as you stand before God, you are a saint. You are holy. He has already seated you in the heavenly realms with Jesus. You have a seat in the heavenly realms, today! Right now, at this moment, your position before God is one of righteousness, or rightness.

This is important for us to know and remember – especially since we do not always feel that way. We know we sin; we do wrong, and we are not always right before God in our actions and thoughts. Our experience is not one of perfection as we live out our lives. And when we sin satan always comes along and accuses us and says, "Oh I know what you have done. Let me point this out to you; you cannot possibly be right before God."

But please remember, positionally, we are right before God. You have received Jesus as Lord and Saviour. He has forgiven you of your sins, justified you, given you a new nature, and lives within you to help you follow Him. You are right before God; you are holy; you are a saint.

Progressive Sanctification

Our position before God is one of being holy, yet our experience of living out this life contradicts what we know about our position. Positionally, through Christ, we are right before God, but experientially we do not always act right. And that leads us to the second aspect of sanctification called experiential or progressive sanctification.

If we ended this chapter right here, you might come to an erroneous conclusion that you are perfect in everything you do and that you do not sin any more. You might be tempted to say, "I am like God: I am perfect, I am holy." That, of course, would not be true because experientially, as we walk through this life, we are not perfect, and we do sin. The fact is, the disciple of Christ still has a sin nature. You and I still have a sin nature. When Christ came into our life He gave us a new nature, but He did not destroy or eradicate our sin nature. We still have that sin nature; it is still part of us. Experientially, as we experience life on earth, we still sin. What Jesus did do, however, was to break the power that sin had over us. We can now experience victory over sin. Because we have a new nature given to us by Christ, we are not bound to sin anymore. That is, we do not *have* to sin. We can choose to say no to temptation and walk away from sin. And as we walk more and more with Jesus, we are able to say no to sin more and more. We progressively become more and more like Him in our character and our actions. This is called progressive sanctification.

> PROGRESSIVE SANCTIFICTION
>
> The ongoing process of the Holy Spirit to bring about Christ-likeness in the life of every Christian.
>
> 2 Corinthians 3:18
>
> 1 Thessalonians 5:23-24

In 2 Corinthians 3:18 we read,

And we, who with unveiled faces all reflect the Lord's glory, are being transformed into his likeness with ever-increasing glory, which comes from the Lord, who is the Spirit.

Paul points to the fact Christ is leading us into an ongoing process of sanctification. Progressive sanctification is the work of the Holy Spirit developing Christ-likeness into our lives. As a result of receiving Jesus as Lord and Saviour, we begin to progress toward Christ-likeness in increasing measures as we walk with Him in obedience and friendship. Jesus continues to sanctify us with every step that we take with Him. Just as He has made us holy positionally, he seeks to make us holy experientially.

We read in 1 Thessalonians 5:23-24,

May God himself, the God of peace, sanctify you through and through. May your whole spirit, soul and body be kept blameless at the coming of our Lord Jesus Christ. [24]The one who calls you is faithful and he will do it.

Paul tells us that God is at work sanctifying us in our spirit, soul, and body. It is God's desire and purpose in our life to make us more and more like Him, to be a person of holiness in our character. God is at work transforming our lives from one of sin to one of holiness. This is the process of experiential or progressive sanctification. It is transformation.

Transformation

Jesus is transforming you today. There is a transformation that is taking place within you, and Jesus is the one who is doing that for you. It is God who transforms you; it is Jesus in you who transforms you. He has both made you holy and is making you holy. I hope that is not terribly confusing. Positionally before God you are holy, you are right. You cannot be any more right before God than you now are through Jesus Christ. Jesus has done the work already. It is not accomplished by your work; it is through His work. It is by His death on the cross. We don't work for our salvation; we are already right before God because of the work of Jesus. In the same way, we do not become more Christ-like by our own efforts and our own work. It is, once again, Jesus who does that for us. It is by the work of Jesus that our lives are transformed to look more and more like Him.

When we received Jesus as Lord and Saviour, we received Him as both Saviour and Lord. He is the one who saves us and has made us positionally right before God, and He is the one who commands us to be progressively right before God. The apostle Peter writes in, 1 Peter 1:16b, "Be holy, because I am holy." There is a responsibility that every

Christian has before God to submit to the process of transformation. By following Jesus our lives are going to change, indeed, our lives must change. That is the very nature of progressive sanctification.

You see, we cannot just receive Jesus as our Lord and Saviour and say, "There! I am done. There is nothing more that I need to do. I will live my life as I please." No, He has given us a new nature and expects us to live by that new nature. He is now teaching and training us in how to live in that new nature. Jesus has both transformed us and is continuing to transform us. We do not receive Jesus as Lord and Saviour and then go back to our old life as if nothing has happened. Something significant did indeed happen. Our position before God changed, therefore, our progression, or experience, before God must change. How we live our life matters because we either reflect Jesus with ever increasing glory, or we reflect another, whether it be self or satan. We as Christians are called to be reflecting Jesus in the way we talk, in the way we think, in the way we act, and in the manner in which we treat people because we are both transformed and are being transformed. Transformation is not an option.

TRANSFORMATION

Romans 12:2a

2 Corinthians 5:17b

Romans 12:1

Romans 12:2a reads, "Do not conform any longer to the pattern of this world, but be transformed by the renewing of your mind." That is sanctification. It is the process and progression of conforming less and less to the world and more and more to the life and teaching of Jesus. It is being transformed in our actions and thoughts to Jesus and His will and ways. It is to look more like Jesus than you look like anybody or anything else. Because we are new creations, we are to live as new creations. As Paul says in 2 Corinthians 5:17b, "The old has gone, the new has come!"

In verse 1 of Romans 12, Paul says, "Therefore, I urge you, brothers, in view of God's mercy, to offer your bodies as living sacrifices, holy and pleasing to God – this is your spiritual act of worship." Paul teaches us that the way we live our life matters, that we are supposed to look more and more like Jesus. He does not say, "It is okay if you do whatever you want with your body. Go ahead and sin; it does not matter." No, that is not the teaching of Scripture. Paul is teaching us that because we have received salvation from Jesus, because we are a changed people, because we are justified, because we are regenerated, and because we have a new nature, we are to offer ourselves as "living sacrifices holy and pleasing to God." And notice that Paul says, "This is your spiritual act of worship." Clearly the way we live, what we do and say, is considered as worship to God. Everything we do should be transformed into worship to God. We no longer worship our old life, we worship Jesus. We have a new life, and we cannot combine the two. We cannot take a bit of this old life because we really quite enjoyed that and try to combine it with this new life that Jesus calls us to. Our old life was in opposition to God. It put us in a wrong relationship with God, therefore, we must leave it and follow Jesus who puts us in a right relationship with God.

Believers in Christ are disciples of Christ and, therefore, followers of Christ. This means transformation – progressively becoming more and more like Jesus as we follow Him. We have received Jesus as Lord and Saviour, therefore, we must be transformed. Transformation has to take place. Jesus will not let us remain the same, He just will not. He did not give you a new nature so you can remain in your old nature. He gave you a new nature so you can learn to live according to your new nature. Sanctification changes your very purpose in life, it changes your focus in life, it changes your words in life, it changes your actions in life, it changes the way you treat people in life, and it changes the way you view life. The process of sanctification changes everything about life. Sanctification is a change of heart.

Sanctification as a Relationship

Sanctification can also be defined in terms of a relationship with Jesus. It is more than a theological term. Sanctification is desiring to walk with Jesus in friendship. It is a desire to want to know Him more and more deeply.

When my wife's parents were still alive and living on a farm in Southern Saskatchewan we would go there to visit. Now, my father-in-law always had cats. Of course, you need cats on the farm. But he only liked black cats or white cats. Not gray, not tan, not a mixture, only black or white cats. As a result, he took measures to ensure that he had only white cats or black cats on the farm. Now there was a particular white cat that I remember most of all because this white cat was deaf, it could not hear at all. If you walked softly enough, you could actually sneak up on this white cat and scare it so that the cat would shoot up in the air in surprise.

As I watched this cat, it seemed evident that it knew that it could not hear. That white cat knew it could not hear and knew it was a problem. So, the white cat compensated for this by staying close to the dog. The white cat was always by the dog. If the dog was sleeping, the white cat could sleep. If the dog went for a walk, the cat went for a walk. When the dog became alerted over some sound, the cat would become alert because it looked to the dog and knew something was alerting the dog. It could not hear, but it knew the dog could hear. If there was danger, the cat knew because the dog knew. If the danger was gone and it was now safe, the cat knew because the dog knew. The cat's life was transformed because it spent its life in relationship with the dog.

Our relationship to Jesus is supposed to be like that: one spent closely watching Jesus so that we would know how to act and respond in every situation and circumstance of life.

If only people knew that we are deaf. When it comes to spiritual things, we are deaf. The only way we hear spiritual truth is in a relationship with Jesus. We need to stay close to Jesus. That is sanctification. It is walking closely with Jesus because we know that we are deaf and need to look to Him to know spiritual truth for our lives. On our own, we are in danger of being snuck up on and overcome with sin. We have to stay in a close relationship with Jesus. That is sanctification.

Conclusion

Positionally, we are right before God. We need to know that we are holy because God has made us holy. But experientially, we know we need to become holy. We still have a sin nature. We need to stay in a close relationship with Jesus. We are spiritually deaf, and we need to be in a relationship with Jesus.

Where are you at with Jesus? Are you still playing around in the old life? Are you taking Jesus as your Saviour, but rejecting Him as your

Lord? Are you saying, "God, thank You for my new nature, but I really like parts of the old one so I am going to play around with the old life?" Do not do it! That is not living the sanctified life. Jesus commands us to be holy. Jesus died for us to be holy. Let God transform you; that is His desire. Walk closely with Him. You are positionally sanctified before God and are being progressively sanctified by Him as well. Let us live as transformed people.

Closing Prayer

Jesus, thank You that You have made us right before God. Thank You that our position before God is one of holiness. I ask that You would be at work progressively sanctifying us. Please transform us. God, be at work in our life, and help us to reflect Your character to those around us. Help us to act like You, to talk like You, respond like You, and to present You to others. May others see the character of Jesus reflected in us when they look at us. Thank You that You have sanctified us, and I ask that You continue to sanctify us as we live this life with You. I ask and pray this in Your name, Jesus.

Amen.

Chapter 8

THE ESSENTIALS

OF

SCRIPTURE

We now turn our attention to the essentials of Scripture. It is through the words of God, the Bible, that we mature and grow in Christ. Indeed, it is by the words of God that we come to know how to be in a right relationship with God in our every day living. Spiritual maturity comes through reading the words of God.

In this chapter, we are going to give a definition of Scripture, show that Scripture is the revealed truth of God, and that these words from God are infallible and inerrant. We will then explore the canonicity of Scripture and briefly delve into the illumination of Scripture by the Holy Spirit.

Definition of Scripture

We will begin with a definition. Simply put, Scripture, the Bible, is God's revelation to humankind. That is to say, the words of the Bible come from God as He revealed them to humanity. The Bible is God's revealed truth. Significantly, the words of God are truth that we could not know on our own. God had to reveal these truths to us. The phrase "that we could not know on our own" is important, because the reality is that we cannot know God on our own. The words that God gave to us were not something that we could discover on our own, by our own devices. Scripture is God's revealed truth about Himself that we could not know on our own, so that we can be in a right relationship with Him and others.

> ## DEFINITION OF SCRIPTURE
>
> God's revealed truth to humankind that we could not know on our own in order to be in a right relationship with Him and others.

Humankind is not able to be in a right relationship with God on our own. God had to both reveal Himself to us and reveal to us how to be in a right relationship with Him. Without God's revelation to us, we could not know Him. God revealed both the problem of sin and the remedy to sin. God revealed to us how we must live in order to receive everlasting life. What we have in the Bible are the revealed words of God so that humanity could know God and could know how to be in a right relationship with God for eternal salvation.

The Revealed Truth of God

It is important to know that the Bible is not a man-made book. The Bible contains the words of God that He Himself revealed to humanity. For that reason, the Bible is distinct from every other book that we have. The Bible is not like Shakespeare; the Bible is not like Plato; the Bible is not like Clancy. The Bible is not like any other book because every other book that is written is a man-made book. Not the Bible. No one person thought up the Bible, nor was it a group project passed down from generation to generation until completed. No, the Bible contains the words of God and only His words that He revealed to humanity to be written down. These are words that we could not know on our own unless He told us.

Let us look at a few Scriptures that show this.

THE REVEALED TRUTH OF GOD

2 Timothy 3:16-17
Hebrews 1:1-2
2 Peter 1:20-21

In 2 Timothy 3:16-17 Paul writes,

> All Scripture is God-breathed and is useful for teaching, rebuking, correcting and training in righteousness, [17]so that the man of God may be thoroughly equipped for every good work.

All Scripture, every bit of what we have, is God-breathed. What does God-breathed mean? It simply means that the words of Scripture came from the breath of God. They are His words, originating from His being. He spoke them so that we now have them. All the words of the Bible are from God and are useful for knowing how to be in a right relationship with Him. Note that there are four ways in which the Bible is useful for being in a right relationship with God.

First, the Bible is useful for teaching. God's words teach us how to understand and live this Christian life. We know how to act and behave as a Christian because we can read God's breathed words to us. It teaches us right from wrong, good from evil, and godliness from selfishness.

Second and third, Scripture is useful for rebuking and correcting us when we are going in the wrong direction. We read the Bible and realize that certain behaviors or activities are wrong according to God, so we had better stop that activity and turn away from it. The Bible instructs us between right and wrong and corrects the wrong in our life.

Fourth, the Bible is also meant for training in righteousness. Training is the process of putting into habit that which we are being taught. It is the repetition of thoughts and behaviors that we learn from His words. Continual reading of the Bible helps us to develop patterns and habits so that we live rightly before God.

All of these functions of Scripture combine so that the disciple of Christ can be thoroughly equipped for doing everything God wants him/her to do. Without the words of God, we cannot follow Christ and mature in our walk with Christ. That is how important the words of the Bible are.

Another Scripture that helps us understand the importance of God's words is Hebrews 1:1-2 which states,

> In the past God spoke to our forefathers through the prophets at many times and in various ways, [2]but in these last days he has spoken to us by his Son, whom he appointed heir of all things, and through whom he made the universe.

We learn from this passage that God speaks to us, that He breathes His words to us, and that He breathes them to us through the Prophets of the Old Testament and through His own son, Jesus. Yes, God speaks to us and has always been speaking to us. He wants us to know Him. Thus, we have His words recorded in His book, the Bible.

In 2 Peter 1:20-21 Peter writes,

Above all, you must understand that no prophecy of Scripture came about by the prophet's own interpretation. [21]For prophecy never had its origin in the will of man, but men spoke from God as they were carried along by the Holy Spirit.

Now, remember Hebrews 1:1-2 just said that God spoke to us in the past through the prophets. Peter follows this up by letting us know that the prophets did not make up their own material. The Bible did not originate with the will of the prophets. The prophets did not say, "I have a great idea! I am going to say this today, and it is going to be God's word." No, the words of the Bible originated from God who said to the prophets, "You are going to write these words from me, not your own." Hence, prophecy never came about by the prophet's own will.

The Bible comes to us because the prophets listened to God and started writing as God spoke to them. All throughout the history of the Bible, God chose people to be His prophets to write down what He wanted humankind to know about Him. God used Moses, Joshua, Samuel, David, Ezra, Nehemiah, Isaiah, Jeremiah, Peter, Paul, John, and many more. These people were moved along by the Holy Spirit.

Divine Inspiration

This is what is called divine inspiration. The Bible is divinely inspired by God. It is different than Shakespeare writing a book. You could say Shakespeare was an inspired guy because he wrote such great literature, or Plato or some of those classics. But they were not divinely inspired. They wrote out of their own will, out of their own mind, out of their own artistry. Their words did not come from God, nor did they ever claim that what they wrote were God's words. They knew they were their own words. The difference between Scripture and all other books is that Scripture claims to be from God because it is from God. The words that these prophets were writing were divine words of God. The writers of Scripture were directed or inspired by God to write.

Now, to be clear, God did not dictate His words to prophets, rather, He divinely inspired them to write the words that He wanted people to know and to adhere to. The prophets were engaged in a relationship with God, listening to Him and writing what God revealed to be true about Himself. That is called divine inspiration. God used their personalities, their intellects, and their circumstances to write the words that He wanted revealed to humankind. This is why the books of the Bible are written in the different styles and genres. They came as a result of the different personalities and artistry of the prophetic writers. Each one wrote his part. Amazingly, there is a unity of thought that runs through the whole Bible, and even more amazingly, there is no contradiction in Scripture at all, especially considering that the Bible was written over centuries of time by thirty or more different authors.

Inerrancy and Infallibility

The Bible is not only divinely inspired by God through the Holy Spirit, it is also inerrant and infallible.

THE INERRANT AND INFALLIBLE WORD OF GOD
Inerrancy – without error or mistake Infallible – without fault, wrong, or contradiction

Inerrancy means to be without error or mistake. There are no errors or mistakes in the Bible. God has never had to rewrite a chapter or come out with a corrected and updated edition. The words of the Bible that we have today are the same words of the Bible that were originally given by God. (Of course the language has been translated from Hebrew and Greek.) No corrections are needed to God's words. They are all truth and without mistake. His words are also infallible. Infallible means to be without fault, without wrong, and without contradiction. This means that when you read the words of God as found in the Holy Bible, you can be sure that it is all true and correct. It all comes from God, there is no error. There is no non-truth in the Bible.

The Bible is both inerrant and infallible. This means that when we read the words of God, we are reading the truth. It also means that when we read the Bible we can conclude that what we just read was neither a mistake nor an error which should never have been written there. (It should be noted that on occasion, an error has arisen as a result of human copying. Yet even these errors are very minor and have not altered or changed any essential doctrines of Scripture.) Every word of God is true and trustworthy. We do not have to decide what is true and what is not true because it is all truth!

If we start picking and choosing what is true and what is not true in the Bible, then we lose the truth of the Bible, and there is no point in reading the Bible. By deciding for ourselves what is true or not true in the Bible, we make ourselves out to be the authority of the Bible and therefore over God! We put ourselves in the position of determining truth. And if that is the case, then we do not need God to do that for us, and therefore, we do not need to read His word.

There is also the ever-present danger of putting our own life experience or desires as the authority over the Bible. We can come to the erroneous conclusion that since, in my own life experience, I have not experienced the truth of some of the words of God, then those words from God must not be true. We then determine the truth of a passage of Scripture based on our own limited experience rather than accepting that God's words are true. We prefer to change God's words than change our own life. Further, if we become the authority over what truth is, then how can we know for certain that Jesus really died on the cross? How do we determine the truth of it? Is it by our own experience or knowledge? If it is up to us to determine truth and error, then we place ourselves as the authority of truth, even above God Himself. When we place ourselves in the position of authority as to what are the words of God or what are not, then we reject that the Bible is inerrant and infallible truth that comes from God Himself.

The Bible is the inerrant and infallible truth of God. The Bible is without error and without contradiction. It is all truth.

It is important to note that there are some scribal inconsistencies such as punctuation or human copying errors. But any good translation will have footnotes that indicate that some ancient manuscripts contain differences that are attributed to scribal inconsistencies. Good and honest scholarship identifies that there are many ancient manuscripts and that some are more dependable than others. As the Bible was copied over the centuries, some minor human copying errors occurred. However, the words we have today are still God's words. The minor scribal errors do not change any theology or doctrine – all the words of Scripture are God's words.

Let's take a look at some more Scriptures that speak about the truth of God's words.

> ## THE INERRANT AND INFALLIBLE WORD OF GOD
>
> Psalm 19:7-8
> Psalm 119:42
> James 1:25

Psalm 19:7-8 states,

> The law of the Lord is perfect, reviving the soul. The statutes of the Lord are trustworthy, making wise the simple. [8]The precepts of the Lord are right, giving joy to the heart. The commands of the Lord are radiant, giving light to the eyes.

The Psalmist, King David, confirms that words of God are perfect. He says that the words of God are right and trustworthy. Psalm 119:42 also says, "then I will answer the one who taunts me, for I trust in your word." Here we see that the Psalmist can trust his life to God's word because he knows it is trustworthy. He puts the entire weight of his life upon the words of God. He can trust the words of God because they are not going to crumble, they are not going to fall, nor are they going to let him down. He will never be led astray by the words of God and can, therefore, put the full weight of his life for his eternal destiny upon the trustworthy words of God simply because they *are* trustworthy.

> Then we have James 1:25 which states,

> But the man who looks intently into the perfect law that gives freedom, and continues to do this, not forgetting what he has heard, but doing it – he will be blessed in what he does.

James speaks of the "perfect law". What law is James talking about? He is talking about the words of God, the perfect written words of God. Not only does James make the claim that the written words of God are perfect, but he goes further to say that if we look intently into the perfect words of God, then we are going to be blessed in what we do. James recognizes that there is no other book like the Bible. You can look into the words of Plato; you can look into the words of Shakespeare; you can look into the words of Tom Clancy; you can look into the words of Louis L'Amour; but you are not going to be blessed in eternity by putting your trust in those words because they are not perfect truth. They do not come from God. Therefore, they are not perfect; they are not infallible and inerrant. Only the Bible is perfect. The Bible is holy. It is set apart as completely other than any other book we have.

There are still more verses that we can look at regarding the inerrant and infallible word of God.

THE INERRANT AND INFALLIBLE WORD OF GOD

John 10:34-35
Matthew 5:17-18
2 Peter 3:15-16

John 10:34-35 says,

Jesus answered them, "Is it not written in your Law, 'I have said you are gods'? [35]If he called them 'gods,' to whom the word of God came – and the Scripture cannot be broken . . ."

In this passage, Jesus is answering the pharisees who want to stone Jesus for blasphemy. Jesus, in answering them uses the Old Testament Scripture as truth because – and this is the point – Scripture is the truth. It can be trusted and relied upon. Jesus says that Scripture cannot be broken. Scripture cannot be torn apart, it cannot be broken apart into bits and pieces, nor can it be separated into truth and non-truth. We cannot claim that some words are from God, but other words are not. Scripture cannot be broken. The words that God spoke are all God's words. You cannot take the Bible and rip pages out, ignore parts of it, and rewrite other parts because, as Jesus says, the words of God cannot be broken. The weight of Jesus' argument against the pharisees rested upon the truth and reliability of God's words, which the pharisees accepted as unbroken truth.

In another verse, Matthew 5:17-18, Jesus says,

> Do not think that I have come to abolish the Law or the Prophets; I have not come to abolish them but to fulfill them. [18]I tell you the truth, until heaven and earth disappear, not the smallest letter, not the least stroke of a pen, will by any means disappear from the Law until everything is accomplished.

Jesus did not come to abolish or get rid of the words of God. Again, Scripture cannot be broken. The words of God can never be erased; they will instead be fulfilled. Thus, Jesus did not come and say, "I am going to get rid of all of that Old Testament stuff because it is wrong, has error, is a little faulty, or needs updating." No, Jesus came and clearly said, "I have not come to get rid of it. They are the words of God; they must be fulfilled, therefore, I have come to fulfill them."

When the Matthew 5 passage and the John 10 passage are taken together, we discover something interesting. In the Matthew passage, Jesus is talking about the Law and the Prophets, and in John 10, Jesus is talking about the Psalms, commonly called the writings. In the Hebrew Bible, there are three major parts: the law, the prophets, and the writings. What Jesus is saying is that all of the Old Testament is the truth of God's words. None of it can be broken. None of it will disappear, nor can be wiped away. The Old Testament was accepted as the divinely inspired words of God. That was already settled by the time of Jesus.

Regarding the New Testament, we have these interesting words from the Apostle Peter. Peter writes in 2 Peter 3:15-16,

> Bear in mind that our Lord's patience means salvation, just as our dear brother Paul also wrote you with the wisdom that God gave him. [16]He writes the same way in all his letters, speaking in them of these matters. His letters contain some things that are hard to understand, which ignorant and unstable people distort, as they do the other Scriptures, to their own destruction.

Peter very clearly says the writings of Paul are on the same level as the writings of the Old Testament; they are Scriptures. Just as the Old Testament was accepted as God's divinely inspired words, we now have Peter accepting that Paul's letters are God's divinely inspired words. Already, during the time of the disciples, there is a clear acknowledgement that what Paul writes are the words of God, that he has been inspired by God to write His words.

By 286 A.D. the Bible was accepted as the Bible as we know it today. The Old Testament was already accepted during the time of Jesus, and then, during the days of the early church fathers the rest of the New Testament was decided upon as to what were God's inspired words and what were not. In fact, by 180 A.D. the Muratorian Canon was already accepted which included 22 of the 27 New Testament books of the Bible today. The only books missing were James, 2nd Peter, 2nd John, 3rd John, and Jude.

Because this topic is so important and because the Bible is under so much attack in our society, a society which seems to believe that the Bible is just another book and that it can be dismissed or chopped up to suit one's lifestyle, or that the words themselves do not matter, we are going to take some more time on this subject. Let's take a look at three more verses regarding the inerrant and infallible truth of God.

THE INERRANT AND INFALLIBLE WORD OF GOD

Revelation 22:18-19
Deuteronomy 4:2
Proverbs 30:5-6

We go first to Revelation 22:18-19. John, the apostle, is writing,

> I warn everyone who hears the words of the prophecy of this book: If anyone adds anything to them, God will add to him the plagues described in this book. [19]And if anyone takes words away from this book of prophecy, God will take away from him his share in the tree of life and in the holy city, which are described in this book.

Clearly, John understands that the words that he is writing are God's words. He knows they are words that cannot be broken or changed. They are the very words of God and therefore must not be added to or taken away from. He believes them to be the inerrant and infallible words of God.

There is some debate about whether John is talking about the Bible as a whole or just the book of Revelation itself when he uses the phrase, "this book of prophecy." It could be argued that the book of Revelation acts as a kind of a bookend to the whole Bible, just as Genesis acts as a bookend. Revelation closes the Bible while Genesis introduces it. So, is

John just talking about Revelation, or is he talking about the whole Bible – Genesis to Revelation? Wherever you land on that question, it is clear that John himself acknowledges and understands that what he, at least, is writing in Revelation is God's divinely inspired words.

In Deuteronomy 4:2, Moses in addressing the Israelites says, "Do not add to what I command you and do not subtract from it, but keep the commands of the Lord your God that I give you." This is similar to what John wrote in Revelation about not adding or taking away from the words that were written. In Deuteronomy, Moses is talking about the Law of the Pentateuch, the first five books of the Bible. He warned the Israelites to not add to His words nor to subtract from them because they are God's divinely inspired words. He warned them to not alter them in any way, because they are truth, and anything altered from truth is falsehood.

Then we have Proverbs. Proverbs 30:5-6 says, "Every word of God is flawless; he is a shield to those who take refuge in him. 6Do not add to his words, or he will rebuke you and prove you a liar." Again, we see the phrase, "do not add to these words." The writer in Proverbs is very clearly saying that the words of God are flawless. They are without error and without mistake. They are inerrant and infallible and should not be altered. The Psalmist warns the readers to not take away from the words of God by rewriting them in any way because they are God's words and must be revered as such.

We have looked at many Scriptures to show that the words of God are truth and without error or mistake. They are words that can be trusted and counted on. A person can place the whole weight of his/her being upon the truth of the words of Scripture without worry of those words failing or proving to be false. They are words that lead us into a right relationship with God. They are words that are both infallible and inerrant. They are the words of God.

The Canon of Scripture

I have briefly mentioned the canon of Scripture in our earlier discussion. Let us now take a deeper look at the concept of the canon of Scripture. Canon is a word that originates from the Greek which simply means rule or authority. So, when we refer to the canon of Scripture, we are referring to the rule or authority of Scripture.

The canon of the Bible came about as the early church met together and came to a consensus about what writings were divinely inspired and what writings were not inspired from God. They came to an agreement about the books that constitute the Holy Bible as we have it today – 66 books, 39 in the Old Testament and 27 in the New Testament.

THE CANON OF THE BIBLE

Canon – rule or authority

66 books in the Bible

39 Old Testament

27 New Testament

The early church had a criterion for determining the canonicity of the Bible, particularly the New Testament books. Jesus already accepted the Old Testament as God's divinely inspired word, and those thirty-nine books of the Old Testament were accepted by the early church fathers.

But what about the New Testament? How were the writings determined as canon or not canon?

In order for any writing to be accepted as divine authority on par with the already accepted 39 books of the Old Testament, the criterion that was established consisted of five proofs. Each writing had to have apostolic authority behind it, it had to have the ring of God's authority in the words, it had to have the ability to transform lives toward God, it could not contradict any other previously recognized divinely inspired words of God, and it had to be accepted by the early church fathers. By 180 A.D. 22 of the 27 books had already been canonized as Scripture, and by the late third century, after much debate and seeking God, the canon of Scripture was finalized into what is now our Holy Bible.

CRITERA FOR CANONICITY

Accepted by the early church fathers

Ring of God's authority

Power to transform lives

Consistent with the rest of Scripture, not contradictory

Prophetic or apostolic authority

As an example of determining canonicity, let us look at some other types of literature. When you read Shakespeare, or Louis L'Amour, or Tom Clancy, it is clear that the words of those writers do not sound like the words of God. They do not have the ring of God's authority in them. Nor would any of those writers say they were trying to make them sound like the words of God. Further, many of their words are contradictory to Scripture, and they do not have any power to transform lives for the purpose of serving God. One does not read these authors for the purpose of changing their life to follow God. They are not words of salvation from God. I have never heard anyone say that the words of eternal salvation are found in the words of these writers! I do not know that I have ever been transformed by reading Louis L'Amour. I enjoy reading Louis L'Amour, but I have never been transformed by any of his books. The first five books of the Sacketts cannot transform me like the first five books of the Bible!

There is clearly a different tone in these books than the tone of the writing of the Bible. When I read God's words in the Bible, I hear Him speak, and my life is transformed. Also, the whole message of the Bible is consistent. Each book is consistent with all of the rest of the books of Scripture. They are not contradictory. God will never contradict Himself. Thus, when the early church fathers were getting together to determine canonicity, if what was written clearly contradicted what the Apostle Paul had written or what was written in the Old Testament, they then concluded that the writing could not be inspired by God and, therefore, could not be accepted into the canon of Scripture. What God said 3000 years ago is true today and will be true 3000 years from now. God is truth, and there is no contradiction in truth; therefore, there can be no contradiction in His word.

Admittedly, though, there are times when we read the Bible and find ourselves wondering what the meaning is of what we just read, or how that makes sense, or how it fits with what we read in a different passage. And there are definitely times when we think that what we read has to be a contradiction. Thankfully, though, God is there to help us in our understanding of His words to us. He provides for us, through His Holy Spirit, illumination of His words.

Illumination of Scripture

> THE ILLUMINATION OF THE BIBLE
>
> The Holy Spirit is at work bringing to light what the words of God mean.
>
> John 14:26
> Ephesians 1:18

Illumination is the Holy Spirit at work bringing to light the words of what God means in His Bible. Just as God inspired His words, making sure that what He wanted written down was written down for us, so He ensures us that as we read it, we will be able to understand it. God illuminates our minds as we read His word by the Holy Spirit. John 14:26 says,

> But the Counselor, the Holy Spirit, whom the Father will send in my name, will teach you all things and will remind you of everything I have said to you.

Jesus promises us that He is going to teach us the word of God. Ephesians 1:18 states,

> I pray also that the eyes of your heart may be enlightened in order that you may know the hope to which he has called you, the riches of his glorious inheritance in the saints.

Paul's prayer is for the eyes of our heart to be enlightened. He is praying for the Holy Spirit to illuminate our minds so that we can know and understand God and His words. Disciples of Christ can be assured that as we read Scripture and seek to understand it, God will help us to understand His words. It is His promise to us. When we dig into the words of God a little bit more and ask for His illumination as we read and study, we gain a greater understanding of what the writer is really saying and what that means for our own lives. In this way, we discover that the apparent contradictions in Scripture disappear, and we come to discern the consistent message of salvation throughout all of God's words.

God's Word as a Plumb Line

> GOD'S WORDS ARE OUR RULE OF FAITH AND
> PRACTICE
>
> Amos 7:8
> Psalm 32:8
> Psalm 119:105

It is important for us to discern and know God's words because they teach us how to live rightly before God and others. The words of the Bible are the rule of faith and practice for the disciple of Christ. The prophet Amos uses the phrase "plumb line". In Amos 7:8 we read,

> And the Lord asked me, "What do you see, Amos?" "A plumb line," I replied. Then the Lord said, "Look, I am setting a plumb line among my people Israel; I will spare them no longer.

The plumb line refers to the words that God had spoken to His people. God's words are a plumb line. Plumb lines are used by carpenters in setting walls or doors to ensure that they are square. A plumb line always hangs level and gives a true perpendicular to that which it is hanging from. The plumb line hangs true to square. By referring to a plumb line, Amos is saying that God's words are always true to square. That is, His words can be counted on as plumb, or truth, for our lives. The Canon of the Bible are the words of truth that we need to line up to or measure our lives with.

Psalm 32:8 says, "I will instruct you and teach you in the way you should go; I will counsel you and watch over you." The words of God instruct us, teach us and counsel us in the way to go.

Psalm 119:105 also says, "Your word is a lamp to my feet and a light for my path." God's words are always true and always right! The words of God will never lead us into darkness. They will always lead us into the light of Christ. If we are lead into the darkness, then we know it did not come from God.

The rule and authority of our life are the words of God, which is why it is so important to know the words of God. Our decisions, the way we live, how we speak and how we act all need to be based upon the rule and authority of God and His words to us.

Conclusion

The Bible is the revealed words of God for all humankind, so that we can live in a right relationship with God and with each other. The Holy Spirit ensures that the words of God were written, preserved, and understood by humanity. The Bible is the rule of faith and practice for the disciples of Christ. You can trust the words of God and depend upon them.

CONCLUSION

The Bible is the revealed words of God for all of humankind so that we can live in a right relationship with God and with each other.

The Holy Spirit ensured that the words of God were written, preserved, and understood by humanity.

The Bible is the rule of faith and practice for the disciple of Christ.

Closing Prayer

Jesus, thank You for Your words. Thank You that You wrote them and made sure that we can understand them so that we can be in a right relationship with You. Jesus, lead us in a right relationship with You in all we do. I ask it in Your name, Jesus.

Amen.

Chapter 9

THE ESSENTIALS

OF

THE SECOND COMING OF CHRIST

In this chapter we turn our attention to the second coming of Christ. We will explore the fact of His return, the manner of His return, and the timing of His return. We will also take a look at the rapture, the Great Tribulation, and the antichrist.

To begin with, it needs to be recognized that there is a fair amount of unknown that surrounds the second coming of Christ. Though there is a fair amount written about the general return of Christ in Scripture, we are left with many questions regarding the details of His return. In fact, Jesus Himself informs us that He does not even know the exact time of His own return! He says in Matthew 24:36, "No one knows about that day or hour, not even the angels in heaven, nor the Son, but only the Father." Yes, not even Jesus knows the exact day and hour of His return! How much less could we? Sometime later, on the day of His ascension, His disciples asked Jesus to fill in some information regarding the time when He was going to come back. Jesus answered them by saying in Acts 1:7, "It is not for you to know the times or dates the Father has set by his own authority." Like us, the early disciples wanted a date for His return so that they could put it on their calendar. But Jesus made it clear that it is not for us to know the times or dates. We can search as much as we want, and we can try to figure out as much as we can, but we will never know the exact times and dates when Jesus will return.

This led to some confusion in the early church just a few short years after Christ's ascension. Some believed that Jesus had already returned, and they missed Him, while others assured them that Christ had yet to return (2 Thessalonians 2:1ff). So, it is not surprising that today there are still many questions about the nature and timing of the second coming of Christ.

We tend to want to know dates, times and events, and when that information is not apparent to us, we begin to wonder if He is really coming after all. We want to know exactly when He is coming, how He is coming and what all the details of His coming are. We look for well-defined signs and occurrences that give us significant probabilities of the details of His coming. But the reality is we cannot know all of these details, though we still keep trying.

It was predicted that Jesus would return in 1984 according to George Orwell's book, 1984. When the world successfully made it past 1984, the Y2K scare of the year 2000 came and went. After that, it was the Inca calendar that was supposed to indicate another end of the world. Prediction after prediction has come and gone. It is as Jesus has said – when it comes to times and dates of His return – we simply cannot know.

Yet there are some things that we can know. So let us turn our attention to what we can know as God has revealed it to us by His words.

The Fact of Christ's Return

We start with the fact that Jesus is coming again! We can know with all surety that Jesus is coming again because we have the promise from Jesus that He is coming again. There are three passages of Scripture that are the major Scriptures for knowing about the second coming of Christ.

JESUS IS COMING AGAIN

The Promise of Jesus	Matthew 24:23-30
The Testimony of the Angels	Acts 1:8-11
The Teaching of Paul	1 Thessalonians 4:13-18

We begin with Matthew 24:23-30. It would be well worth your time to read all of Matthew 24 and 25 as these passages constitute the bulk of Jesus' teaching on His second coming. In this chapter, however, we are just going to go through parts of those chapters. In Matthew 24:23-30 we have the promise from Jesus that He will, in fact, be coming back to earth again.

> At that time if anyone says to you, 'Look, here is the Christ!' or, 'There he is!' do not believe it. [24]For false Christs and false prophets will appear and perform great signs and miracles to deceive even the elect – if that were possible. [25]See, I have told you ahead of time.
>
> [26]So if anyone tells you, 'There he is, out in the desert,' do not go out; or, 'Here he is, in the inner rooms,' do not believe it. [27]For as lightning that comes from the east is visible even in the west, so will be the coming of the Son of Man. [28]Wherever there is a carcass, there the vultures will gather.
>
> [29]Immediately after the distress of those days 'the sun will be darkened, and the moon will not give its light; the stars will fall from the sky, and the heavenly bodies will be shaken.'

> [30]At that time the sign of the Son of Man will appear in the sky, and all the nations of the earth will mourn. They will see the Son of Man coming on the clouds of the sky, with power and great glory.

Jesus promises, twice, that He is coming again.

The angels also give their testimony that Jesus is coming again and pronounce this to the disciples. We read this in Acts 1:8-11.

> But you will receive power when the Holy Spirit comes on you; and you will be my witnesses in Jerusalem, and in all Judea and Samaria, and to the ends of the earth.
>
> [9]After he said this, he was taken up before their very eyes, and a cloud hid him from their sight.
>
> [10]They were looking intently up into the sky as he was going, when suddenly two men dressed in white stood beside them. [11]"Men of Galilee," they said, "why do you stand here looking into the sky? This same Jesus, who has been taken from you into heaven, will come back in the same way you have seen him go into heaven."

The message here is to not focus on when Jesus is coming back, nor is it to spend our energy in trying to figure out when Jesus is coming back. Rather, the message is to spend our energy in telling people about Jesus because we *know* that He is coming again. Jesus will come back again; there is to be no doubt about that. There is, however, doubt about the day and the hour. Let us then tell others what we know about and not what we can only speculate about.

Both Jesus and the angels have given testimony that He is coming back. To add to that, we have the preaching of the apostle Paul. 1 Thessalonians 4:13-18 says,

> Brothers, we do not want you to be ignorant about those who fall asleep, or to grieve like the rest of men, who have no hope. [14]We believe that Jesus died and rose again and so we believe that God will bring with Jesus those who have fallen asleep in him.

When Paul mentions those who have fallen asleep, he is speaking about those who have died. His purpose in writing these words is to encourage the Thessalonian believers about those who have died. Paul wants them to know and understand that Jesus is coming back again. As a result of that, those who have died will be seen again when Christ comes back! Paul tells them to not grieve like the rest of men who have no hope. Jesus is coming again, and all who have received Jesus as Lord and Saviour, whether dead or living, will come again with Jesus. They will live.

> [15]According to the Lord's own word, we tell you that we who are still alive, who are left till the coming of the Lord, will certainly not precede those who have fallen asleep. [16] For the Lord himself will come down from heaven, with a loud command, with the voice of the archangel and with the trumpet call of God, and the dead in Christ will rise first. [17]After that, we who are still alive and are left will be caught up together with them in the clouds to meet the Lord in the air. And so we will be with the Lord forever. [18]Therefore encourage each other with these words.

Paul makes it clear that Jesus is coming again. Jesus promised it, the angels testified to it, and Paul's teaching confirms it.

Besides the three major Scriptures that we have just worked through, there are some other supporting Scriptures that help to firm up this truth. One of those is Hebrews 9:28, "so Christ was sacrificed once to take away the sins of many people; and he will appear a second time, not to bear sin, but to bring salvation to those who are waiting for him." Jesus will appear a second time.

Then there is the book of Revelation that declares the second coming of Jesus. Jesus Himself says in Revelation 22:20a, "Yes, I am coming soon." Once again, Jesus confirms His return to the earth.

The second coming of Jesus cannot be denied. There is coming a day when Jesus will return, and all those who have believed in Him, who have received Him as Lord and Saviour, dead or living, will be raised up with Him in the clouds to be with Him. And so we say, "Come, Lord Jesus. Come!"

The Manner of Christ's Return

Now that we know Jesus is definitely coming again, we turn our attention to know the manner in which He will return. There will be a time that He will return, and we certainly do not want to miss that event! What does Scripture have to tell us about the manner of Christ's return?

THE MANNER OF CHRIST'S COMING	
Visible by the whole world	Matthew 24:23-30
To judge the world	Matthew 25:31-46 2 Thessalonians 1:5-10
In the same way He left	Acts 1:9-11 1 Thessalonians 4:13-18

There are three truths that we need to know about the second coming of Jesus to the earth.

1. Visible to the Whole World

First, the return of Jesus will be visible by the whole world so that the whole world will know that it is Jesus who has come. We turn again to Matthew 24:23-27.

At that time if anyone says to you, 'Look, here is the Christ!' or, 'There he is!' do not believe it. [24]For false Christs and false prophets will appear and perform great signs and miracles to deceive even the elect – if that were possible. [25]See, I have told you ahead of time.

[26]So if anyone tells you, 'There he is, out in the desert,' do not go out; or, 'Here he is, in the inner rooms,' do not believe it. [27]For as lightning that comes from the east is visible even in the west, so will be the coming of the Son of Man.

Jesus uses the example of lightning because lightning can be seen from a long way away. Lightning is unmistakable, especially in the dark. When there is lightning you know there is lightning! It could be miles and miles away, yet you recognize it as lightning. Having spent time on the prairies, I know something about lightning. Some of the most magnificent lightning displays happen over the vastness of the prairies because on the prairies you can see for what seems like forever. During those storms, the lightning will light up the whole sky even during the day. At night, the light is almost too intense to even look at; it overwhelms the senses. Sometimes lightning will strike like a sheet across the sky as far as you can see. East to west, the sky is lit up. There is not a single person who is unaware of lightning like that during a prairie storm. This is what it will be like when Jesus comes again. His return will be unmistakably visible, even more visible than a good prairie lightning storm.

It will not go unnoticed, nor will it happen in private. The second coming of Christ will be visible to the whole world. This is why Jesus warns us that if somebody says He has already come, do not believe it, because we are going to know when He comes. The whole world is going to know. It is not going to happen by accident or in private. Jesus further elaborates in Matthew 24:28-30,

> Wherever there is a carcass, there the vultures will gather.
>
> [29]Immediately after the distress of those days 'the sun will be darkened, and the moon will not give its light; the stars will fall from the sky, and the heavenly bodies will be shaken.'
>
> [30]At that time the sign of the Son of Man will appear in the sky, and all the nations of the earth will mourn. They will see the Son of Man coming on the clouds of the sky, with power and great glory.

The whole world is going to convulse. All of creation is going to proclaim that Jesus has come. You will not miss it. It is going to be visible, it is going to be public, and it is going to be a world-wide event! All the nations will see Jesus return! His return will not be limited to a certain area. When Jesus comes, the whole world will know, not just one or two nations. It is not just going to be a North American phenomenon, it is not just going to be a Middle Eastern phenomenon, it is not just going to be a Far Eastern phenomenon; it is going to be the whole entire world phenomenon!

2. To Judge the World

The second fact that we need to know about the return of Jesus is that Jesus is coming back to judge the people of the world.

An interesting element of Christ's return is what Jesus says in verse 30 of chapter 24, "all the nations of the earth will mourn." Why will they mourn? What does Jesus mean by this? In the New Testament, generally speaking, the use of the phrase, "nations of the earth" denotes the unbelieving nations or the unbelieving people of the world, that is, those who do not believe and have not received Jesus as Lord and Saviour. When Jesus says, "At that time the sign of the Son of Man will appear in the sky, and all the nations of the earth will mourn," he is referring to those who have not believed in Him and received Him as Lord and Saviour. It is the non-Christian population who will mourn at the coming of Christ.

Christians, however, will have a different reaction to the return of Jesus. There is a distinction made between believers and the world or nations. Jesus makes this clear from Matthew 25:31-46 where Jesus says,

> When the Son of Man comes in his glory, and all the angels with him, he will sit on his throne in heavenly glory. [32]All the nations will be gathered before him, and he will separate the people one from another as a shepherd separates the sheep from the goats. [33]He will put the sheep on his right and the goats on his left.
>
> [34]Then the King will say to those on his right, 'Come, you who are blessed by my Father; take your inheritance, the kingdom prepared for you since the creation of the world. [35]For I was hungry and you gave me something to eat, I was thirsty and you gave me something to drink, I was a stranger and you invited me in, [36]I needed clothes and you clothed me, I was sick and you looked after me, I was in prison and you came to visit me.'
>
> [37]Then the righteous will answer him, 'Lord, when did we see you hungry and feed you, or thirsty and give you

something to drink? [38]When did we see you a stranger and invite you in, or needing clothes and clothe you? [39]When did we see you sick or in prison and go to visit you?'

[40]The King will reply, 'I tell you the truth, whatever you did for one of the least of these brothers of mine, you did for me.'

These verses speak of those who are disciples of Christ. Jesus speaks of those who, by their actions and words toward others are both serving Jesus and reflecting that Jesus is Lord and Saviour of their life. Putting others first is really putting Jesus first. This group of people are those who are right with Jesus and will look forward to His return.

Jesus then addresses another group, those who are not right with Jesus. He says,

[41]Then he will say to those on his left, 'Depart from me, you who are cursed, into the eternal fire prepared for the devil and his angels. [42]For I was hungry and you gave me nothing to eat, I was thirsty and you gave me nothing to drink, [43]I was a stranger and you did not invite me in, I needed clothes and you did not clothe me, I was sick and in prison and you did not look after me.'

[44]They also will answer, 'Lord, when did we see you hungry or thirsty or a stranger or needing clothes or sick or in prison, and did not help you?'

[45]He will reply, 'I tell you the truth, whatever you did not do for one of the least of these, you did not do for me.'

[46]Then they will go away to eternal punishment, but the righteous to eternal life.

These verses speak about those who are not disciples of Christ. These are people who have chosen not to serve Jesus nor to reflect Him in their lives. Not everybody receives Jesus. This is the reason there is going to be mourning when He comes back. Jesus is returning to judge the unbelieving world for not believing in Him and serving Him. There are consequences for rejecting Jesus.

There is a heaven, and there is a hell, and the eternal destiny of every person is determined by our response to Jesus: to believe in and receive Him or to reject Him. God, of course, wants all people to come unto salvation and everlasting life. That is the heart of God. We see that in 2 Peter 3:9 where Peter assures us that "The Lord is not slow in keeping His promise, as some understand slowness. He is patient with you, not wanting anyone to perish, but everyone to come to repentance." God does not want anyone to perish. The reality, however, is that not every single person chooses to follow Jesus. This is why there will be mourning when Jesus comes again.

The Apostle Paul also confirms this in 2 Thessalonians 1:5-10 where he writes,

> All this is evidence that God's judgment is right, and as a result you will be counted worthy of the kingdom of God, for which you are suffering. 6God is just: He will pay back trouble to those who trouble you 7and give relief to you who are troubled, and to us as well. This will happen when the Lord Jesus is revealed from heaven in blazing fire with his powerful angels. 8He will punish those who do not know God and do not obey the gospel of our Lord Jesus. 9They will be punished with everlasting destruction and shut out from the presence of the Lord and from the majesty of his power 10on the day he comes to be glorified in his holy people and to be marveled at among all those who have believed. This includes you, because you believed our testimony to you.

We see again that there are two responses to the coming of Jesus. There is the response of those who will be mourning because they have not received Jesus as Lord and Saviour, and there is a response of marvel and praise for those who have received Jesus as Lord and Saviour.

The reality is this: Jesus is coming again. He is coming again, and the whole world will be accountable to Him. Every person has a choice to make before He comes. There are consequences for following and consequences for not following. We must make a choice! Will you follow Him?

3. In the Same Way He Left

The third fact that we need to know about the second coming of Christ is that Jesus will come in the same way that He left the world. Acts 1:9-11 says,

After he said this, he was taken up before their very eyes, and a cloud hid him from their sight.

[10]They were looking intently up into the sky as he was going, when suddenly two men dressed in white stood beside them. [11]"Men of Galilee," they said, "why do you stand here looking into the sky? This same Jesus, who has been taken from you into heaven, will come back in the same way you have seen him go into heaven."

The angels make it clear to the disciples that Jesus has ascended, or gone up, into heaven. There is no need to continue to keep looking up; He is gone. But, they say, He will come back again. And, importantly, He will come down from heaven just as He ascended up into heaven. Jesus will return by visibly descending from the clouds in the sky because He visibly ascended into the clouds.

This truth is also taught in 1 Thessalonians 4:13-18.

> Brothers, we do not want you to be ignorant about those who fall asleep, or to grieve like the rest of men, who have no hope. [14]We believe that Jesus died and rose again and so we believe that God will bring with Jesus those who have fallen asleep in him. [15]According to the Lord's own word, we tell you that we who are still alive, who are left till the coming of the Lord, will certainly not precede those who have fallen asleep. [16]For the Lord himself will come down from heaven, with a loud command, with the voice of the archangel and with the trumpet call of God, and the dead in Christ will rise first. [17]After that, we who are still alive and are left will be caught up together with them in the clouds to meet the Lord in the air. And so we will be with the Lord forever. [18]Therefore encourage each other with these words.

Here the apostle Paul writes that Jesus will come with a loud command. It is not certain who will give this command. Is Paul telling us that the voice of the archangel is the same as the loud command? Or is Paul indicating that the voice of the archangel will be in addition to the loud command? It might be the voice of the archangel who gives that loud command, or it may take some other form, but certainly everybody on earth will hear the loud command.

When thunder sounds, everyone in the area hears it; there is no mistaking thunder. Similarly, on July 4th in the United States of America, fireworks are shot off everywhere across the country. The whole country hears those fireworks and understands what they mean. There is no missing those fireworks across the country. In an even more magnified way, everyone in the whole world will hear the shout of the loud command when Jesus returns.

But that is not all; there will also be a trumpet call. I wonder who will be blowing the trumpet! Likely an angel as the book of Revelation indicates. But no matter who is blowing the trumpet, it is certainly going to be a noticeable trumpet call! At this trumpet call, both Christians who have been dead and Christians who are alive will be caught up in the air together. This is certain to make people of the world notice! This event is not going to happen in a small enclosed space. The whole world will hear and see and know that Christ has returned. Yes, Jesus is coming again, and He is coming again for the whole world to see and hear, in a manner so that the whole world will know. It will certainly not be a silent or private event.

The Rapture

This leads us to the essentials of the rapture. The phrase "caught up in the air," or "taken up" is what has been termed "the rapture". When Jesus returns to earth again, Christians will be caught up in the air with Christ. Jesus speaks about this in Matthew 24:36-42.

> No one knows about that day or hour, not even the angels in heaven, nor the Son, but only the Father. [37]As it was in the days of Noah, so it will be at the coming of the Son of Man. [38]For in the days before the flood, people were eating and drinking, marrying and giving in marriage, up to the day Noah entered the ark; [39]and they knew nothing about what would happen until the flood came and took them all away. That is how it will be at the coming of the Son of Man. [40]Two men will be in the field; one will be taken and the other left. [41]Two women will be grinding with a hand mill; one will be taken and the other left.

⁴²Therefore keep watch, because you do not know on what day your Lord will come.

This describes the rapture: Christians being taken up in the air to meet Jesus. Non-Christians are going to watch Christians being taken up into the air when Jesus comes. They are going to watch the rapture, and they are going to mourn because they did not receive Jesus as their Lord and Saviour when they had the chance.

We know that Jesus is definitely coming again. We also know, according to God's word, that Jesus is coming again in conjunction with something called the Great Tribulation.

The Great Tribulation

THE GREAT TRIBULATION

It is a seven year period of tribulation that will affect the whole world at the same time.

Matthew 24:1-22

Revelation 3:10

The Great Tribulation is a seven-year period of tribulation that will affect the whole world at the same time. This great tribulation will be a time of intense tribulation of which the world has never seen, nor will ever see again. This will be a significant period of time on the earth that marks the end of the world as we know it. Jesus talks to His disciples about this in Matthew 24:1-8.

Jesus left the temple and was walking away when his disciples came up to him to call his attention to its buildings. ²"Do you see all these things?" he asked. "I tell you the truth, not one stone here will be left on another; every one will be thrown down."

[3]As Jesus was sitting on the Mount of Olives, the disciples came to him privately. "Tell us," they said, "when will this happen, and what will be the sign of your coming and of the end of the age?"

[4]Jesus answered: "Watch out that no one deceives you. [5]For many will come in my name, claiming, 'I am the Christ,' and will deceive many. [6]You will hear of wars and rumors of wars, but see to it that you are not alarmed. Such things must happen, but the end is still to come. [7]Nation will rise against nation, and kingdom against kingdom. There will be famines and earthquakes in various places. [8]All these are the beginning of birth pains."

Now, I don't know where we are in terms of "the beginning of birth pains," but I do know that we, as a world, have been in the end times ever since the ascension of Jesus 2000 years ago. The end times began with the ascension of Jesus, and we are definitely closer now to the Great Tribulation than we were before. As to where we now are on that timeline no one really knows. Are we still somewhere in the beginning? Are we midway through, or are we close to the end? It is very difficult to discern. Predictions have abounded as to the timing of the end of the world for hundreds of years, yet they have all been proven false. No one really knows the times and dates. We do know, however, that there have been, and continue to be, earthquakes, volcanoes, famines, tornadoes, wars and rumors of wars, just as Jesus said. We know that the signs of the end times are all around us, and we are moving closer to the end.

Jesus continued his teaching on what will happen in the end times in Matthew 24:9-12,

Then you will be handed over to be persecuted and put to death, and you will be hated by all nations because of me. [10]At that time many will turn away from the faith and will betray and hate each other, [11]and many false prophets will appear and deceive many people. [12]Because of the increase of wickedness, the love of most will grow cold,

As part of this build up to the Great Tribulation, there is coming a time when Christians will be hated by the rest of the world, even to the point, as Jesus says, that some Christians will not continue to follow Him. They will walk away from Jesus because they will determine that it is too difficult to follow Jesus and that the cost is too high.

Also, because of the increase of wickedness, the love of most will grow cold. That is a scary statement – the love of most will grow cold. This means that people are not going to love each other anymore, or at least not very much. There will be a great lack of love in this world. We already see this in society today. People are rude, uncaring, disrespectful, and plain old mean to one another. Fewer and fewer people consider the needs of others, and that is because love is growing cold.

The end times will certainly give opportunity to set Christians apart from the rest of the world because Christians are called to love. When others do not love, Christians will still love. Caring, kindness, compassion, and concern for others will come through Christians. The love that Christians have through Christ should never grow cold. Jesus reminds the church of Ephesus in Revelation 2:1-7 to remember their first love – their love for Christ and others. The Christian's first love is Jesus, and through Jesus, to love others. The only people showing love in this world during the end times and the Great Tribulation are going to be Christians.

Jesus, in Matthew 24:13-22, continues the teaching of the Great Tribulation,

> but he who stands firm to the end will be saved. [14]And this gospel of the kingdom will be preached in the whole world as a testimony to all nations, and then the end will come.
>
> [15]So when you see standing in the holy place 'the abomination that causes desolation,' spoken of through the prophet Daniel – let the reader understand – [16]then let those who are in Judea flee to the mountains. [17]Let no one on the roof of his house go down to take anything out of the house. [18]Let no one in the field go back to get his cloak. [19]How dreadful it will be in those days for pregnant women and nursing mothers! [20]Pray that your flight will not take place in winter or on the Sabbath. [21]For then there will be great distress, unequaled from the beginning of the world until now – and never to be equaled again. [22]If those days had not been cut short, no one would survive, but for the sake of the elect those days will be shortened.

Jesus says that there will be a time of unequaled distress throughout the whole world. He is referring to the Great Tribulation, a time of unequaled distress from the beginning of the world until now.

Jesus also says in Revelation 3:10, "Since you have kept my command to endure patiently, I will also keep you from the hour of trial that is going to come upon the whole world to test those who live on the earth." Jesus confirms that a time is coming that will affect the whole world. There will be a Great Tribulation.

But notice the good news. Jesus will be with us during those last days. He says He will "keep us from the hour of trial." There is some difference in opinion as to what those words from Jesus mean. In fact, there are three views on when Jesus will come again and rapture His people out of the world.

There is a pre-tribulation rapture view, a mid- tribulation rapture view, and a post-tribulation rapture view. The pre-tribulation view proposes that Christians are raptured before the Great Tribulation. This view proposes that Christians will not experience any of the Great Tribulation, but that Jesus will take them up out of the world before it happens. The mid-tribulation view proposes that Christians are raptured in the middle of the Great Tribulation so that they will experience only the first half of the Great Tribulation and be taken up out of the world to miss the second half. Finally, the post-tribulation view proposes that Christians will go through the entire Great Tribulation – all seven years of it. There are also many variations of these views as well.

Whatever view one might take, we can be sure that Jesus promises to be with us through, and in, whatever part of the Great Tribulation we might have to experience, if any. His presence will always be with us, even during those terrible days. He will never leave or forsake His own.

THREE VIEWS ON THE RAPTURE

Pre-tribulation View   Christians are raptured before the Great Tribulation

Mid-tribulation View   Christians are raptured in the middle of the Great Tribulation

Post-tribulation View   Christians are raptured after the Great Tribulation

The Antichrist

The final topic that we need to talk about in this chapter is the biblical teaching on the antichrist.

THE ANTICHRIST

Matthew 24:15
Daniel 9:27
1 John 2:18
Revelation 13:1-5

During those days of the Great Tribulation, the antichrist appears. Jesus mentions him in Matthew 24:15 as, "the abomination that causes desolation." This phrase, "abomination that causes desolation" is also spoken of in Daniel 9:27 where Daniel is referring to the antichrist. The Apostle John also writes about the antichrist in 1 John 2:18. John writes, "Dear children, this is the last hour; and as you have heard that the antichrist is coming, even now many antichrists have come. This is how we know it is the last hour."

It is interesting to note that John calls it the last hour. Clearly he felt that time was getting very short before Christ would come again. Of course, the question needs to be asked, "How long does the hour last?" John wrote those words in about 94 A.D. so this last hour has been about 1900 years so far. How much longer do we have left before the antichrist is revealed, the Great Tribulation is upon the world, and Jesus returns to rapture His people? The answer: we don't know. But we do know that the antichrist is coming. Notice John says, "you have heard that the antichrist is coming." The antichrist is a real person whom John fully expected would come into the world. He writes in Revelation 13:1-5,

And the dragon stood on the shore of the sea.

> And I saw a beast coming out of the sea. He had ten horns and seven heads, with ten crowns on his horns, and on each head a blasphemous name. ²The beast I saw resembled a leopard, but had feet like those of a bear and a mouth like that of a lion. The dragon gave the beast his power and his throne and great authority. ³One of the heads of the beast seemed to have had a fatal wound, but the fatal wound had been healed. The whole world was astonished and followed the beast. ⁴Men worshiped the dragon because he had given authority to the beast, and they also worshiped the beast and asked, "Who is like the beast? Who can make war against him?"
>
> ⁵The beast was given a mouth to utter proud words and blasphemies and to exercise his authority for forty-two months.

The antichrist will be revealed so that the whole world will know and even worship him. This will be a significant world event – just like the rapture of the saints, the revealing of the antichrist will not be done in private. Furthermore, the antichrist will be known by his actions and words. The antichrist will be the exact and complete opposite of Jesus. The antichrist's character will be opposite of the character of Christ, yet he will pretend to the world that he is the Christ. That is why the antichrist is going to do signs and wonders and miracles, so that the whole world, those who do not know the truth through Jesus, will believe that he must be Jesus, and therefore will worship him.

This, by the way, is why it is so important to know who Jesus is and to have a strong relationship with Jesus now. For if the antichrist came tomorrow, you would recognize him as not being Jesus because you would already know the real Jesus. Paul encourages us to know Christ and to remain in Him in 2 Thessalonians 2:1-12.

> Concerning the coming of our Lord Jesus Christ and our being gathered to him, we ask you, brothers, [2]not to become easily unsettled or alarmed by some prophecy, report or letter supposed to have come from us, saying that the day of the Lord has already come. [3]Don't let anyone deceive you in any way, for that day will not come until the rebellion occurs and the man of lawlessness is revealed, the man doomed to destruction. [4]He will oppose and will exalt himself over everything that is called God or is worshiped, so that he sets himself up in God's temple, proclaiming himself to be God.
>
> [5]Don't you remember that when I was with you I used to tell you these things? [6]And now you know what is holding him back, so that he may be revealed at the proper time. [7]For the secret power of lawlessness is already at work; but the one who now holds it back will continue to do so till he is taken out of the way. [8]And then the lawless one will be revealed, whom the Lord Jesus will overthrow with the breath of his mouth and destroy by the splendor of his coming. [9]The coming of the lawless one will in accordance with the work of Satan displayed in all kinds of counterfeit miracles, signs and wonders, [10]and in every sort of evil that deceives those who are perishing. They perish because they refused to love the truth and so be saved. [11]For this reason God sends them a powerful delusion so that they will believe the lie [12]and so that all will be condemned who have not believed the truth but have delighted in wickedness.

The antichrist is coming to pretend that he is Jesus, but he is not. He will be the opposite of Jesus; he will be the anti-Jesus. His power and work will come from satan, not God. He will deceive and lie; there will be no truth in him.

We are living in the end times. Jesus is coming back again. His followers will be raptured up to heaven with Him. The Great Tribulation is coming and so is the antichrist. In the second to last verse of the Bible, Jesus gives us a promise. It is, "Behold I am coming soon."

Jesus is coming soon. He could come at any time. His return is imminent. He is coming like a thief in the night, and no one knows exactly when. But He is coming. Have we passed springtime? Have we passed the final hour? I don't know. Jesus could return today. The question is, "Are you ready for Jesus to return today?" Where are you at with Jesus? Do you know Jesus as your Lord and Saviour? Jesus, right now, offers His free gift of salvation to you. He does not want anyone to perish but all to have everlasting life. Have you received Jesus as Lord and Saviour? Will you receive Jesus as Lord and Saviour?

We have a choice now, to follow or not to follow Jesus.

Closing Prayer

I am going to pray a prayer, and it is a prayer that simply says, "Jesus, I want You to be my Lord and my Saviour." If you have never prayed that, and you don't know for sure if Jesus is in your life and that you are going to heaven for eternal life, pray this after me:

Dear Jesus, I know that I am a sinner, and I ask You to forgive me of my sins. I believe You died on the cross for my sins, and I believe You were raised on the third day. Jesus, come into my life; be my Lord, and be my Saviour. Help me to live for You for eternity. I ask this in Jesus' name.

Amen.

Chapter 10

THE ESSENTIALS

OF

THE RESURRECTION

We now turn our attention to the topic of the resurrection. We will cover the resurrection of Christ, the resurrection of believers, and the resurrection of unbelievers.

The resurrection is a topic that, beyond Easter and communion, is not taught in churches very often. Yet the resurrection is an essential doctrine. In fact, I would suggest to you that the resurrection is one of the central and most important doctrines of the Christian faith. I make that statement based upon what the apostle Paul says in 1 Corinthians 15. This is commonly referred to as the resurrection passage. 1 Corinthians 15:1-4 reads,

> Now, brothers, I want to remind you of the gospel I preached to you, which you received and on which you have taken your stand. [2]By this gospel you are saved, if you hold firmly to the word I preached to you. Otherwise, you have believed in vain.

Paul is talking about the gospel and what the gospel is. He is going to give us his version of the essentials of the gospel. He continues,

> [3]For what I received I passed on to you as of first importance: that Christ died for our sins according to the Scriptures, [4]that he was buried, that he was raised on the third day according to the Scriptures.

Paul uses the phrase, "he was raised on the third day." He is speaking about the resurrection of Jesus. The gospel, for Paul, includes the resurrection. To put it another way, the resurrection of Jesus is part of the gospel message. The message of salvation is incomplete without the resurrection of Jesus. Paul says that Jesus died for our sins, that He was buried, and that He was raised again on the third day. The resurrection is central to our faith.

As Paul continues, in verses 12-20, he clearly tells us that without the resurrection of Jesus our faith is in vain. The resurrection of Jesus Christ is essential for our faith to have any meaning at all. The fact is that if Jesus was not raised from the dead, then we should close the doors of the church because the church does not make any difference without the resurrection of Jesus from the dead. We read this in 1 Corinthians 15:12-20.

> But if it is preached that Christ has been raised from the dead, how can some of you say that there is no resurrection of the dead? [13]If there is no resurrection of the dead, then not even Christ has been raised. [14]And if Christ has not been raised, our preaching is useless and so is your faith. [15]More than that, we are then found to be false witnesses about God, for we have testified about God that he raised Christ from the dead. But he did not raise him if in fact the dead are not raised. [16]For if the dead are not raised, then Christ has not been raised either. [17]And if Christ has not been raised, your faith is futile; you are still in your sins. [18]Then those also who have fallen asleep in Christ are lost. [19]If only for this life we have hope in Christ, we are to be pitied more than all men.
>
> [20]But Christ has indeed been raised from the dead, the firstfruits of those who have fallen asleep.

Paul clearly teaches that of central importance to our faith is the resurrection. Our faith has meaning and power because of the death and resurrection of Christ. Because Jesus was resurrected from the dead, we can know that our faith is not futile.

Without the resurrection of Christ, there is no salvation. That is how essential the resurrection of Jesus Christ is for our faith. Jesus has been raised from the dead, and because Jesus has been resurrected from the dead, so too will the believer be resurrected from the dead. Furthermore, because the resurrection of Jesus is true, there is also a resurrection of sinners. Every person on earth will be resurrected from the dead. Because of the resurrection of Jesus, there will be a resurrection of the saints, that is the believers, and a resurrection of the sinners, that is non-believers.

Definition

DEFINITION OF THE RESURRECTION
Resurrection – To rise again (from the dead)
1 Corinthians 15:44

Let us first start with a definition of resurrection. The term resurrection, as used in the Bible means to rise again, almost always from the dead. Furthermore, the resurrection always includes a body. We will be raised again in bodily form. In 1 Corinthians 15:44 it says, "it is sown a natural body, it is raised a spiritual body. If there is a natural body, there is also a spiritual body."

Paul goes on to show that the resurrection will include a new body. Just as Jesus was raised with a new body, we will be raised with a new body after we die.

In Corinthians 15:35-45 Paul argues that there are many types of bodies that God has created for animals, fish, and birds. God not only created earthly bodies, He also created heavenly bodies such as the moon and the stars. The apostle's point is that there are many types of bodies, and God is not limited to just one body type. Therefore, He is able to create new imperishable bodies for the resurrection from the dead. They will be different bodies than what we have now, in that they will be spiritual and imperishable bodies, but they will be bodies nonetheless. There will definitely be a resurrected body of some sort.

Resurrection of Jesus

RESURRECTION OF JESUS	
Attestation of the angels	Matthew 28:5-7
Appeared in bodily form	1 Corinthians 15:3-6
Seated in the heavenly realms	Ephesians 1:19b-20

We turn first to the resurrection of Jesus. In regard to the resurrection of Jesus, the angels, in Matthew 28:5-7, attest to the fact that Jesus has been raised from the dead. Matthew writes,

> The angel said to the women, "Do not be afraid, for I know that you are looking for Jesus, who was crucified. [6]He is not here; he has risen, just as he said. Come and see the place where he lay. [7]Then go quickly and tell his disciples: 'He has risen from the dead and is going ahead of you into Galilee. There you will see him.' Now I have told you."

The two Marys were at the tomb early in the morning, and they were met by an angel. The angel knew that they were looking for the body of Jesus, and they told the women, "Jesus is not here, He has risen just like He said... He has risen from the dead." The women were not going to find the body of Jesus in the tomb because Jesus had risen from the dead and was now alive! Jesus was walking to Galilee, not in his beat up and broken body, but with a new revived body. The angels testify to the resurrection of Jesus with a new body.

The apostle Paul also testifies to the resurrection of Jesus. As we have already read in 1 Corinthians 15:3-6,

> For what I received I passed on to you as of first importance: that Christ died for our sins according to the Scriptures, ⁴that he was buried, that he was raised on the third day according to the Scriptures, ⁵and that he appeared to Peter, and then to the Twelve. ⁶After that, he appeared to more than five hundred of the brothers at the same time, most of whom are still living, though some have fallen asleep.

Jesus appeared to Peter, the twelve, and to five hundred of the disciples with His new body. There could be no doubt that Jesus had been raised from the dead as there were over five hundred witnesses to His resurrection. The resurrection of Jesus did not happen in secret, nor did it not happen alone. The resurrection of Jesus took place publicly for all to see and confirm.

Paul then went on to write, in 1 Corinthians 15:7, that Jesus appeared to James, to all the apostles, and last of all He appeared to Paul himself (Acts 9:1-9). The apostle Paul gives personal testimony that he saw Jesus in bodily form after the crucifixion. He saw Jesus alive, resurrected from the dead, and living in His resurrected body. Jesus had indeed been resurrected from the dead.

For more proof of Christ's resurrection, we turn to Ephesians 1:19b-20. Here we read that Jesus is seated in the heavenly realms. Paul writes, "That power is like the working of his mighty strength, [20]which he exerted in Christ when he raised him from the dead and seated him at his right hand in the heavenly realms." Paul is clear that Jesus is alive and is dwelling in heaven, sitting on his throne. He has been raised from the dead and sits enthroned in heaven today. He is indeed alive; He has been raised from the dead.

Resurrection of the Saints

The resurrection of Jesus is good news for Christians because, as a result of Christ's resurrection from the dead, Christians too are going to be raised from the dead. Let's take a look at the resurrection of the saints. As a side note, I use the word "saint" as Paul used the word "saint" to refer to Christians. Paul indicates that Christians are saints, meaning holy ones, set apart ones and those who have believed in and received Jesus as Lord and Saviour. If you are a disciple of Christ, you are a saint. It does not, however, mean you are perfect; it just means you have believed in Jesus and are following Him. Paul and the rest of Scripture never use the word "saint" to indicate perfection, or without sin. It is a word that indicates a new and changed life because of the life of Christ in them.

THE RESURRECTION OF THE SAINTS

1 Thessalonians 4:13-18
1 Corinthians 15:35-54

Let's look at the teaching about the resurrection of the saints by starting with 1 Thessalonians 4 which is probably the second major body of Scripture that talks about the resurrection. Let us read 1 Thessalonians 4:13-18.

Brothers, we do not want you to be ignorant about those who fall asleep, or to grieve like the rest of men, who have no hope. [14]We believe that Jesus died and rose again and so we believe that God will bring with Jesus those who have fallen asleep in him.

In other words, Jesus was raised from the dead and so too will everyone who believes in Jesus Christ as Lord and Saviour be raised from the dead.

[15]According to the Lord's own word, we tell you that we who are still alive, who are left till the coming of the Lord, will certainly not precede those who have fallen asleep. [16]For the Lord himself will come down from heaven, with a loud command, with the voice of the archangel and with the trumpet call of God, and the dead in Christ will rise first. [17]After that, we who are still alive and are left will be caught up together with them in the clouds to meet the Lord in the air. And so we will be with the Lord forever. [18]Therefore encourage each other with these words."

These are indeed encouraging words. These are words that give promise to all believers in Jesus Christ that they will be raised again! Those who have already died, being believers in Christ, will be raised again. When Jesus comes back, they will be raised up with Him in the clouds, and we will meet them. What a great truth to be encouraged by! Death is not the end; there is a resurrection to life, to eternal life for the believer in Christ Jesus. It is a truth from God which you can count on. It is a guarantee because He has promised it. This essential doctrine of the resurrection is so important to our faith in Christ because it guarantees that death does not defeat life. It means we have hope and a future; it means that we have life after death. There is everlasting life, or eternal life. We, as Christians, have that guarantee of eternal life because we believe in Jesus as Lord and Saviour and follow Him.

Going back to the teaching of 1 Corinthians 15, Paul also talks about the reality of the resurrection of the saints. In 1 Corinthians 15:35-54, Paul makes the case for the resurrection of the dead in order to refute those who did not really believe in the resurrection. And, of course, people continue to say that today. They continue to deny the resurrection of Christ and the resurrection of people. We read in 1 Corinthians 15:35-39,

> But someone may ask, "How are the dead raised? With what kind of body will they come?" [36]How foolish! What you sow does not come to life unless it dies. [37]When you sow, you do not plant the body that will be, but just a seed, perhaps of wheat or of something else. [38]But God gives it a body as he has determined, and to each kind of seed he gives its own body. [39]All flesh is not the same: Men have one kind of flesh, animals have another, birds another and fish another.

In arguing for the resurrection, Paul, in essence, says, "Look, there are different kinds of bodies. Wheat, when it grows, does not look like barley, which does not look like corn, which does not look like oats. They are all different; they all have different bodies. Furthermore, fish do not look like birds, birds do not look like people, and people do not look like animals. There are different bodies that God has given to each one." In 1 Corinthians 15:40-41 we read,

> There are also heavenly bodies and there are earthly bodies; but the splendor of the heavenly bodies is one kind, and the splendor of the earthly bodies is another. [41]The sun has one kind of splendor, the moon another and the stars another; and star differs from star in splendor.

Again, Paul argues that even in the heavens, if you look up there, you are going to see different bodies. So why would we doubt that we are going to have a resurrected body? There are different kinds of bodies all over the place, therefore, God is perfectly capable of creating a resurrected body for us. Continuing, Paul writes in 1 Corinthians 15:42-44a,

> So will it be with the resurrection of the dead. The body that is sown is perishable, it is raised imperishable; [43]it is sown in dishonor, it is raised in glory; it is sown in weakness, it is raised in power; [44a]it is sown a natural body, it is raised a spiritual body.

The resurrected body is certainly going to be different from this earthly body. God is going to create a body that is going to be imperishable. It is going to be indestructible. It is going to be a body that is made in honor and glory. And it is going to be a body that is raised in power. The resurrected body is not going to be a natural body that we have now on this earth, rather, it will be a spiritual body that is meant for eternity. It is not a body that will be given over to weakness, nor given over to sickness or disease or ill health. The resurrected body is going to be an imperishable body! Imperishable! I don't know what that is going to feel like, but I am certain that I am going to love that kind of a body. I love to run and jump and play, but I am limited in what I can do and will be even more limited as the years go by. I get tired and worn out, and I have to rest. But when I get a new imperishable body, I will not have to worry about getting tired and having to rest and recover. My knees will never be in danger of giving out, nor will there ever be any back pain, or hip pain, or muscle pain… at all! I could be running and jumping and playing forever. This is the kind of body that I want! And I will get it one day because of Christ's resurrection.

Paul continues to cement his argument of the resurrected body. He states in 1 Corinthians 15:44b-49,

If there is a natural body, there is also a spiritual body. [45]So it is written: "The first man Adam became a living being"; the last Adam, a life-giving spirit. [46]The spiritual did not come first, but the natural, and after that the spiritual. [47]The first man was of the dust of the earth, the second man from heaven. [48]As was the earthly man, so are those who are of the earth; and as is the man from heaven, so also are those who are of heaven. [49]And just as we have borne the likeness of the earthly man, so shall we bear the likeness of the man from heaven.

In other words, because Jesus has received His resurrected body, the perfect new resurrected body, the disciple of Christ will also receive his/hers. He/she will receive the resurrected body just as surely as he/she has received an earthly body.

Paul brings his argument to a close with verses 50-54,

I declare to you, brothers, that flesh and blood cannot inherit the kingdom of God, nor does the perishable inherit the imperishable. [51]Listen, I tell you a mystery: We will not all sleep, but we will all be changed – [52]in a flash, in the twinkling of an eye, at the last trumpet. For the trumpet will sound, the dead will be raised imperishable, and we will be changed. [53]For the perishable must clothe itself with the imperishable, and the mortal with immortality. [54]When the perishable has been clothed with the imperishable, and the mortal with immortality, then the saying that is written will come true: "Death has been swallowed up in victory."

Christians have the victory! And this victory is secured in Jesus Christ because of His resurrection. Every single believer who has believed in and received Jesus as Lord and Saviour will be raised from the dead and will be given a new spiritual, imperishable, and glorified body that will last for an eternity.

The resurrection is clearly central to Christianity. It is the hope we know, and it is the victory we have. This knowledge and victory in Christ has the power to take away our fear and our worry. Because Jesus has been resurrected from the dead for eternity, we can know that we too will be resurrected from the dead and live forever in eternity with Him. This is the reality of heaven. Unfortunately though, we live in a day and age when people declare that heaven and hell are not real. Many also declare that Jesus is not real either. The Bible declares it differently. We know the reality of Jesus, the reality of heaven and the reality of hell.

The Reality of Heaven

THE REALITY OF HEAVEN	
Jesus is preparing a place for us	John 14:1-3
Where Jesus dwells	Hebrews 9:24
Where God the Father dwells	Matthew 6:9
Where our inheritance is	1 Peter 1:3-5
Where sin does not exist	Revelation 21:1-7

Jesus Himself tells us that heaven is a real place. John records these words of Jesus in John 14:1-3,

> Do not let your hearts be troubled. Trust in God; trust also in me. [2]In my Father's house are many rooms; if it were not so, I would have told you. I am going there to prepare a place for you. [3]And if I go and prepare a place for you, I will come back and take you to be with me that you also may be where I am.

Jesus promises us that there is a real place called heaven and that He is preparing a place for everyone who believes in Him and receives Him as Lord and Saviour. He is preparing your place for you right now. Then, one day, He is going to come back to earth and take every believer to that place that He has been preparing. Jesus is our realtor; He has a property for you, and you are the only one who can make an offer on it. It is not for anyone else, just for you. And it gets better – that place has already been paid for! Jesus has already paid for your house/mansion/home in heaven. All you have to do is move in. And I can guarantee that you are going to love it! It is going to be your dream house! Jesus is preparing it for you already. Heaven is a real place where Jesus currently is, preparing a home for us. He will come back and take us to be there with Him forever.

Another verse that speaks about heaven is Hebrews 9:24 which says, "For Christ did not enter a man-made sanctuary that was only a copy of the true one; he entered heaven itself, now to appear for us in God's presence."

Again, Jesus is in heaven and heaven is real. Scripture would not say that He entered heaven if heaven was not a real place. Matthew 6:9 states that God the Father dwells in heaven. Matthew 6:9 is the start of the Lord's Prayer, "Our Father in heaven." The King James version says, "Our Father which art in heaven" and the New American Standard version puts it this way, "Our Father who is in heaven." Clearly, heaven is a real place where God dwells.

We also learn from 1 Peter 1:3-5 that we have an inheritance in heaven. Peter writes,

> Praise be to the God and Father of our Lord Jesus Christ! In his great mercy he has given us new birth into a living hope through the resurrection of Jesus Christ from the dead, ⁴and into an inheritance that can never perish, spoil or fade – kept in heaven for you, ⁵who through faith are shielded by God's power until the coming of the salvation that is ready to be revealed in the last time.

Every Christian has an inheritance in heaven. We have an inheritance that will never perish, that will never spoil, that will never fade, that will never diminish, that will never be affected by inflation, and that will never be threatened by the stock market. We have an inheritance that is secure and set in place for us. It is the place that Jesus is now preparing. It is real and it is the inheritance of every follower of Christ. You are going to receive it one day.

Another writer who speaks about our inheritance is the apostle John. In the book of Revelation 21:1-2 John writes,

> Then I saw a new heaven and a new earth, for the first heaven and the first earth had passed away, and there was no longer any sea. ²I saw the Holy City, the new Jerusalem, coming down out of heaven from God, prepared as a bride beautifully dressed for her husband.

I was once asked, "Are there going to be cities in heaven?" Well, there is certainly going to be one we know of; there is going to be the city of Jerusalem. John continues with verse 3,

> And I heard a loud voice from the throne saying, "Now the dwelling of God is with men, and he will live with them. They will be his people, and God himself will be with them and be their God."

As part of heaven, God is going to restore the earth to the perfect state as it was when God created the earth, like it was in the Garden of Eden. God will once again walk with people as He did with Adam and Eve in the cool of the day (Genesis 3:8). But since Adam and Eve sinned, God could not physically walk with them in the garden anymore. But once sin is done away with and death has been done away with, God will once again physically walk with us in the garden, in the city, or wherever we are on the new earth in heaven. Now that is an amazing inheritance which is saved up and waiting for all those who have believed in and received Jesus as Lord and Saviour.

There is another piece of information that we need to know about regarding our inheritance in heaven. John writes in Revelation 21:4,

> He will wipe every tear from their eyes. There will be no
> more death or mourning or crying or pain, for the old order
> of things has passed away.

How many of you reading this had to take medication today because you have some sort of pain, or sickness, or disease? In heaven there will be no need of any type of medication because we will all have a body that is without pain and will never experience any type of pain again. Pain and even the idea of pain are going to be gone forever. There are not going to be any tears or any crying. You will never have anything that hurts you or that is emotionally painful. In heaven, we will never experience any depression, any despondency, or any discouragement. There will be nothing negative in heaven at all. There will only be celebration and perfection.

John tells us that the old order of the earth will have passed away. There will be no more sin, no more death, no more satan, nor anything associated with sin, death and satan. We will have perfect bodies and live in a perfect world – forever. We have God's word on that. We have his written promise. It is found in Revelation 21:5-7.

> He who was seated on the throne said, "I am making everything new!" Then he said, "Write this down, for these words are trustworthy and true."

> ⁶He said to me: "It is done. I am the Alpha and the Omega, the Beginning and the End. To him who is thirsty I will give to drink without cost from the spring of the water of life. ⁷He who overcomes will inherit all this, and I will be his God and he will be my son."

God Himself has given us His word that heaven is a real place that holds a real inheritance for His people.

Often the question is asked, "Where is the Christian who dies now? Where are they right now?" That answer can be found in Luke 23:39-43.

> One of the criminals who hung there hurled insults at him: "Aren't you the Christ? Save yourself and us!"

> ⁴⁰But the other criminal rebuked him. "Don't you fear God," he said, "since you are under the same sentence? ⁴¹We are punished justly, for we are getting what our deeds deserve. But this man has done nothing wrong."

> ⁴²Then he said, "Jesus, remember me when you come into your kingdom."

> ⁴³Jesus answered him, "I tell you the truth, today you will be with me in paradise."

When we die as Christians we are at that moment of death with Jesus. Jesus did not say, "Once you go through purgatory you will be with me."

Or, "Once you wait there for a while and, when I have decided if you are good enough, you can come with me." No, Jesus clearly said, "Today you will be with me in paradise." Today, indicating that upon the death of the thief on the cross, he would immediately be in heaven. Paradise, by the way, is another Greek word used for "heaven".

Christians who die are in heaven, in paradise, with Jesus right upon the time of their death. It does not seem that they will have a resurrected body yet, because these are received only when Jesus returns, but their spirit is in heaven with Jesus. The spirit, that which makes us, is with Jesus so that we can enjoy paradise.

That is the good news about the resurrection of Jesus. But there is some bad news regarding the resurrection from the dead. There is the whole gospel of God. The resurrection of the saints is only part of the gospel message. The resurrection of the sinner is the other part of the gospel that needs to be spoken about.

The Resurrection of the Sinner

> THE RESURRECTION OF THE SINNER
>
> Daniel 12:1-2
>
> John 5:28-29

There is a resurrection of the sinner. Both the believer and non-believer will be raised again. Everybody on earth will be raised again.

We start in the book of Daniel 12:1-2 which states,

At that time Michael, the great prince who protects your people, will arise. There will be a time of distress such as

> has not happened from the beginning of nations until then. But at that time your people – everyone whose name is found written in the book – will be delivered. ²Multitudes who sleep in the dust of the earth will awake: some to everlasting life, others to shame and everlasting contempt.

Daniel is speaking about the second coming of Christ, the Great Tribulation, and the resurrection of the dead, both Christians and non-Christians. The book spoken of is the book of life – a book which holds the names of everyone who has believed in and received Jesus as Lord and Saviour. The words, "multitudes who sleep in the dust of the earth will awake," refers to all people who have ever died in the past. Daniel tells us that there will be a resurrection from the dead; they "will awake, some to everlasting life others to shame and everlasting contempt." This means that the believer will be resurrected into heaven, and the unbeliever resurrected into hell.

John 5:28-29 says,

> Do not be amazed at this, for a time is coming when all who are in their graves will hear his voice ²⁹and come out – those who have done good will rise to live, and those who have done evil will rise to be condemned.

This is the resurrection. This is what both 1Thessalonians 4 and 1 Corinthians 15 speak about. A time is coming when all who are in their graves will hear His voice and come out. All people will be judged by Christ and either receive eternal life or eternal death.

The Reality of Hell

> THE REALITY OF HELL
>
> A place of weeping and gnashing of teeth
> Matthew 24:45-51
>
> Eternal punishment
> Matthew 25:46
>
> Lake of burning sulfur, a place of torment
> Revelation 20:7-15

There is the reality of hell. Everybody will be raised – both the sinner and the saint. In Matthew 24:45-51, while teaching on end times, Jesus says,

> Who then is the faithful and wise servant, whom the master has put in charge of the servants in his household to give them their food at the proper time? [46]It will be good for that servant whose master finds him doing so when he returns. [47]I tell you the truth, he will put him in charge of all his possessions. [48]But suppose that servant is wicked and says to himself, 'My master is staying away a long time,' [49]and he then begins to beat his fellow servants and to eat and drink with drunkards. [50]The master of that servant will come on a day when he does not expect him and at an hour he is not aware of. [51]He will cut him to pieces and assign him a place with the hypocrites, where there will be weeping and gnashing of teeth.

Jesus teaches that there is a real place, a place in which those who do not follow Jesus and have rejected Jesus, will be assigned to for eternity. They will be resurrected to an eternal separation from God forever. Matthew 25:46 states, "Then they will go away to eternal punishment, but the righteous to eternal life." Jesus is talking about those who did not believe in Him and receive Him as Lord and Saviour. They will go away to eternal punishment while those who are righteous, those who believed in Him and received Him, are resurrected unto eternal life.

Hell is a reality. In Revelation 20:7-15 we read the following,

When the thousand years are over, Satan will be released from his prison [8]and will go out to deceive the nations in the four corners of the earth – Gog and Magog – to gather them for battle. In number they are like the sand on the seashore. [9]They marched across the breadth of the earth and surrounded the camp of God's people, the city he loves. But fire came down from heaven and devoured them. [10]And the devil, who deceived them, was thrown into the lake of burning sulfur, where the beast and the false prophet had been thrown. They will be tormented day and night for ever and ever.

[11]Then I saw a great white throne and him who was seated on it. Earth and sky fled from his presence, and there was no place for them. [12]And I saw the dead, great and small, standing before the throne, and books were opened. Another book was opened, which is the book of life. The dead were judged according to what they had done as recorded in the books. [13]The sea gave up the dead that were in it, and death and Hades gave up the dead that were in them, and each person was judged according to what he had done. [14]Then death and Hades were thrown into the lake of fire. The lake of fire is the second death. [15]If anyone's name was not found written in the book of life, he was thrown into the lake of fire.

This is a part of the gospel. The reality is heaven exists and hell exists. There are many books out there that will try to convince you that hell does not actually exist, that the teaching of hell in the Bible is a euphemism for just a bad place where you do not want to go. No, it is not a euphemistic place; it is a real place. Both Jesus and the apostles taught that hell was a real place. God's word is very clear. But I want to tell you this, hell is not a place that God desires any person to go to.

Both 1Timothy 2:3-4 and 2 Peter 3:9 tell us that God wants all people to come unto salvation. God does not want anyone to perish.

1Timothy 2:3-4 reads, "This is good, and pleases God our Savior, 4who wants all men to be saved and to come to a knowledge of the truth." And Peter writes, "The Lord is not slow in keeping his promise, as some understand slowness. He is patient with you, not wanting anyone to perish, but everyone to come to repentance."

Furthermore, hell is a place that was made for the devil and his angels, for those who rebelled against God. Hell was never intended for human beings. God created satan to be good, but satan and some of the angels rebelled against God. Thus, God is reserving a place for them where they will be punished for eternity. But God does not want you and me to go there! Certainly not! He does not want any of the people he created to go there. That is the very reason that Jesus died on the cross: to save humankind from their sin and give them everlasting life.

Salvation is the solution to hell given by a loving God. Jesus, who knew no sin, died on the cross for us. He took our sins so that anyone and everyone who believes in Him and receives Him as Lord and Saviour will have everlasting life. It is easy to go to heaven. It is a free gift. We do not have to work for it – we just simply have to receive it. We have to say, "Yes, Jesus I believe in you; I receive you as Lord and Saviour, help me to live for you." God made it easy because He does not want anyone of us to perish. Salvation is a free gift. It is not by works; it is by the death and resurrection of Jesus Christ. That is the gospel. That is the love of God. He wants all of us to come to salvation.

The full gospel story includes both heaven and hell, sin and salvation. To say there is no hell is to say there is no heaven, and to say there is no heaven is to say there is no salvation. There is salvation from sin through the death and resurrection of Jesus Christ. And Jesus wants everybody to come to salvation. That is the worldwide all encompassing, inclusive word of God. He wants everybody to come unto salvation no matter who you are, where you live, what you have done, or what color you are – He wants all people to come unto salvation. That is who God is. That is the result of the resurrection of Jesus: salvation for everybody on earth.

Conclusion

Perhaps most reading this have received Jesus as Lord and Saviour. Most of you have your inheritance in heaven. Most of you know that if you were to die today, you know that you have everlasting life. You know that because you received Jesus as Lord and Saviour. Some of you, however, might not be that sure. Some of you might wonder if you were to die today where would you go, heaven or hell? What would you say to God when God says, "Why should I let you into my heaven?" The answer to that question is, "Because I believed in Jesus and received Him as my Lord and Saviour."

Can you say that today? If you can't I invite you to ask Jesus into your life today through a simple prayer. It is a prayer that asks Jesus into your life. If you need to pray that prayer and ask Jesus in, pray it after me.

Prayer of Salvation

Jesus, I believe You died on the cross for me. I believe You were raised again on the third day. I know that I have sin in my life, and I ask You to forgive me of my sins. Jesus, come into my life, be my Saviour, be my Lord, and grant me everlasting life. In Jesus' name, Amen.

Closing prayer

Jesus, I thank You for those who have received You as Lord and Saviour. They know You because they have just asked You in. You have given them everlasting life. God, let them know that they are secure in You, that they have an assured inheritance, that they can be confident that they have everlasting life, and that You are preparing a place for them. Jesus, thank You for Your resurrection, that we, too, will be raised again, and we have a place in heaven with You – guaranteed. Thank You, Jesus. In Your name we pray.

Amen.

Chapter 11

THE ESSENTIALS

OF

THE GIFTS OF THE HOLY SPIRIT

AND

FRUIT OF THE HOLY SPIRIT

This chapter actually contains two essential doctrines of Scripture, but I have combined them together because, well, they really do belong together in the life of a disciple of Christ. We are going to cover the essentials of both the gifts of the Holy Spirit and the fruit of the Holy Spirit. There is often a fair amount of confusion surrounding the gifts and the fruit of the Spirit. It is the purpose of this chapter to bring some clarity about these two essential teachings of Scripture. We will define both the gifts of the Spirit and the fruit of the Spirit and show the difference between them. Yes, the gifts are not the same as the fruit. They are different works of the Holy Spirit in the life of the believer. We will look first to the gifts of the Spirit and then move on to cover the fruit of the Holy Spirit.

Definition of the Gifts of the Holy Spirit

We begin with a definition of the gifts of the Holy Spirit. The gifts of the Holy Spirit are supernatural enablings, given to Christians, by God's Holy Spirit for the purpose of accomplishing the works that God has given each Christian to do in bringing about His kingdom and His glory. Many times, people refer to spiritual gifts as talents or abilities, but they are more than abilities that we are born with and talents that we have acquired. These natural talents and abilities can certainly be enhanced by the Holy Spirit, but the gifts of the Holy Spirit, as we learn about them in Scripture, are supernatural enablings that we would not have on our own if it were not for the Holy Spirit in us. Non-Christians do not have the gifts of the Holy Spirit because non-Christians do not have the Holy Spirit in them. Remember that a person cannot be a Christian apart from the Holy Spirit because it is the Holy Spirit who regenerates people with the new nature of Christ. Thus, when any person receives Christ, he is made new by the Holy Spirit, and it is then that the Holy Spirit gives to each new believer a spiritual gift or gifts. Thus, the gifts of the Spirit are supernatural enablings given by the Holy Spirit of God.

Perhaps it would help to give a quick list of the gifts of the Holy Spirit. The mention of the gifts of the Holy Spirit are found in three major Scripture passages:

1. Romans 12:3-8 – prophesying, serving, teaching, encouragement, giving, leading, and mercy.

2. 1 Corinthians 12:7-11 – wisdom, knowledge, faith, healing, miracles, prophecy, discernment, speaking in tongues, and interpretation of tongues.

3. Ephesians 4:7-13 – apostle, prophet, evangelist, pastor, and teacher.

These are the gifts of the Holy Spirit. Again, they are gifts that are given to believers by the Holy Spirit that are different, or separate, from natural talents and abilities that we have on our own.

Purpose of Spiritual Gifts

Now that we have the definition of a spiritual gift, we need to know what the purpose of a spiritual gift is. Why does the Holy Spirit give each believer a spiritual gift? Let's take a look at a number of Scripture passages to help us discover the purpose of spiritual gifts.

THE GIFTS OF THE HOLY SPIRIT

    Ephesians 2:10

    Ephesians 4:11-15

    Romans 12:4-8

    1 Corinthians 12:1-31

In Ephesians 2:10 Paul tells us that God has created us to do the works that He has already prepared in advance for us to do. The apostle Paul writes, "For we are God's workmanship, created in Christ Jesus to do good works, which God prepared in advance for us to do." God has prepared works for us to do. When we received Jesus as our Lord and Saviour, God already had plans for us! Disciples of Christ are to be actively engaged in building His kingdom and, in order to do that, God has tailored the works of our life for each one of us individually! He knows exactly who we are, exactly what He has made us to do, and exactly what we need from Him to do those works! God is not going to tell us to go and do these works in our own strength and by our own talents and abilities. No! God prepares *us* for the work that He has prepared *for us*! God Himself will empower us, by the gifting of His Spirit, to accomplish His purposes. We are not left on our own to accomplish the works that He is asking us to accomplish. We do the works of God by God's supernatural enabling, both to us, and through us. It is not by our efforts, nor by our striving; it is, rather, by the power of the Holy Spirit in us.

In Ephesians 4:11-15, Paul gives a list of Spiritual gifts and then instructs us about God's purpose for these gifts.

> It was he who gave some to be apostles, some to be prophets, some to be evangelists, and some to be pastors and teachers, [12]to prepare God's people for works of service, so that the body of Christ may be built up [13]until we all reach unity in the faith and in the knowledge of the Son of God and become mature, attaining to the whole measure of the fullness of Christ.

> [14]Then we will no longer be infants, tossed back and forth by the waves, and blown here and there by every wind of teaching and by the cunning and craftiness of men in their deceitful scheming. [15]Instead, speaking the truth in love, we will in all things grow up into him who is the Head, that is, Christ.

Paul lists five spiritual gifts in this passage: apostles, prophets, evangelists, pastors, and teachers. Note that each of these gifts is used for the purpose of making God's words known to others. Furthermore, they are given by the Holy Spirit for the purpose of preparing others for their own works of service, so that the body of Christ will be built up and become mature in knowledge and service to God. The gifts of the Holy Spirit are given for the benefit of the body of Christ. Their purpose is to build up the church and bring spiritual maturity to those in the church by making the words of God known and understandable. It is important to understand that the essential purpose of the gifts of the Holy Spirit is to bring others to spiritual maturity in Christ. These five gifts, in particular, are given to help others understand God's words so that they can connect more with

God, know who He is, and therefore know what works He is calling them to do.

When the people of God are fulfilling their purpose from God, the church is built up, and the gospel is made more widely known. This is the reason that God gives spiritual gifts – so that His word will be promoted and proclaimed for all to hear and come unto Jesus in a personal saving relationship. In a way, Christians are like Legos; those little building blocks that click together. Do you remember playing with Legos and connecting them together to build things? God's people are like Legos in the sense that we all have a part to play in 'clicking' together to build the Kingdom of God. All of the different gifts work together to create one thing: the Kingdom of God. Each Christian has his/her own works to do that are important to fitting in with the works that another has to do. They all fit together by God's plan and purpose. And they all build the kingdom together. Every Christian has a spiritual gift, a supernatural enabling given by the Holy Spirit to fulfill the work of God in building His kingdom.

Another list of spiritual gifts is found in Romans 12:4-8. It reads,

> Just as each of us has one body with many members, and these members do not all have the same function, [5]so in Christ we who are many form one body, and each member belongs to all the others. [6]We have different gifts, according to the grace given us. If a man's gift is prophesying, let him use it in proportion to his faith. [7]If it is serving, let him serve; if it is teaching, let him teach; [8]if it is encouraging, let him encourage; if it is contributing to the needs of others, let him give generously; if it is leadership, let him govern diligently; if it is showing mercy, let him do it cheerfully.

This is a different list of spiritual gifts. There are more than the five given in Ephesians. This passage lists another five spiritual gifts besides prophecy and teaching.

There are a few things to note about this passage. First, Paul says we all have different gifts according to what God gives us. We are given these gifts by God's determination, not our own. We do not demand gifts from God. We can ask, but ultimately, we need to accept that what we receive is up to God. God gives spiritual gifts to each person that best suit him/her for the work that God knows He has already prepared for us. God fits us with exactly what we need, not what we think we need, or decide we need, or even desire to have. God has made each of us differently and has called us to different works, therefore we have different gifts, gifts that He knows we will need to accomplish His will for our life.

Paul teaches us more in this passage about spiritual gifts. He tells us that these gifts are to be used with our whole being, with passion and with diligence in serving God. God expects us to be faithful with the gifts that He gives to us. We are expected to be using those gifts. We cannot say, "Well, I know God has given me that gift, but I am not going use that gift because I am not happy about it, or because I don't want to, or because I don't feel like it." What is the reaction to a child who will not share his/her toys because he/she is not happy, or does not feel like it, or simply does not want to? Do we not expect our children to share? Do we not encourage them to share? Do we not teach them to share with others? Yes, we expect them to share with others what we have given them. We expect that they will take their toys and play with others. Similarly, God expects us to share our spiritual gifts for the benefit and building up of others and His kingdom. Remember the words of Paul in Romans 12:7-8,

> If it is serving, let him serve; if it is teaching, let him teach; [8]if it is encouraging, let him encourage; if it is contributing to the needs of others, let him give generously; if it is leadership, let him govern diligently; if it is showing mercy, let him do it cheerfully.

Paul is teaching us to accept the gifts that God has given to us and to use them with all of our hearts. He is telling us to serve others with those gifts and to serve with the fullness of our whole being. Let us not be casual about serving with the gifts that He has given us. If your gift is teaching, then you had better teach. Put your whole being into teaching. If it is encouraging, then be an encourager with effort and passion. Do not just encourage once in a while; make a practice of it; make a lifestyle of it.

As an aside, have you noticed that we tend to use the "gift of discouragement" with all of our hearts? If we are not happy about something, or we want to discourage someone or tear them down, because that is in our sinful nature, we put our hearts into it, don't we? If we are going to tear someone down then we really tear them down. We don't just put a partial effort into it, we go all the way. We tend to want them to know that "man, I have dealt with you, and you have been schooled, buddy." Why do we do that so fully, but not the gift of encouragement, or teaching, or serving, or giving?

The Bible tells us to use the gifts of the Holy Spirit to school people; to school people with blessing, to build them up, and to bring spiritual maturity. Using our spiritual gifts is to contribute to the well-being of others and to the well-being of the Kingdom of God. Our attitude should be one that says, "Whatever God has given me I will give to others. Whatever flows into my life from God will flow out to others."

To recap, the gifts of the Holy Spirit are given to Christians. They are supernatural enablings that we are to use with our whole being. We are to be thankful to God for them, recognizing that His power is at work in us to accomplish the works that He has given us to do.

One more major passage on spiritual gifts remains, 1 Corinthians 12:1 -11.

> Now about spiritual gifts, brothers, I do not want you to be ignorant. [2]You know that when you were pagans, somehow or other you were influenced and led astray to mute idols. [3]Therefore I tell you that no one who is speaking by the Spirit of God says, "Jesus be cursed," and no one can say, "Jesus is Lord," except by the Holy Spirit.
>
> [4]There are different kinds of gifts, but the same Spirit. [5]There are different kinds of service, but the same Lord. [6]There are different kinds of working, but the same God works all of them in all men.
>
> [7]Now to each one the manifestation of the Spirit is given for the common good. [8]To one there is given through the Spirit the message of wisdom, to another the message of knowledge by means of the same Spirit, [9]to another faith by the same Spirit, to another gifts of healing by that one Spirit, [10]to another miraculous powers, to another prophecy, to another distinguishing between spirits, to another speaking in different kinds of tongues, and to still another the interpretation of tongues. [11]All these are the work of one and the same Spirit, and he gives them to each one, just as he determines.

What we need to learn from this is that all of the gifts are given by the same Spirit, God's Holy Spirit. The gifts of the Spirit are given in unity, for the unity of the body of Christ. Spiritual gifts all work together; they click together. If spiritual gifts are not clicking, or working together, then someone is not using their spiritual gift the way God would have them use it. Gifts given from the Holy Spirit never create division and dissension in the body of Christ. Spiritual gifts are never used for tearing down. Rather, spiritual gifts are always used for the building up of the body and creating unity.

The apostle Paul uses the metaphor of the human body as he continues his teaching in 1 Corinthians 12:12-31. Each of us has a body with toes and fingers, and arms, and elbows, a nose, and a mouth, etc . . . They are different parts of the body, but they all work together for the good of the body. If one part ceases to work as it should, it affects the rest of the body. The parts of the body are not independent of each other. We all need all the parts of the body in order to fully function correctly. If you break your finger on your right hand and you are right-handed, then you will not be able to write so well anymore. That finger affects more than itself. It affects the hand and the ability of the whole body to function as it should. Paul tells us that, in a similar way, the body of Christ is negatively affected by one of the parts of the body not functioning as it should. Every Christian has a spiritual gift from God which needs to be used, put into use together with the gifts that have been given to other Christians. If one person is not using his/her spiritual gift for the building up of the body of Christ, then that body will not fully function as it should. Thus, the promotion and proclamation of the gospel of Jesus Christ will not be as effective as it ought to be.

Spiritual gifts are vitally important. It is essential to the spread of the gospel that each disciple of Christ knows his/her spiritual gift and is using that spiritual gift for the encouragement and building up of the body of Christ. God works powerfully through His body when the gifts of the Holy Spirit are working together as they should. The church is unstoppable when the body of Christ works together in unity by the power of the Holy Spirit. Jesus declared to us that He is building His church and the gates of hell will not prevail against it; nothing can stop the building of the church through the body of Christ as each part uses the spiritual gift that God has given him/her.

The Fruit of the Spirit

We now turn our attention to the essentials of the fruit of the Spirit. The questions we want to address are, "What is the fruit of the Spirit?" "And how is that different from the gifts of the Spirit?" The answer to those questions begins with a definition of the fruit of the Spirit.

Definition

> **THE FRUIT OF THE HOLY SPIRIT**
>
> Character qualities that are developed in a Christian's life by the Holy Spirit as a Christian walks in relationship with Jesus.
>
> Galatians 5:22-23a

The fruit of the Spirit can be defined as character qualities that are developed, or produced, in a Christian's life by the Holy Spirit as a Christian walks in a right relationship with Jesus. The most important fact to remember is that the fruit of the Spirit is about character qualities. Whereas the gifts of the Spirit are supernatural enablings given to us to accomplish the work that God has prepared for us to do, the fruit of the Spirit is about producing Christ-like character in our lives. It is what is produced when the Holy Spirit presses into our lives. This is important because, not only do we need to accomplish the works of God through His power that is given to us as a gift, it is equally important that our character reflects the character of Jesus as we go about accomplishing His works. These character qualities are called the fruit of the Spirit. They are the character qualities that the Holy Spirit produces in us as we walk in obedience to Jesus.

Let's have a look at the fruit of the Spirit as found in Galatians 5:22-23a. "But the fruit of the Spirit is love, joy, peace, patience, kindness, goodness, faithfulness, [23a] gentleness and self-control."

The apostle Paul lists nine character qualities that make up the fruit of the Spirit. Note that these nine words all describe character qualities. These are character qualities that at some point in time will define the character of a Christian. As we walk with Jesus and mature in Him, we will begin to look more and more like Jesus. We will love more, be more joyful, more peaceful, more faithful, and have a greater degree of goodness, gentleness and self-control in our lives. Our character – who we are, what defines us – becomes more like Jesus.

An important fact to note is that these character qualities are not qualities that we, ourselves, work at or initiate by ourselves. They are, rather, characteristics that the Holy Spirit presses into our lives as we grow in maturity with Jesus. The Holy Spirit is continually seeking to mold and shape our character so that we reflect all of these character qualities.

NOTE!
The fruit of the Spirit is singular!
It is a single fruit, not nine separate fruits.

A very common mistake is to refer to the fruit of the Holy Spirit in the plural – as "fruits". They are not "fruits" but one fruit. The word fruit is singular, not plural. All these character qualities work together to create one piece of fruit. There are not nine fruits of the Spirit, only one fruit – singular. To describe what this fruit looks like and tastes like takes all nine character qualities. If even just one characteristic is missing, then it is not the fruit of the Holy Spirit, but some other fruit. It may be close to it, or similar to it, but not the fruit that comes from the Holy Spirit. The fruit of the Holy Spirit must have all nine character qualities to be the fruit of the Holy Spirit and nothing less or more. Those who are non-Christians can have different aspects of this fruit, but every quality must be present in order to be the fruit of the Spirit.

It should also be noted that the fruit takes time to mature, just as natural fruit does. Thus, a Christian can have these qualities is some measure, but likely they are not fully mature. Each quality takes time to mature and develop so that, eventually, the fruit ripens and becomes mature in all of its nine qualities. Do not become discouraged, or think you are not a Christian because you are not experiencing these nine character qualities in your life to any great or full degree. The fruit takes time to ripen. Keep walking with Jesus and allow the Holy Spirit to transform and shape your character. It is important to keep obeying, keep following, and keep seeking. Do not stop or believe you are mature enough. Also, allow God to develop all nine qualities of the fruit in your life.

The fruit of the Spirit is not a smorgasbord where we decide which qualities we want and how much of that quality we want or do not want. We cannot take a little bit of gentleness, a large portion of love, a small amount of self-control, a dash of some of the other qualities, but no patience because we really do not like that dish. No, there are nine character qualities that are essential to making up the one fruit of the Spirit; they all have to be present to be the fruit of the Holy Spirit.

Again, it is certainly true that we will display each quality in different measures because we are growing in Christ. We are not perfect. These qualities are developed in us as we follow Christ, spend time with Christ, and mature in Christ. We will not display these qualities in perfection because we will not attain perfection in this life. However, we need to be continually growing in these qualities as we walk with Jesus and learn from Him. They must be part of our character.

If we claim to be disciples of Christ, we have to start looking more and more like those nine character qualities. What I am talking about here is transformation; transformation of character that comes from the work of the Holy Spirit. It is the Holy Spirit who transforms us. We cannot do it on our own. We can make changes here and there on our own, but we cannot transform the heart. Heart transformation comes only from Christ's Spirit in us. Paul writes about this in Galatians 5:16-26,

> So I say, live by the Spirit, and you will not gratify the desires of the sinful nature. [17]For the sinful nature desires what is contrary to the Spirit, and the Spirit what is contrary to the sinful nature. They are in conflict with each other, so that you do not do what you want. [18]But if you are led by the Spirit, you are not under law.
>
> [19]The acts of the sinful nature are obvious: sexual immorality, impurity and debauchery; [20] idolatry and witchcraft; hatred, discord, jealousy, fits of rage, selfish ambition, dissensions, factions [21a] and envy; drunkenness, orgies, and the like.

This is quite a list! It may cause us some despair as we read through this list. Yet, he continues in verses 21b-23a to give us another list,

> I warn you, as I did before, that those who live like this will not inherit the kingdom of God.
>
> ²²But the fruit of the Spirit is love, joy, peace, patience, kindness, goodness, faithfulness, ²³ᵃ gentleness and self-control.

The second list, the list of the fruit of the Spirit is a list of opposites from the first list. Paul purposely contrasts these lists so that we can see how important the work of the Holy Spirit is to transforming our character. Without the Holy Spirit in us, we will tend toward the character qualities of the first list. Only the Holy Spirit can transform character.

The first list is discouraging. It is a list of character qualities that you would not likely desire in a good friend. But the second list! This is the kind of person that you do want as a friend, and, hopefully, the type of person that you would like to be as well. Paul then follows up with these words,

> ²³ᵇAgainst such things there is no law. ²⁴Those who belong to Christ Jesus have crucified the sinful nature with its passions and desires. ²⁵Since we live by the Spirit, let us keep in step with the Spirit. ²⁶Let us not become conceited, provoking and envying each other.

The key here is this phrase, "Let us keep in step with the Spirit." The only way to be the kind of person that Paul is talking about, with all nine character qualities, is to keep walking, to keep in step, with the Spirit of Jesus. It is to walk beside Jesus, matching my steps to His. When we start realizing that some of the characteristics in our life look more like those in the first list, we know we are not walking with Jesus. It is then that we know we have to stop what we are doing and have to get right with Jesus. We have to get back in step with the Holy Spirit and with the transforming power that comes only from Him.

I want to give you a note of encouragement here. We can often get discouraged because our life can often look more like the first list than the second list. And that can sometimes make us want to give up or give in. We may wonder if we can ever change, if God can ever transform our lives to look more like the second list. I want to tell you that you can and will be transformed into the image of Christ! No matter what your character was or is now. You may have even heard people say things about you such as, "That person will never change." Do not believe that! That is a lie and a false statement. You will be transformed and changed into the image of Jesus, because that is what God does! That is His specialty! Jesus transforms lives – all lives can be changed. It does not matter what you have done, where you have been, how bad you are, or how bad people say you are, your life can be transformed by the power of Jesus through His Spirit in you. He died on the cross for our transformation.

Take for an example the apostle Paul. Paul was a murderer. He pursued Christians in order to arrest them and have them killed. He himself gave approval to the stoning of Stephen! His life was given over to eradicating Christians and the message of Christ. Yet, Jesus revealed Himself to Paul and transformed Paul's life. Paul became a gentle, kind, good, self-controlled, faithful, fruit-of-the-Spirit kind of guy. He became a completely opposite person. He was not perfect, but he was passionately following Jesus to become more and more like Him. Paul learned to keep in step with the Spirit for the transformation of his character.

We, too, can be transformed like the apostle Paul. People will say of us, "I know that person; he/she used to be like that, but now acts differently. Why has that person changed so much? Why is that person transformed?" The answer is that Jesus has taken over your life as Lord and Saviour, and the Holy Spirit is developing His fruit in your life.

The Holy Spirit loves to transform lives, and He has the power to do it. He transforms people so that alcoholism is no longer a characteristic of their life, that rage is no longer a characteristic of their life. Bitter people become better people, angry people become gentle people, unfaithful people become faithful people, and people with no joy in their lives find joy in their lives no matter what the situation. That is the power of the Holy Spirit, and He is ready to transform your life.

Conclusion

Transformation comes from the power of the Holy Spirit. He transforms our character so that we use the gifts that He gives us for the purpose of building His kingdom. It is the Holy Spirit that sets us anew with new purpose and transforming character. It is no longer about us – it is now all about Jesus. It is about building His kingdom with the gifts that He gives us in the transformed character of the fruit of the Spirit. Let us seek to keep in step with the Spirit of Jesus. Let us seek Jesus in greater measure, so that when others look at us, they see love, joy, peace, patience, kindness, goodness, gentleness, faithfulness, and self-control. And let us be at work, doing the works that God has prepared in advance for us to do, using the spiritual gifts that He has given us to do them with. We have a kingdom to build, God's kingdom, and it is done only through the power of Jesus, who gives both the spiritual gifts and the spiritual character qualities to use those gifts effectively.

Closing Prayer

Jesus, thank You that You love to transform people. That is why You died; for the transformation of peoples' lives, from bondage in sin to freedom in You for everlasting life and the forgiveness of sins. Jesus, transform us, change us, mold us, shape us, help our character to be defined by Your fruit and not by the unfruitful list. God, we do not want to be doing the deeds of darkness; we want to be doing the deeds You prepared in advance for us to do, the deeds of light. Help us to live by the fruit of the Spirit so that the work we do for You is building Your kingdom. I ask and pray in Your name, Jesus.

Amen.

Chapter 12

THE ESSENTIALS

OF

PRAYER

Prayer is a rather large topic in the Bible. If we were to explore the exhaustive teaching on prayer – that would make for a very long book, never mind one chapter. I will hopefully get you started with the essentials of prayer, and you can study the topic of prayer on your own or perhaps in a Bible study group. In this chapter we will look at a simple definition of prayer and discuss how prayer is communication with God for the purpose of knowing Him. We will also take a look at prayer as a lifestyle, not just an event, and how prayer connects us with God. After that, we will discuss some hindrances to prayer and then move on to show how God helps us in prayer.

Definition

A simple definition of prayer is this: communication with God through both audible and inaudible means. Or, to put it another way, prayer is communicating with God through our voices and our thoughts.

DEFINITION OF PRAYER

Communication with God – both audibly and inaudibly

We often think of prayer as an out-loud kind of talking to God, but we don't always pray out loud, nor do we *have* to pray out loud. Quite often, maybe even usually, we pray silently, in our minds. Because God is all knowing, we can communicate with God through our thoughts. God is able to hear our thoughts and answer those prayers that we silently pray in our minds.

We may sometimes wonder if this is a valid way of praying or wonder if God can really know our thoughts. The Bible answers this for us. According to Psalm 139:23, the answer is yes! In this verse the Psalmist writes, "Search me, O God, and know my heart; test me and know my anxious thoughts." How would God know the Psalmist's thoughts are anxious? Because God knows our thoughts. They are not hidden from Him because He is omniscient, or all knowing. There is nothing that He does not know, including our thoughts. In the New Testament, Luke twice tells us that Jesus "knew their thoughts".

Luke 6:8 says, "But Jesus knew what they were thinking and said to the man with the shriveled hand, "Get up and stand in front of everyone." So he got up and stood there. And in Luke 9:47 we read, "Jesus, knowing their thoughts, took a little child and had him stand beside him." God hears our thoughts and knows exactly what we are thinking, including our prayers to Him. That is why prayer is communication with God, both audibly and inaudibly.

Prayer as Communication

Prayer is communication with God. I use the word communication purposely because communication is more than just talking. It is more than a one-way monologue. Communication is also listening. Prayer is listening. If you are not listening to God but only talking to God, then you are missing half of the purpose of prayer! Prayer is both speaking to God and taking time to listen to what God has to say.

Prayer is sometimes silence. Prayer may begin with, "Hello, God" and then simply remain silent. Prayer does not have to be filled with noise from our mouth. Sometimes prayer is 15, 20, 30 minutes spent in silence, listening for God's voice. We can say to God, "Here I am; I am listening," and then wait in expectant silence for Him to speak.

Prayer is much more than speaking to God. Certainly, making petitions and requests of God is part of prayer, but it really might even be the smallest part of prayer. Prayer is larger than just asking things from God. Prayer is communication with God for the purpose of knowing God. Prayer is an awareness of God. Prayer is a relationship with God. Prayer is to know Him more, to know Him better, and to know Him more fully.

When we wake up in the morning, when we eat our meals, when we travel to work, when we are working, when we are at play, when we are walking or sitting, or whatever it is we are doing, we can be communicating with God through being aware of what God is doing around us. Prayer is being aware of the presence of God in our life, wherever we are and whatever we are doing.

There is a wonderful little book called "Practicing the Presence of God" by Brother Lawrence. Brother Lawrence was a monk. His job in the monastery was to cook for the other monks so he was constantly peeling and cooking potatoes in the kitchen. His work was not very exciting. He wanted to be out there preaching or teaching the word of God, instead he was inside making food for the rest of the monks. He, at first, lamented his duties as not very "godly" but later learned that he could know God just as well peeling potatoes as he could preaching the gospel. He learned to continually pray while he was cooking. He learned to continually practice the presence of God. It did not matter what he was doing; he was always aware of where God was in his life and who he was before God. That is prayer. Whatever we do, wherever we go, and whatever is happening around us, we can continually have an awareness of God through a lifestyle of prayer.

Prayer as Bible Reading

Prayer can also take the form of reading our Bible. When we ask God to speak to us, He often does that through His written word. Prayer may start with, "Good morning, God, what do you have for me this morning? Let's talk." Then, we read what He has written to us in order to allow Him to talk to us. You may have never thought of reading the Bible as prayer, but it *can* be. It *can* be prayer if we read the words of God with the anticipation of hearing from God.

We are communicating with God when we read His words of communication with us. God *wants* us to get to know Him, He *wants* to speak to us, and He *wants* to reveal Himself to us. Yes, He desires our company and wants us to communicate with Him through both speaking and listening.

Whatever form prayer takes, prayer is always seeking the thoughts of God. Perhaps an even simpler definition of prayer is: seeking the thoughts of God. The Psalmist says in Psalm 139:17, "How precious to me are your thoughts, O God! How vast is the sum of them!" The Psalmist wanted to know God more. His prayer was to know the thoughts of God! Knowing the thoughts of God is really what we are after. Prayer is seeking to know God.

Prayer as Knowing God

If we are going to know God, we are going to have to both spend time listening and reading to hear and know the thoughts of God. Prayer is not just presenting our list of requests to God, though it may include that. Prayer is so much more. Prayer is recognizing that more important than the list of requests we bring is the One to whom we bring the list. Our lists do not matter as much as knowing God matters. This is why Paul can encourage us to "pray continually" in 1 Thessalonians 5:17.

Paul is not telling us to continually present our requests to God over and over and over without stopping. No, he is telling us to continually be in communication with God, wherever we are and whatever we are doing, so that we might know Him better – so that we might know His word, His will, and His ways for us.

Prayer as a Lifestyle

Prayer is a lifestyle. Prayer is not something we merely do as an event, nor an action that we take at a certain time. Prayer is more than an event; prayer is a lifestyle that we continually practice throughout time. Prayer is being aware of God in every circumstance of our life. Prayer is an awareness of who God is, of what God is doing, and where He is at work around us in our life. Prayer is a lifestyle of constant awareness of God.

Awareness of God is communication with God. My wife and I would often find ourselves in the same room, each reading our own books. We were not talking to each other; we were reading our books. Yet, we had an awareness of the other person. We knew where each other was and what each other was doing. There was a communication between us because of our awareness of each other. This is the way it is between us and God. When we are aware of God's presence, there is a communication that takes place.

We often use the phrase "let's go to prayer". What do we mean by that? It seems that we use that phrase because we are referring to the act of prayer as an action that takes place at a certain time. Now, that is certainly true; prayer is an action that takes place at a certain time, but when we are done praying at that time, we should not believe that we are done communicating with God. Because we say "Amen" and open our eyes does not mean our time with God is over so that we can move on with the rest of life. No, communicating with God does not end as an event or action might end. When Paul encourages us to pray continually, he is encouraging us to be continually aware of what God is doing around us and continually aware of God's presence in our life. Prayer is not just an action or an event that begins and ends according to a specified time period.

The Primary Purpose of Prayer

As has been mentioned before, the primary purpose of prayer is to know God more deeply. It is not primarily to petition God, it is not primarily to ask God for things, nor is it to seek God for blessings or to change material circumstances in our life. That is not the primary purpose of prayer. The primary purpose of prayer is to know God more deeply. It is first and foremost for simply knowing God. It is for connecting us with God.

> ### THE PRIMARY PURPOSE OF PRAYER
> Prayer is first and foremost for the purpose of knowing God.
>
> Prayer is to know God more deeply.

If prayer is only for seeking God for the purpose of receiving answers to requests or changing our life circumstances, then you have only half a prayer. Prayer as only petition and request is a monologue to God, not communication with God. Prayer is a wonderful opportunity that God gives us to know Him. Prayer is God saying to us, "Why don't you come and spend time in my space and my presence so that we can walk life together?" The opportunity to pray is God inviting us to know Him and spend time with Him.

Prayer as Connecting With the Power of God

The God of the universe who created everything, who has power beyond our imagination, who speaks a word and it is done is the very same God who wants to spend time with "little 'ole' us". Imagine! The God of all power seeking our company and desiring that we seek His company! Matthew 6:33 says, "But seek first his kingdom and his righteousness, and all these things will be given to you as well." Jesus is exhorting us to seek His company first, and then allow Him to take care of the rest of our needs. Because He is all powerful He can answer our prayers of request and petition. But before He does that, He requests our company. Jesus knows that prayer connects us with the power of God. God knows we need things; God knows we live in a life where circumstances often conspire against us. He knows that there is disease, sicknesses and illness. He knows that there are strains and stresses in life. God knows and understands about all these effects of sin in this world that affect us directly. He knows and He says, "Seek me first." Don't seek the solutions first; don't seek the answers first. Don't seek the gifts first; seek the giver first. Prayer is seeking the giver – it is seeking God. It is knowing that when we seek God, we seek the controller of the universe who, with a word, can change our circumstances. Through prayer, God invites us to be recipients of His great power.

Prayer as Connecting With the Peace of God

Not only does prayer connect us with the power of God, prayer connects us with the peace of God. Prayer brings the peace of God into our lives through His presence.

> Prayer brings the peace of God into our lives through His presence.

> Philippians 4:4-7

In writing to the Philippian church, Paul says in 4:4-6,

> Rejoice in the Lord always. I will say it again: Rejoice! [5]Let your gentleness be evident to all. The Lord is near. [6]Do not be anxious about anything, but in everything, by prayer and petition, with thanksgiving, present your requests to God.

We do get anxious about things in life; we do have things in life that we do not know how to deal with. There are plenty of anxieties, stresses and situations in life where we need to find solutions or fixes. It is during these times that Paul encourages us to bring our requests to God because Paul knows what God will do for us. He knows that even though we may not receive everything we ask for, or that God may answer differently than we have requested, God will give us His peace. God does promise that no matter what our request may be, and no matter what His answer to our request will be, He *will* give us His peace. God's will is always to give us His peace in every situation that we find ourselves in. In Philippians 4:7, we find God's promise, "And the peace of God, which transcends all understanding, will guard your hearts and your minds in Christ Jesus."

The result of our seeking God for our requests is the peace of the presence of God in our lives. It may not mean He is going to take away your sickness, it may not mean He is going to heal you of your disease, it does not mean the person you are praying for will never die, it may not mean forest fires will stop, it does not mean the world will all be perfect, but it does mean that when we pray, what we will always receive from God is the peace of His presence. Every time, guaranteed! God's promise is to give us His peace to replace our anxiety. The peace that God gives us will guard our hearts and minds from anxiety and worry. God desires to keep us from undue anxiety and strain and stress. He places His peace within our hearts and minds to give us a confidence and assurance that He is at work taking care of us and those around us. The peace of God allows us to rest in confidence with Him. The storms rage on, and sickness and disease take lives, but God says, "I will be there *for* you. I will be there *with* you. I will be there *in* you. I will give a peace that you cannot explain to anybody else unless they know God." Real peace – real peace of heart and peace of mind – comes only from a relationship with Jesus Christ. We, as human beings, can find a peace that comes from God when we seek to communicate with Him in prayer.

PURPOSE OF PRAYER

The purpose of prayer is not to get things from God but to know God.

To hear from God
To be changed by God
To enjoy the peace of His presence

In summary, the primary purpose of prayer is not to get things from God, nor is it to manipulate God or to somehow force God into doing what we want him or demand of him to do. The primary purpose of prayer is to simply know God. Then, when we know who God is, we receive from Him the peace of His presence. And, strangely, the stuff we asked for does not matter as it used to because His presence is more important than His provision. Prayer is for us to know God, to hear from God, to be changed by God, and to enjoy the peace of the presence of God. That is why we pray. That is the purpose of prayer.

Hindrances to Prayer

There are, however, some hindrances to prayer. Scripture is pretty clear about that. Now, just to be clear, whenever we pray God always hears us. It is not a matter of God not hearing us; He always does, but He is not always willing and inclined to answer us because of the hindrances that we bring to prayer.

HINDRANCES TO PRAYER

Anger and dispute	1 Timothy 2:8
The treatment of our wives	1 Peter 3:7
Undealt with sin in our lives	1 Peter 3:8-12

Anger and Dispute

A major hindrance to prayer is anger and dispute. In 1Timothy 2:8, Paul says, "I want men everywhere to lift up holy hands in prayer, without anger or disputing." Paul uses the phrase, "lift up holy hands". What does that mean, and what does that mean for prayer?

Holy means to be separate, or to be like God in His perfection. So, to lift up holy hands is to lift up hands that are separated to do God's will, hands (the actions of living) that are given over to accomplishing the works of God, His perfect works that serve to build and promote His kingdom. To lift up holy hands indicates a person's desire to see the perfect will and ways of God being lived out in them and around them. The actions of anger and disputing are almost always opposed to the perfect way and will of God. Anger leads us into dispute, and dispute feeds anger. When we are angry and we do not resolve our anger with forgiveness that comes from God, and when we do not resolve our disputes with the forgiveness and grace of God, then our prayers do not get very far with God. We cannot be in a wrong relationship with others and claim to be in a right relationship with God. God cannot honor prayers that come from unrepentant and unforgiving hearts. We need to be right with each other to be right with God, at least to the degree that it depends on us as Romans 12:18 tell us, "If it is possible, as far as it depends on you, live at peace with everyone."

Mistreatment of Our Wife

This hindrance to prayer is one that is particular to men, but I wonder if it might not pertain to the way a woman would treat her husband as well. 1 Peter 3:7 says,

> Husbands, in the same way be considerate as you live with your wives, and treat them with respect as the weaker partner and as heirs with you of the gracious gift of life, so that nothing will hinder your prayers.

Did you catch that?! "So that nothing will hinder your prayers!" Evidently, the way we treat our wife has an effect upon our prayer life. Husbands, if you are not in a right relationship with your wife, then your prayers are hindered. We cannot pretend, men, that we are great with God when we are wrong with our wife. According to 1 Peter 3:7, any and every husband should not think that he has peace with God when he is in conflict with his wife. A clear hindrance to prayer is the mistreatment of our wife. Men, how do you treat your wife? Do you respect her? Are you considerate of her? Are your prayers being hindered? We need to be in a right relationship with our wife so that we can be in a right relationship with God.

Unconfessed Sin

Another hindrance to prayer is the sin that we allow to remain in our lives without dealing with it. We find this in 1 Peter 3:8-12,

> Finally, all of you, live in harmony with one another; be sympathetic, love as brothers, be compassionate and humble. [9]Do not repay evil with evil or insult with insult, but with blessing, because to this you were called so that you may inherit a blessing. [10]For,
>
> "Whoever would love life and see good days must keep his tongue from evil and his lips from deceitful speech.
>
> [11]He must turn from evil and do good; he must seek peace and pursue it.
>
> [12]For the eyes of the Lord are on the righteous and his ears are attentive to their prayer, but the face of the Lord is against those who do evil."

Now, none of us would say that we are evil or that we purposely take actions that are evil, but the apostle Paul suggests that we all do evil when we sin. Sin is evil because it is never good. By definition, sin can never be good; it is always evil because sin is anything which is in opposition to the will, ways, and words of God. In these verses, Paul mentions the sins of deceitful speech, insults, pride, disunity, and a lack of care, or love, for others. These are all the works of evil that sin undertakes. And these are all actions that hinder our prayers from being answered by God.

Example of Israel

We have an example of ancient Israel. In Isaiah 1: 2-4, God says,

Hear, O heavens! Listen, O earth! For the Lord has spoken: "I reared children and brought them up, but they have rebelled against me. ³The ox knows its master, the donkey his owner's manger, but Israel does not know, my people do not understand."

In a rebuke to the people of Israel, God tells them that even the donkey knows his owner's manger. The stubborn and not-so-smart donkey knows where he gets fed. The ox also knows who his master is. Yet the people of Israel, those chosen by God, do not understand that God is the One who feeds and cares for them. They have chosen to wander away and rebel against God, their master, and not listen to Him. Isaiah goes on to say in verse 4,

Ah, sinful nation, a people loaded with guilt, a brood of evildoers, children given to corruption! They have forsaken the Lord; they have spurned the Holy One of Israel and turned their backs on him.

Now, jumping to verse 10 we read,

Hear the word of the Lord, you rulers of Sodom; listen to the law of our God, you people of Gomorrah!

The people of Israel had sinned so much and gone so far away from God that God calls them Sodom and Gomorrah. That is pretty serious. Sodom and Gomorrah are the epitome of sin or the "gold standard" of sin. Yet, God calls His own nation Sodom and Gomorrah because they have walked away from Him and turned to walking in their own ways and will. Continuing further in chapter 1 of Isaiah, in verses 11-15,

"The multitude of your sacrifices – what are they to me?" says the Lord. "I have more than enough of burnt offerings, of rams and the fat of fattened animals; I have no pleasure in the blood of bulls and lambs and goats.

[12]When you come to appear before me, who has asked this of you, this trampling of my courts?

[13]Stop bringing meaningless offerings! Your incense is detestable to me. New Moons, Sabbaths and convocations – I cannot bear your evil assemblies.

[14]Your New Moon festivals and your appointed feasts my soul hates. They have become a burden to me; I am weary of bearing them.

[15]*When you spread out your hands in prayer, I will hide my eyes from you; even if you offer many prayers, I will not listen.* Your hands are full of blood;

God clearly says there comes a point when the rebelliousness of our sin, and our continual unwillingness to deal with that sin causes a break in our relationship with God, so that He no longer listens to our prayers. Willing, continual, undealt with sin results in God saying, "You can pray all you want, but I am not even listening." That is pretty serious – to have our prayers no longer move God to take any action for us. That is what

God did to Israel, and that is what God does to us. Because of undealt with or unconfessed sin, God hides His eyes from us.

Yet, not all is lost. God does not want this condition of ours to last for long. Therefore, He gives us a solution. The solution is found in verses 16-18,

> [16]wash and make yourselves clean. Take your evil deeds out of my sight! Stop doing wrong,
>
> [17]learn to do right! Seek justice, encourage the oppressed. Defend the cause of the fatherless, plead the case of the widow.
>
> [18]"Come now, let us reason together," says the Lord. "Though your sins are like scarlet, they shall be as white as snow; though they are red as crimson, they shall be like wool."

Because sin hinders our prayers before God, we need to get right with God. We need to say, "Yes, God, I am a sinner. God, forgive me of my sins, and God, I forgive those who sinned against me."

In Proverbs 1:23-33, we have the poetic version of what is in Isaiah 1. These verses tell us that when we listen to God and repent at His calling He will take time to listen to us and help us. But, if we do not repent at His calling, if we refuse to listen to His rebukes, then He will refuse to listen to us when we call out to Him.

> If you had responded to my rebuke, I would have poured out my heart to you and made my thoughts known to you.
>
> [24]But since you rejected me when I called and no one gave heed when I stretched out my hand,

[25]since you ignored all my advice and would not accept my rebuke,

[26]I in turn will laugh at your disaster; I will mock when calamity overtakes you –

[27]when calamity overtakes you like a storm, when disaster sweeps over you like a whirlwind, when distress and trouble overwhelm you.

[28]"Then they will call to me but I will not answer; they will look for me but will not find me.

[29]Since they hated knowledge and did not choose to fear the Lord,

[30]since they would not accept my advice and spurned my rebuke,

[31]they will eat the fruit of their ways and be filled with the fruit of their schemes.

[32]For the waywardness of the simple will kill them, and the complacency of fools will destroy them;

[33]but whoever listens to me will live in safety and be at ease, without fear of harm."

The writer of Psalms, King David, also knew this truth when he wrote in Psalm 66:18, "If I had cherished sin in my heart, the Lord would not have listened;" David is essentially saying, "If I have willful, continual, and unconfessed sin in my life, God is not going to listen to me." The Bible is clear: we cannot live in continual, unconfessed sin and claim to be right with God. God clearly says that it does not work that way. Continual, unconfessed, unrepentant sin is a barrier to prayer, so much so that Jeremiah was commanded by God to *not* pray for Israel because God was repulsed at their continual wickedness and unrepentance.

Jeremiah 7: 9-16,

Will you steal and murder, commit adultery and perjury, burn incense to Baal and follow other gods you have not known, [10]and then come and stand before me in this house, which bears my Name, and say, "We are safe" – safe to do all these detestable things? [11]Has this house, which bears my Name, become a den of robbers to you? But I have been watching! declares the Lord.

[12]'Go now to the place in Shiloh where I first made a dwelling for my Name, and see what I did to it because of the wickedness of my people Israel. [13]While you were doing all these things, declares the Lord, I spoke to you again and again, but you did not listen; I called you, but you did not answer.

God said, "I tried to get your attention when you were living in the wickedness of your sin. I wanted you to repent so I kept putting things in your way that would cause you to see the truth of your actions and turn from them. But, you did not."

[14]Therefore, what I did to Shiloh I will now do to the house that bears my Name, the temple you trust in, the place I gave to you and your fathers. [15]I will thrust you from my presence, just as I did all your brothers, the people of Ephraim.'

[16]So *do not pray for this people nor offer any plea or petition for them; do not plead with me, for I will not listen to you.*

That is an alarming statement from God to Jeremiah in verse 16. The Israelites had come to a point where they would not admit to the sin in their lives. They continually disobeyed God and disregarded His words, ways, and will. Therefore, God instructed his shepherd Jeremiah to not bother to pray for them because his prayers would just be a waste of his time and breath. God was not going to listen to any prayers until true repentance took place in the lives of His people.

Can this ever be the case with Christians today? Most certainly. Christians can disobey and disregard God just as Israel had done, perhaps all too commonly. Thankfully though, God is gracious, slow to anger, and abounding in love. He is willing and waiting to forgive us of our sins. 1 John 1:9 says, "If we confess our sins, He is faithful and just and will forgive us our sins and purify us from all unrighteousness." It is essential for fruitful prayer life to be right with God. Before we pray, make sure we are right with God and others. Confess and repent of any and all sin.

Praying to Impress

Another hindrance to prayer is praying in order to impress God and others. Jesus addresses this in Matthew 6:1. Here we read, "Be careful not to do your 'acts of righteousness' before men, to be seen by them. If you do, you will have no reward from your Father in heaven."

If prayer is simply to know God, then you do not have to try to impress God. You cannot, by the way, impress God. God is never impressed with us in the sense that He responds to us in a, "Whoa, wow, Michael, you are really impressive!" kind of way. Not only do we not pray to impress God, neither do we pray in order to impress others. Let us continue in Matthew 6 with verses 2-5,

> So when you give to the needy, do not announce it with trumpets, as the hypocrites do in the synagogues and on the streets, to be honored by men. I tell you the truth, they have received their reward in full. 3But when you give to

the needy, do not let your left hand know what your right hand is doing, [4]so that your giving may be in secret. Then your Father, who sees what is done in secret, will reward you.

[5]And when you pray, do not be like the hypocrites, for they love to pray standing in the synagogues and on the street corners to be seen by men. I tell you the truth, they have received their reward in full.

Jesus is talking about the pharisees. They loved to stand up in public to pray for all to listen to them. They took the posture of, "Hey look at me; listen to that. Did you hear that prayer, did you see how great that was, did you see what I did; did you see? Wow! Look at me!" These are self-aggrandizing prayers. They are not prayers of sincerity to know God and strengthen a relationship with Him. They are prayers designed to impress others and God, if that were possible. But God is not impressed. In fact, God says, "Well, you got your reward; people are impressed. Congratulations, but you get nothing from me."

Notice that hypocrites can pray. Anybody can pray. Not everybody who prays, though, is praying to God. Not everyone who prays is sincere. And not everybody who prays is going to be listened to by God. Prayers to impress are no prayers at all. Praying is not about impressing God or others. Praying is about you and God.

Jesus says this in Matthew 6:6, "But when you pray, go into your room, close the door and pray to your Father, who is unseen. Then your Father, who sees what is done in secret, will reward you." Prayer is a conversation, a communication between you and God, and does not need to have anyone else as an audience.

Now, this does not mean that you should never pray out loud in front of others, or in a group with others. Jesus is not banning praying with others. No, Jesus is simply giving us a warning to be careful about our motivation for praying. Public prayer is hard. Anytime you stand in front of somebody or sit with someone and you pray out loud, immediately your mind says, "Oh-oh, people are listening and somebody is going to judge me so I better make sure I get the right words." It is not that you are trying to impress them necessarily, but you are nervous about being unimpressive. You do not want to stumble around words and sound unimpressive. The reality is, however, prayer is between you and God, even when others are around listening to you. When you pray with others, you are giving them a glimpse of your relationship with God through your communication with Him. You are inviting those you are praying with into your relationship with Jesus. Public prayer, in a sense, is to say, "God, here I am, with these folks whom you have called me in community with, so I want to bring us all together to commune with you." Public prayer is going, as a community, into God's presence. That is why we pray together. It is never about impressing God or others. It is simply about communing with God together.

There is yet one more lesson that we need to learn from Jesus about prayer in the Matthew 6 passage. Jesus teaches in verse 7-8,

> And when you pray, do not keep on babbling like pagans, for they think they will be heard because of their many words. [8]Do not be like them, for your Father knows what you need before you ask him.

Jesus again, is teaching that prayer is not about impressing, impressing with length of prayer and repetition of prayer. God is not impressed with vocabulary, or length, or the use of repetitive phrases, as if continually repeating something gains a favorable answer from God. Once again, prayer is not primarily about what we are asking for; prayer is primarily about communing with the One we pray to. It is about knowing the Giver more than seeking His gifts.

Help For Prayer

With all of these hindrances to prayer, it may seem almost impossible to pray successfully. We might be tempted to say, "How can I pray successfully? Is there any help that I can receive in order to pray successfully?" Thankfully, yes!! Jesus Himself helps us to pray. His own disciples asked Him to teach them how to pray. Out of that question comes the instruction from Jesus on how to pray. We can find His teaching in Matthew 6: 9-15.

This, then, is how you should pray:

Our Father in heaven,

hallowed be your name,

[10]your kingdom come,

your will be done,

on earth as it is in heaven.

[11]Give us today our daily bread.

[12]Forgive us our debts,

as we also have forgiven our debtors.

[13]And lead us not into temptation,

but deliver us from the evil one.

There are a number of helps that we need to take notice of in this model prayer from Jesus.

First, in our prayers, we need to recognize who God is, and then, who we are not. The phrase, "Our Father in heaven, hallowed (holy) be your name", recognizes who God is and admits to who we are not. We are proclaiming that He is God and we are not God. This phrase also leads us to recognize that we are in a relationship with Him. He is our Father who dwells in heaven. We do not pray to an unknown spirit or an unknown God, nor do we pray to an impersonal God. We pray to a God with whom we have a family relationship. Prayer is always a relationship with God, our Father.

Second, in our prayers, we recognize that we are seeking His will on this earth, not our own. We are not self-seekers, but God seekers. We desire His kingdom to come and not our own kingdom. We are not praying to use God to build our kingdom; rather, we are praying for God to use us to build His kingdom. We recognize who God is, we recognize our relationship with God, and we recognize that it is God's will that we pray for.

This model prayer then goes on to lead us to recognize God's provision in our life, "Give us our daily bread." This is the third help. Now, you and I have money. We go to the grocery store, and we buy our food to make what we want to eat. It seems that we are not in need of God to do that for us; we have it covered. So why is "give us our daily bread" part of this prayer that Jesus teaches? What is Jesus teaching us?

Jesus is teaching us that we need to recognize that everything we have, including even the ability to buy food, comes from God. We are recognizing that God provides for us; we do not do it ourselves. Any provision that we can gain is first provided for by God. We can only provide if God first provides for us. This phrase is a way in which we humble ourselves before God and recognize what He does for us in providing.

The fourth help that God gives us is to recognize our own sin and our own sinfulness; "Forgive us our sin." The Greek word clearly indicates it is sin that we are seeking forgiveness of. The words, "debts" and "trespasses" are another way of indicating that it is debt to God and trespass against God; it is sin. We are to recognize our sin and to seek forgiveness of that sin, whether it is against God or against others.

Then, we need to recognize that we have an obligation to forgive others. It is not only forgiveness that we need from God; it is also forgiveness that we need to extend to others, to those who sin against us.

It is important to notice the relationship between being forgiven by God and forgiving others. Matthew 6:14-15 says,

> For if you forgive men when they sin against you, your heavenly Father will also forgive you. [15]But if you do not forgive men their sins, your Father will not forgive your sins.

These words of Jesus seem kind of strange, and the first reaction might be to say, "That cannot be right! God always forgives me – He has to!" Yet, the teaching from Jesus here is that we are expected to forgive others. God says, "If you expect me to forgive you, if you are claiming to be a disciple of Christ and you want my forgiveness, you have to act like a disciple of Christ and forgive others."

We can neither harbor bitterness against others, nor can we harbor un-forgiveness against people and then go to God and say, "God forgive me but not them." And notice, it does not depend on another person's actions. The phrase, "I will forgive them *if*", is not biblical. God did not say that forgiveness is conditional; there is no "if". When Jesus was hanging on the cross He did not say, "Father forgive them *if* they meet my expectations." No! He forgave unconditionally. We are asked to do the same.

Forgiveness is expected. Forgiveness is about getting right before God, getting ourselves right before God. Through prayer we recognize our need for forgiveness and the need to forgive others.

HELP FOR PRAYER

The teaching of Jesus – Matthew 6:9-15

RECOGNIZE:

Who God is and who we are not

Our relationship with Him

His will for this earth; get rid of our own will

His provision for our life

Our own sin and sinfulness

Our need for his forgiveness

Our need to forgive others

This model of prayer is given by Jesus in order to help us to stay in a right relationship with God. It is given to us so that we might know Him more through communicating with Him through both speaking and listening. The primary purpose of prayer is for us to talk to God and to hear God. It is for us to walk with God in His presence and in His peace in each and every circumstance. It is not primarily about asking or receiving. Prayer is about humbling ourselves before God because God is God, and we are not. Prayer is primarily about knowing God.

PRIMARY PURPOSE OF PRAYER

Prayer is for us to communicate with God in order to walk with God in His presence and His peace in every circumstance in life.

Closing Prayer

Thank You, God, for Your love. Thank You that You love us enough to give us the opportunity to be in Your presence. Here we are before Your throne in Your presence. Forgive us our sins and cleanse us from all unrighteousness. God, we do not claim to be perfect, especially in Your presence. We do claim to be needy and in need of great help from You, so Father provide for us and help us. Draw us into a closer relationship with You. Help us to pray so that we might know You more. We ask this in Your name, Jesus.

Amen.

Chapter 13

THE ESSENTIALS

OF

THE CHURCH

The last essential doctrine that we will cover in this book is the doctrine of the church. In this chapter we will look at various ways to define the church, dividing them into "spiritual" and "physical". For the church is both a physical organization and a spiritual living organism. We will begin with the spiritual definitions of the church using biblical metaphors and words and then move onto the physical definitions. After that, we will explore the purpose of the church and finish with the future of the church.

Church – The Spiritual Side

The Founding and Foundation of the Church

A major way of defining the church is through the metaphor of building. All buildings are built upon a foundation that is set in the ground. Then, once the foundation is set, the actual building arises unto completion. With buildings that are built with brick or stone (as was common in the days of Jesus), the first brick or stone to be laid was called the cornerstone. This stone was set upon the foundation so that it was square and would give reference to the way the whole building would arise. It would ensure that the walls could be set straight and square from then on. Buildings existed because of the foundation and the cornerstone; it is where they had to start.

In a similar way, the church exists and began because of Jesus. Without Jesus there would be no church. In fact, before Jesus, there was no such thing as "church". Jesus is the founder and foundation of the church. In Matthew 16:13-18, Jesus asks the disciples to tell Him who they think He is. They tell Him that other people have referred to Him as John the Baptist, Elijah, Jeremiah, or one of the other prophets. Then Peter answers in verse 16 by saying, "You are the Christ, the Son of the living God." This is the answer that Jesus was leading them to, as we see in His reply in verses 17 and 18,

> Blessed are you, Simon son of Jonah, for this was not revealed to you by man, but by my Father in heaven. [18]And I tell you that you are Peter, and on this rock I will build my church, and the gates of Hades will not overcome it.

This response from Jesus is important for a couple of reasons. One, this is the first time that the word "church" is used in the Bible. It has never been used before, but Jesus uses it now. Jesus is the one who begins the idea of church; it started with Him. Furthermore, the response of Jesus is important because He says that the foundation of the church, the rock, that which it will be built on, is the confession that Peter makes of Jesus being the Messiah, or Son of God. In other words, Jesus says that the church will be founded upon who He, Himself, is, the Saviour of the world. The church is built upon the fact that Jesus is the Saviour of the world. Jesus is the Messiah, or God with skin on. He is God who has come down to pay the penalty of sin so that anyone who believes in Him and receives Him will have forgiveness of sin and everlasting life. Thus, Jesus is both the founder of the church and the foundation of the church!

The Apostle Paul also teaches that Jesus is the foundation of the church. In 1 Corinthians 3:10-11, Paul writes,

> By the grace God has given me, I laid a foundation as an expert builder, and someone else is building on it. But each one should be careful how he builds. [11]For no one can lay any foundation other than the one already laid, which is Jesus Christ.

Jesus is the foundation of the church. Without Jesus, the church does not exist. He both founded the church and is, Himself, the foundation of the church. In his letter to the Ephesians, Paul uses another term to describe Christ's importance to the existence of the church. Paul refers to Jesus as the cornerstone of the church in Ephesians 2:20b-22,

> with Christ Jesus himself as the chief cornerstone. [21]In him the whole building is joined together and rises to become a holy temple in the Lord. [22]And in him you too are being built together to become a dwelling in which God lives by his Spirit.

This teaching about Jesus not only comes from Paul, but the apostle Peter also teaches that Jesus is the cornerstone of the church. 1 Peter 2:4-6 says,

> As you come to him, the living Stone – rejected by men but chosen by God and precious to him – [5]you also, like living stones, are being built into a spiritual house to be a holy priesthood, offering spiritual sacrifices acceptable to God through Jesus Christ. [6]For in Scripture it says: "See, I lay a stone in Zion, a chosen and precious cornerstone, and the one who trusts in him will never be put to shame."

The whole church is built upon and according to Jesus as its foundation and cornerstone. The church exists only because Jesus brought it into being.

The Body of Christ

Another way of defining the church is through the metaphor of the human body. In both Ephesians 4 and 1 Corinthians 12, the apostle Paul uses the metaphor of a human body to refer to Jesus and those who follow Him in discipleship. Paul refers to Jesus as the head of the church and His disciples as the body of Christ. Ephesians 4:4-6 says,

> There is one body and one Spirit – just as you were called to one hope when you were called – [5]one Lord, one faith, one baptism; [6]one God and Father of all, who is over all and through all and in all.

Paul also writes in Ephesians 4:15-16,

> Instead, speaking the truth in love, we will in all things grow up into him who is the Head, that is, Christ. [16]From him the whole body, joined and held together by every supporting ligament, grows and builds itself up in love, as each part does its work.

We see from these verses that Jesus is the head of the body, or church, and all those who believe in Him and receive Him as their Lord and Saviour are part of His body. In 1 Corinthians 12:12-14 Paul also writes,

> The body is a unit, though it is made up of many parts; and though all its parts are many, they form one body. So it is with Christ. [13]For we were all baptized by one Spirit into one body – whether Jews or Greek, slave or free – and we were all given the one Spirit to drink.
>
> [14]Now the body is not made up of one part but of many.

It is important to note that the body of Christ is made up of all who believe in Christ and receive Him into their lives. Only Christians are part of the body of Christ. Those who are not Christians are not part of the body of Christ, and that is because, as we read, a person is made to be part of the church by the power and work of the Holy Spirit. It is the Holy Spirit that baptizes us into the body of Christ. Please note that this is a spiritual baptism, not a water baptism. Water baptism is different than the baptism of the Spirit. The baptism of the Spirit takes place when we receive Jesus as Lord and Saviour. (Baptism means to immerse in or make part of something.) It is at the point of believing in and receiving Jesus that, according to Titus 3:3-6, we are washed and given new life. Titus 3:3-6 says,

> At one time we too were foolish, disobedient, deceived and enslaved by all kinds of passions and pleasures. We lived in malice and envy, being hated and hating one another. [4]But when the kindness and love of God our Savior appeared, [5]he saved us, not because of righteous things we had done, but because of his mercy. He saved us through the washing of rebirth and renewal by the Holy Spirit, [6]whom he poured out on us generously through Jesus Christ our Savior.

When a person receives Jesus as Lord and Saviour, he/she becomes part of the body of Christ, the church, by the work, or baptism, of the Holy Spirit. Thus, every believer in the whole world is part of the one and same body of Christ.

Called Out Ones

In fact, the word church itself means, "called out ones". The word "church" in the Bible refers to those who have been "called out" by God through believing in and receiving Jesus as their Lord and Saviour.

The church is made up of people who are called by God to come out of the world. Coming out of the world does not mean leaving the planet or going to live in a commune in the jungle. No, to be called out by God simply means to no longer live by the principles or lifestyle of the world. Disciples of Christ live a different lifestyle and by different principles than those who are not disciples of Christ. And that is because the disciple of Christ is not only called to come out of something, in this case the world: disciples of Christ are also called *to* something. Disciples of Christ are called *to* follow Jesus, called *to* live by the teaching and example of Jesus Christ. God calls His disciples to live according to His words, His ways, and His will.

The "called out ones" are all people who have believed in and received Jesus as Lord and Saviour and who now follow His ways rather than the ways of the world. They are those people who are committed to following Christ and His teachings on how to love God and love others. The Apostle Paul writes in Ephesians 5:8, "For you were once darkness, but now you are light in the Lord. Live as children of light."

The church is called to live differently, to love differently, to respond differently, to react differently, and to act differently than those who have not believed in and have not received Jesus as Lord and Saviour. The church is made up of those who recognize that Jesus is indeed the Lord, or Master, of their lives and therefore must follow His teaching and His example of how to act and interact in this world.

Yet, too many disciples of Christ today do not act or interact any differently than the world around them; they look the same as those who are not the "called out ones". Disciples of Christ, the Church, is commanded to be different. Who commands them? Jesus does. Jesus is the one who died for the church, He is the one through whom the church exists. He is the founder and the foundation. He is the cornerstone by which the whole building takes its direction.

So, the church exists because Jesus brought it into existence by His death and resurrection. He is the founder and the foundation. His disciples are the building that arises according to His direction and plan. The church is also the body of Christ, with Christ Himself being the head of the church. Paul says in 1 Corinthians 12:27, "Now you are the body of Christ, and each one of you is a part of it." Every disciple becomes part of the body of Christ through the regenerating work of the Holy Spirit. He/She is called out of a life of sin and darkness into a life of salvation and light. Disciples of Christ are the "called out ones". They are the church, the body of Christ, followers of Jesus.

Church – The Physical Side

What we have just covered can be referred to as the "spiritual" side of the church. That is, defining the spiritual working of the church. But there is more to the definition of the church; there is also a physical side of church, and this, perhaps, is what is most commonly thought of when we use the word "church". Let's take a look at three ways that we define the church as a physical entity.

A Building or Place of Meeting

The church is often referred to as a building or a place of meeting. When a person says they are going to church, they are saying that they have a particular building or place where they are going. When you tell someone that you are going to the Baptist church or the Presbyterian church, those you tell will know exactly where you are going because the church has an address, a locality, or a physical presence. It is a particular place with a particular location.

```
CHURCH

A specific building or place of meeting

Romans 16:3-5a, 16, 23
```

Romans 16:3-5a says, "Greet Priscilla and Aquila, my fellow workers in Christ Jesus. [4]They risked their lives for me. Not only I but all the churches of the Gentiles are grateful to them." Paul refers to "all the churches" as particular places with particular locations. Paul has definite churches or congregations in mind. They are places that he has travelled to and visited. They are definite and physical places on the map.

Furthermore, he writes, [5a]"Greet also the church that meets at their house." Paul identifies the local church that meets at their house. The house is the church. It is not only their house, it also serves as the church.

We get more examples of the local church in Romans 16:16 when Paul writes, "Greet one another with a holy kiss. All the churches of Christ send greetings." And in 16:23 he writes, "Gaius, whose hospitality I and the whole church here enjoy, sends you his greetings." What is he saying? He is saying that there is a group of people that meet for church in this space, in this time, and in this place, which is called church. The building, or place, is called the church.

So, the church can be defined as a building or a particular place of meeting, but it has another definition. The word "church" can also refer to a larger entity defined by its beliefs and doctrines, often referred to as the universal church.

The Universal Church

The term for all believers being part of the one body of Christ is called the universal church. All believers everywhere during all ages are part of the same and one body of Christ. There is only one Jesus, one Saviour, one God, one Spirit and one church. This is the universal church. We go back to Ephesians 4:4-6,

> There is one body and one Spirit – just as you were called to one hope when you were called – [5]one Lord, one faith, one baptism; [6]one God and Father of all, who is over all and through all and in all.

Every single person in this whole entire world, who has believed in Jesus as Lord and Saviour and has received Him into their life, in the past, present or future, is part of the universal church. All believers all over the world during all ages are part of the body of Christ. Those in India, in the Philippines, in Mexico, in Finland, in all parts of the world are all part of the body of Christ. It is a physical entity that you can see and touch. It is the universal church.

So, the church is defined as the "called out ones" who are all part of the universal body of Christ. But there is more. There is also the local church.

The Local Church

Believers all over the world come together in certain localities to worship God together. These places are referred to as local congregations.

The apostle Paul refers to local churches when he addresses his letters to local churches – to the church in Corinth, to the church in Ephesus, to the church in Philippi, etc. Though Paul recognizes that the church of Jesus is a universal church, he also recognizes the local congregation.

LOCAL CHURCH

Disciples of Christ meeting in specific places

The church in Philippi, the church in Ephesus, the church in Corinth, etc.

Your particular church where you meet is the local church. The local church is the body of Christ located in a particular place. It is localized. Believers are part of the universal church and are also part of the local church at the same time. The local church is a specific place – it is where you meet.

The church can be defined by both spiritual aspects and physical aspects. It is the place in your locality where you meet with its own specific name, such as First Baptist. It is the world-wide group of all believers in Christ who have a common faith in Jesus as Lord and Saviour. It is a building, or the place of meeting. The church is also the "called out ones". It is the body of Christ who is the head, and it is built upon the foundation and cornerstone of Jesus Christ Himself – the Saviour of the world.

Purpose and Function

Let us now turn our attention to the purpose and function of the church. When we use the word "church", we are also identifying purpose and function. When you say that you are going to the grocery store, the name "grocery store" identifies what it is and what it does. You know its purpose and function. When you go to the post office, you know where you are going and what you are going for. It is not to buy groceries or to see a movie; it is for mail purposes. You know the purpose and function of the building or entity because its name tells you what it is and what to expect there.

In the same way, the word "church" indicates its function and purpose. When you go to church, you know you are not going for the purpose of buying groceries, nor are you going in order to send and receive letters. No, you are going for the purpose that the church is made for.

Purpose

What then is the purpose that the church is made for? Why does the church exist? What is the church called out to do?

To begin answering this question, let's turn to Matthew 28:18-20. These words of the Bible are often referred as to the "Great Commission". They are the great purpose of the church.

> Then Jesus came to them and said, "All authority in heaven and on earth has been given to me. [19]Therefore go and make disciples of all nations, baptizing them in the name of the Father and of the Son and of the Holy Spirit, [20]and teaching them to obey everything I have commanded you. And surely I am with you always, to the very end of the age."

The Great Commission, or purpose, of the church is to make disciples. This is what Jesus commands the church to do. Note that this is not a suggestion from Jesus, but a command. He is more telling us than asking us. He is the head of the church, and He tells the body what to do. The purpose of the church is to make disciples.

Disciple Making

That, of course, causes one to ask, "What is a disciple? And what does it mean to make a disciple?" Perhaps the simplest definition of a disciple is that a disciple is a follower of Christ. A disciple is someone who believes in Jesus, who has received Jesus as Lord and Saviour and who will follow Jesus. A disciple puts Jesus as his/her commander-in-chief. If Jesus says "go", then the disciple must go. If Jesus says "stay", then the disciple must stay. That which Jesus commands is followed.

A disciple puts Jesus as his/her commander-in-chief.

A disciple is a follower of Jesus, who, in following Jesus, will be one who makes other disciples. A disciple of Jesus makes other disciples of Jesus. In Romans 10:13-15 Paul writes,

> for, "Everyone who calls on the name of the Lord will be saved."
>
> [14]How, then, can they call on the one they have not believed in? And how can they believe in the one of whom they have not heard? And how can they hear without someone preaching to them? [15]And how can they preach unless they are sent? As it is written, "How beautiful are the feet of those who bring good news!"

In order to make a disciple of Christ, you have to tell people about Christ. The purpose of every disciple of Christ is to tell other people about Christ in order that the people you tell may be able to make a decision to follow Christ. People cannot be "called out ones" if they do not know the One who is calling. The church must tell people about Jesus. This is what disciples do because of Jesus' command to, "Go and make disciples."

It is interesting to note that the Greek word "go" is a verbal noun. A more direct translation in English would be "as you are going" or "the one who is going". It is a noun that is doing something. It is a disciple that is going and telling wherever he/she goes. There is no doubt that the disciple is going somewhere, and there is no doubt that he/she is speaking about Jesus wherever he/she goes. Further, it is not something that just happens in a particular place. Making disciples happens wherever and whenever we are going! If you are at work, your task and purpose as a part of the body of Christ is to make disciples. As disciples of Christ, we are consciously aware that we are the called out ones commanded to call others to the called out life.

Evangelism

This action of making disciples wherever we go is commonly called evangelism. The purpose of the church is evangelism. The word evangelism simply means to tell others about the good news of Jesus Christ.

Jesus says in Acts 1:8, "But you will receive power when the Holy Spirit comes on you; and you will be my witnesses in Jerusalem, and in all Judea and Samaria, and to the ends of the earth." As you are going to Jerusalem – be a witness of Jesus; as you are going to Judea be a witness of Jesus; as you are going to Samaria be a witness of Jesus; and as you are going the ends of the earth be a witness of Jesus. This is disciple-making! Wherever your feet take you be a witness of who Jesus is; make disciples. The church is called to evangelism, to telling people about

Jesus. A function and the purpose of the church is to make disciples, to preach the "good news", and to tell people about who Jesus is so they too can become one of the called out ones.

Pillar and Foundation of the Truth

Another function and purpose of the church is to be the pillar and foundation of truth. In 1 Timothy 3:15 Paul says to Timothy, "if I am delayed, you will know how people ought to conduct themselves in God's household, which is the church of the living God, the pillar and foundation of the truth." Paul tells Timothy that God's household, the church, is to be the pillar and foundation of the truth.

What does a foundation do? For the building of houses or other large structures, the foundation is critically important. The foundation holds up the house or the structure. It gives it stability and security. If the foundation cracks or the foundation shifts, then the whole house is in danger of shifting and collapsing. The foundation supports the building. Paul calls the church the foundation of truth in the world. The church holds the foundational truth of God. No other organization has the foundation of the words of truth except the church because the foundation of the church itself is the embodiment of truth – Jesus. God gave His foundations of truth to the church in order for the church to proclaim the truth to everybody else. This is how the church is to be the foundation of God's truth in the world.

Not only is the church the foundation of God's truth, it is also the pillar of truth. What do pillars do? If you build a roof over the porch of your house, pillars are needed to secure and support the roof. Pillars hold up the roof. The pillars are attached to the foundation, and the roof is attached to the pillars. If the pillars are not put up correctly or there are not enough pillars to support the weight of the roof, then it is very likely that the roof will eventually come crashing down. The church, then, is to be a pillar of truth to the world. It is to hold up the truth to society so that people can build their lives upon it without fear of it all crashing down upon them.

The purpose and function of the church is to be the pillar and foundation of the truth – of God's truth. For the world to operate correctly before God, the world needs to be built upon the foundation and pillars of God's truth, and the church is commanded to make that truth known to the world. The church is to present the gospel of Jesus Christ so that the world will know and understand truth, thus affording every person the opportunity to build his/her life upon this firm foundation.

One of the most difficult subjects for parents to think about is what is going to happen to their children when they leave home. Will they make good decisions? Will they make good friends? Will they be able to stand up under the pressure of the world upon them? Will their lives come crashing down, or will they stand? Will the foundation and pillars of truth that they received from their parents be discarded, or will they be cherished and kept? Every parent desires to give good foundations and pillars to their children to build upon. In the same way, God has given the world the foundation and pillars of truth for the world to know Him and build their life upon Him. The church is charged with proclaiming the foundation and pillars of truth to the world. That is the job of the church. That is the purpose of the church – to tell the world about the truth of God. Thus, we must know the truth of God. The writer of Hebrews 5:11-14 says,

We have much to say about this, but it is hard to explain because you are slow to learn. [12]In fact, though by this time you ought to be teachers, you need someone to teach you the elementary truths of God's word all over again. You need milk, not solid food! [13]Anyone who lives on milk, being still an infant, is not acquainted with the teaching about righteousness. [14]But solid food is for the mature, who by constant use have trained themselves to distinguish good from evil.

The writer is saying that we have to know truth and mature in our knowledge of the truth so that we can have a good foundation of truth. This is how important the truth of God is! We need it to distinguish good from evil. We need it to train ourselves to distinguish good from evil. The church is to be the pillar and foundation of the truth so that the world can know God; therefore the church must know the truth and be maturing in the truth. Every disciple of Christ must be maturing and growing in their knowledge of God's truth in order to tell this truth to others around them wherever it is they are going.

To Know God

This leads us to another function and purpose of the church. It is found in Acts 2:42 which says, "They devoted themselves to the apostles' teaching and to the fellowship, to the breaking of bread and to prayer." The purpose of the church is to help people to know God with increasing measure. The early Christians devoted themselves to the apostles' teaching which is the word of God, or the pillar and foundation of the truth. They also devoted themselves to meeting together, to the breaking of bread, or communion, and to prayer.

They wanted to know God more and more. Notice that they devoted themselves to this end. Devoted is an amazing word – to give oneself over to the pursuit of something. In this case it is the pursuit of God. The purpose of the church is to help people to pursue God, to become devoted followers of Jesus. In Hebrews 10:25 disciples of Christ are exhorted to continue to not let go of meeting together but to commit themselves to it so that they can encourage each other to keep pursuing God in relationship with Jesus. We read this in Hebrews 10:24-25, "And let us consider how we may spur one another on toward love and good deeds. [25]Let us not give up meeting together, as some are in the habit of doing, but let us encourage one another – and all the more as you see the Day approaching."

The purpose of the church is to meet together, using prayer, communion, fellowship, and the teaching of the Word of God to pursue a deeper relationship with Jesus.

The Future of the Church

The last topic we want to cover in this chapter is the future of the church. To begin, we turn to Matthew 16:18, which we have read before, "And I tell you that you are Peter, and on this rock I will build my church, *and the gates of Hades will not overcome it."* According to Jesus' own words, the church will not be overcome by satan, and I might add, ever. The church will be victorious! In Romans 16:20a, Paul tells the church these words, "The God of peace will soon crush satan under your feet." Satan will never overcome the body of Christ because Jesus is the head of the church! Jesus is the one who will crush satan under His feet. Paul also tells the church in Galatia, that Jesus triumphed over satan and his forces when He died on the cross. Paul writes in Colossians 2:15, "And having disarmed the powers and authorities, he made a public spectacle of them, triumphing over them by the cross." The church will succeed and be victorious because Jesus has ensured her success and victory by His death and resurrection.

Not only will the church never fail, but the church has a glorious, eternal future awaiting it. In 1 Thessalonians 4:15-18, the apostle Paul tells the church that Jesus will come again and gather the church to be with Him for eternity.

> According to the Lord's own word, we tell you that we who are still alive, who are left till the coming of the Lord, will certainly not precede those who have fallen asleep. [16]For the Lord himself will come down from heaven, with a loud command, with the voice of the archangel and with the trumpet call of God, and the dead in Christ will rise first. [17]After that, we who are still alive and are left will be caught up together with them in the clouds to meet the Lord in the air. And so we will be with the Lord forever. [18]Therefore encourage each other with these words.

Furthermore, the book of Revelation speaks of the church as the "bride of Christ". We read in Revelation 19:6-8,

> Then I heard what sounded like a great multitude, like the roar of rushing waters and like loud peals of thunder, shouting: "Hallelujah! For our Lord God Almighty reigns. [7]Let us rejoice and be glad and give him glory! For the wedding of the Lamb has come, and his bride has made herself ready. [8]Fine linen, bright and clean, was given her to wear."

The wedding of the Lamb refers to the day in which Jesus will return for His church and judge all the people of the world. After that, those who are the body of Christ, His church, will be rewarded for their belief and following of Jesus. They will receive eternal life and celebrate their reward of eternal life with a great wedding feast. It will be a time of exalting in the greatness of God and celebrating the victory of the church that Jesus has given through His death and His resurrection.

The church has a great and glorious future. It is the only organization on earth that has the promise of God for its protection and eternal victory. The church wins! The church overcomes! The church survives and thrives in eternity.

Conclusion

The church is the "called out" people of God who follow Jesus in their local church for the purpose of calling other people to follow and pursue Jesus through the teaching and building upon the foundational words of God's truth. Nobody else in the world can do this, only the church.

Closing Prayer

Jesus, thank You for establishing the church by Your death and resurrection. Thank You that we can be the "called out ones". Help us to pursue You more fully and passionately. Help us to know You more, and help us to help others to come and know You more so they too might become part of the body of Christ with us. Jesus, You are the head of the church and the head of me, Your disciple. Help me to follow Your command to make disciples wherever I go.

Amen.

SCRIPTURE INDEX

Chapter 3

John 16:7-13

John 14:16-17

1 Corinthians 12:11

Ephesians 4:29-30

Hebrews 10:29

John 14:26

Acts 5:2-4

Acts 5:8-9

1 Corinthians 2:11

John 14:17b

Titus 3:5-6

Matthew 28:18-19

2 Corinthians 13:14

Genesis 1:2

John 14:26

Psalm 32:80

John 16:8

John 16:14-15

Acts 1:8

Romans 8:26

1 Corinthians 12:11

Titus 3:4-7

John 3:3

Galatians 5:16-25

Chapter 4

Deuteronomy 6:4

John 10:30

Acts 5:3-4

Genesis 1:26-27

2 Corinthians 13:14

1 Corinthians 8:4-6

1 Timothy 2:5-6

James 2:19

Hebrews 1:8

John 14:9-10a

Matthew 1:23

Matthew 28:19

2 Corinthians 13:14

1 Peter 1:1-2

Isaiah 57:15

Psalm 90:2

John 8:58

Exodus 3:14

Isaiah 9:6

Genesis 1:1-2

1 John 3:20b

John 6:64b

1 Corinthians 2:10b-11

Matthew 19:26

Jeremiah 32:17

Matthew 28:18b

Luke 1:35a

Ephesians 4:6

Matthew 18:20

Psalm 139:7-12

John 3:33

Hebrews 6:18b

John 14:6

John 14:16-17a

John 16:13a

Genesis 1:1

John 1:1-3

Genesis 1:2

2 Timothy 3:16-17

Hebrews 1:1-2

2 Peter 1:20-21

Ephesians 2:8b

John 14:6

Titus 3:4-6

Romans 11:33

Chapter 5	Chapter 6	Chapter 7
Romans 3:23	Romans 3:23	1 Peter 1:13-16
Romans 3:9-24	James 2:10	Romans 5:1-2
Ecclesiastes 7:20	Romans 6:23a	Romans 8:1-4
Luke 11:7-13	Romans 5:8b	Titus 3:3-5
Psalm 51:5	2 Corinthians 5:21	John 3:7b
Ephesians 2:3	John 14:6	2 Corinthians 5:17
Romans 5:12-21	Acts 4:12b	1 Corinthians 1:1-2
Romans 3:12	1 John 4:9-10	1 Corinthians 6:11
1 John 1:8	John 10:17-18	Hebrews 10:10
Galatians 5:16-23	Ephesians 2:8-9	Ephesians 2:4-6
Romans 7:14-25a	Romans 6:23	2 Corinthians 3:18
Galatians 5:25	Romans 10:9-10	1 Thessalonians 5:23-24
Romans 6:23a	1 John 1:9	1 Peter 1:16b
Genesis 3:1-12	Titus 3:3-6	Romans 12:2a
Ephesians 2:1-2	2 Corinthians 5:17	Romans 12:1
John 3:16	Revelation 3:20	
1 John 5:12	Ephesians 2:1-5	
Revelation 20:11-16	Colossians 2:13-15	**Chapter 8**
1 Timothy 2:3-4	Romans 5:1-2	
2 Peter 3:9	Romans 8:1-2	1 Timothy 3:16-17
Romans 5:8b	1 Corinthians 15:51-57	Hebrews 1:1-2
Romans 6:23	Revelation 21	2 Peter 1:20-21
	2 Peter 3:9	Psalm 19:7-8
		Psalm 119:42

James 1:25

John 10:34-35

Matthew 5:17-18

2 Peter 3:15-16

Revelation 22:18-19

Deuteronomy 4:2

Proverbs 30:5-6

John 14:26

Ephesians 1:18

Amos 7:8

Psalm 32:8

Psalm 119:105

Chapter 9

Matthew 24:36

Acts 1:7

2 Thessalonians 2:1ff

Matthew 24:23-30

Acts 1:8-11

1 Thessalonians 4:13-18

Hebrews 9:28

Revelation 22:20a

Matthew 25:31-46

2 Peter 3:9

2 Thessalonians 1:5-10

Acts 1:9-11

Matthew 24:36-42

Matthew 24:1-22

Revelation 3:10

Matthew 24:15

Daniel 9:27

1 John 2:18

Revelation 13:1-5

2 Thessalonians 2:1-12

Chapter 10

1 Corinthians 15:1-4

1 Corinthians 15:12-20

1 Corinthians 15:44

Matthew 28:5-7

1 Corinthians 15:3-6

1 Corinthians 15:7

Ephesians 1:19b-20

1 Thessalonians 4:13-18

1 Corinthians 15:35-54

John 14:1-3

Hebrews 9:24

Matthew 6:9

1 Peter 1:3-5

Revelation 21:1-7

Genesis 3:8

Luke 23:39-43

Daniel 12:1-2

John 5:28-29

Matthew 24:45-51

Revelation 20:7-15

1 Timothy 2:3-4

2 Peter 3:9

Chapter 11

Romans 12:3-8

1 Corinthians 12:7-11

Ephesians 4:7-13

Ephesians 2:10

Ephesians 4:11-15

Romans 12:4-8

1 Corinthians 12:1-31

Galatians 5:22-23a

Galatians 5:16-26

Chapter 12

Psalm 139:23

Luke 6:8

Luke 9:47

Psalm 139:17

1 Thessalonians 5:17

Matthew 6:33

Philippians 4:4-7

1 Timothy 2:8

Romans 12:18

1 Peter 3:7-12

Isaiah 1:2-4

Isaiah 1:10-18

Proverbs 1:23-33

Psalm 66:18

Jeremiah 7:9-16

1 John 1:9

Matthew 6:1-15

Chapter 13

Matthew 16:13-18

1 Corinthians 3:10-11

Ephesians 2:20b-22

1 Peter 2:4-6

Ephesians 4:4-6

Ephesians 4:15-16

1 Corinthians 12:12-14

Titus 3:3-6

Ephesians 5:8

1 Corinthians 12:27

Romans 16:3-5a

Romans 16:16

Romans 16:23

Matthew 28:18-20

Romans 10:13-15

Acts 1:8

1 Timothy 3:15

Hebrews 5:11-14

Acts 2:42

Hebrews 10:24-25

Matthew 16:18

Romans 16:20a

Colossians 2:15

1 Thessalonians 4:15-18

Revelation 19:6-8